The College Classroo Compendium

The College Classroom Assessment Compendium provides new and seasoned instructors with comprehensive strategies, perspectives, and solutions for the daily challenges and issues involved in student assessment. Composed of cross-referenced, research-based entries organized for effective and immediate access, this book provides systematic explanations of assessment policies and practices, including guidelines for classroom implementation. Situated beyond the techniques covered in most instructor training and preparation, these practical entries draw from a variety of disciplines and offer an invaluable reference for college instructors interested in developing coherent, reliable classroom assessment climates.

Jay Parkes is Chair of the Department of Individual, Family, and Community Education and Professor of Educational Psychology in the College of Education at the University of New Mexico, USA.

Dawn Zimmaro is Director of Learning Design and Assessment at the Open Learning Initiative at Stanford University, USA.

Tiana,

Happy Assessing!

Jay

The College Classroom Assessment Compendium

A Practical Guide to the College Instructor's Daily Assessment Life

Jay Parkes and Dawn Zimmaro

Routledge
Taylor & Francis Group

NEW YORK AND LONDON

First published 2018
by Routledge
711 Third Avenue, New York, NY 10017

and by Routledge
2 Park Square, Milton Park, Abingdon, Oxon, OX14 4RN

Routledge is an imprint of the Taylor & Francis Group, an informa business

Library of Congress Cataloging-in-Publication Data
A catalog record for this book has been requested

ISBN: 978-1-138-24024-7 (hbk)
ISBN: 978-1-138-24026-1 (pbk)
ISBN: 978-1-315-28385-2 (ebk)

Typeset in Bembo
by Apex CoVantage, LLC

Jay would like to dedicate this book to your students and ours, and to those mentors and colleagues who taught him how to teach. He would also like to dedicate this book to Morag, William, and Sarah, his very best teachers.

Dawn would like to dedicate this book to her mom, Lois, who showed her how hard work, commitment, and constantly challenging yourself will take you wherever you want to go. She also would like to dedicate this book to all the instructors with whom she collaborated over the years who asked the tough questions about assessment that formed the foundation of this book!

Contents

Illustrations

Figure

Tables

1   Introduction

Who Has Time for This?!?!?

As a 21st-century college instructor, you know what a crush teaching can be! You face a maze of issues: technology, diverse students, helicopter parents, outcomes assessment, shrinking budgets, rapidly changing fields, etc. Assessing your own students in your own classes is definitely part of that mix. It is most likely a part of your job, though, on which you haven't had systematic education or training. Perhaps you've been to a workshop on using clickers in your classroom, or you've read a book about e-portfolios. But we'd wager you've not had sustained, integrated study regarding student assessment.

That's a lot to take on. You spend a large percentage of your teaching time with assessment-related tasks and issues: writing exams, grading papers, talking with students about their work during office hours, filing course grades. A study of K–12 teachers in the 1980s found that they spent a quarter to a third of their time in assessment-related activities (Stiggins & Conklin, 1992). That was educational epochs ago; we suspect that in their reality and yours those numbers are still valid, or now a little low! Spending that much of your teaching time working on all of those activities and issues without a coherent philosophy and sense of purpose is very grueling.

There are plenty of issues you encounter, too: ever-changing course management systems; new educational technologies to support in-class, blended, and online teaching approaches; changing policies and procedures from upper administration; and disgruntled students, intrusive parents, well-meaning colleagues, department chairs, etc. These are issues and people which we can perceive as challenging to our decisions as an instructor. We seem constantly to need either to make a decision or to explain a decision to someone.

You paradoxically need just-in-time information, in an easily accessible and digestible format, that will guide you in what to do, yet you also require a comprehensive approach to addressing assessment issues in your daily life. For these reasons, we've decided to write a compendium of college classroom assessment.

We are deliberately structuring this book into short, encyclopedia-like entries so that it serves as an off-the-shelf reference for you. *Compendium*, according to the Oxford English Dictionary, means "giving the sense and substance, within smaller compass" or "an embodiment in miniature." We've tried to do that for you. Are you writing your syllabus for the next term and are wondering what to do about **attendance***? Did you just make an appointment with a student who wants to know "what else I can do" to better her grade (see **extra credit***)? Was the average on your last exam lower than you and your students were expecting (see **low test scores***)? We offer this volume as some assistance in those situations.

We have constructed this compendium, though, fully acknowledging that assessment policies and practices are driven by your own philosophies (see **assessment philosophy***), which are often as determinative of what you choose to do as any "best practice" recommendation. You need to have, and this compendium has, an underlying framework of philosophy, evidence, and best practice recommendations. *Compendium*, also from the OED, derives from the Latin *compendere*, which means "to weigh together." Each of the entries in this volume cannot be taken in isolation. You might consult an entry to solve a time-sensitive issue, but we hope that, once the immediate crisis is over, you'll take additional time to consider how that issue fits into larger ones.

How to Use This Book

First and foremost, we intend this compendium as a resource for just-in-time learning. As you're preparing a syllabus, as you read a student's e-mail asking about her grade, after you've had a conversation with a colleague about, say, **groupwork***, you can pull this off your shelf and, in a few minutes, have some details and perspectives about that issue. That's why we've broken it into brief, topical entries which are organized alphabetically.

If you can't find exactly what you're looking for immediately, there are several other ways you can look up topics. There is a traditional index at the end of the book. Furthermore, most entries include a "see also" list of other related entries in this book. So if you've found an entry but it isn't exactly what you're looking for, glance down at the "see also" list.

Second, we've designed the book deliberately to aid more systematic learning on your part, too. Every entry includes references which we've used to prepare the entry, resources on the topic which would provide you with more in-depth discussions related to that topic, and a "see also" list of other related entries in this book. Another technique we've adopted is that we will bold-face and asterisk any term in the text which has its own entry in this book. So when you're done reading the entry on **extra credit***, you may decide that you also need to consult the entry for **assessment plan***, or what to say when a **grade feeding frenzy*** occurs. You can use the book in *Choose Your Own Adventure*® style, moving from entry to entry.

Create Your Personal Classroom Assessment Mosaic

Third, you do not actually tackle your assessment issues in isolation. Your own teaching philosophy, your own professional and personal values, and the policy and practice environment in which you work affect many of these decisions and practices. So we invite you here to work on integrating your assessment policies and practices into an explicit framework. Create your own Personal Classroom Assessment Mosaic.

There are lots of ways to do this. Writing about assessment in your statement of teaching philosophy is definitely one option. Assessment of students is routinely considered a portion of what one should address in a statement of teaching philosophy (Schönwetter, Sokal, Friesen, & Taylor, 2002). We would upend the traditional logic, however, which tends to suggest that you write about your values, beliefs, and philosophy first and then write about how that plays out in your instruction. We actually suggest that you think about what you do with assessment first because assessment is usually your values, beliefs, and philosophy *enacted*.

When Jay teaches classroom assessment to K–12 teachers, one of their assignments is to write a Personal Grading Plan (Frisbie & Waltman, 1992). Frisbie and Waltman propose questions like, "What should *failure* mean in your course?," "What does an A+ signify?," and "Should **borderline grade cases*** be reviewed?" The Frisbie and Waltman article is thought-provoking and may prove a useful starting point. We include these and other questions in the **assessment philosophy*** entry.

In conversations with instructors about their course design, Dawn advises them to first develop an **assessment plan*** that not only outlines the number of assessments but defines how they will be used (see **formative and summative assessments***) and to which learning objectives they will align (see **align assessments to learning objectives***). This process helps you explicitly define the alignment between your assessment, learning objectives, and instructional activities that ultimately reflect your overall **assessment philosophy*** as an instructor.

When should you do this? Perhaps you'll start on Spring Break, or when you are next required to submit your teaching philosophy for your formal faculty review, or during the summer when you have some time to read, think, and study. But start soon. Do something now. Regardless of the method(s) you choose to think through and capture your assessment philosophy, beliefs, and values, do take some time to do this. Perhaps you could even get started by writing in the margins of this book. Feel free to make marginal notes like, "Yes!" or "Are you crazy!?!?!?!" next to what you find in this book. But then have some system for articulating to yourself, and then to your students and other constituents, why you think so.

We refer to this as a mosaic because any assessment decision has subcomponents to it. In a mosaic, if you're standing back far enough, you can't actually see those small tiles individually, you see only the whole picture. But if you examine a mosaic closely enough, you can differentiate those subcomponents. The same thing is true of your assessment practices. What decision you make regarding a flawed multiple-choice item on a test (see **drop a question***) draws on your positions on values like **fairness***, **equity***, and **beneficence***; on your philosophy regarding student motivation and learner-centeredness; on your knowledge of educational measurement principles; and on best practice guidelines for multiple-choice use and, perhaps, a research base on those issues.

For some of those issues, like fairness, there are different, reasonable positions and thus actions which different instructors may adhere to. For some of those issues, like educational measurement principles, there are best practice, sense-of-the-field, consensuses on better or worse choices. And for some of those issues, there is a right answer, or at least a research-derived conclusion to the question. You owe it to yourself, to your students, and to your institution to know which of those kinds of foundations on which you're building your assessment practice.

As we wrote these entries in this book, we also drew on this mosaic approach. So for some entries, like **attendance***, we will make a recommendation for your practice and tell you why that's our recommendation. For other entries, like **compensatory and conjunctive grading***, the options rely a bit more on philosophical stance. There, we will provide best practice suggestions for the different options.

Let's Go!

Now that you have some sense of how this book is organized and how we anticipate you will use it, let's go! Use it the way it serves you best as you tackle the challenges that come with assessing student learning each day.

References

Frisbie, D. A., & Waltman, K. K. (1992). Developing a personal grading plan. *Educational Measurement: Issues and Practice, 11*(3), 35–42.

Schönwetter, D. J., Sokal, L., Friesen, M., & Taylor, K. L. (2002). Teaching philosophies reconsidered: A conceptual model for the development and evaluation of teaching philosophy statements. *International Journal for Academic Development, 7*(1), 83–97.

Stiggins, R. J., & Conklin, N. (1992). *In teachers' hands: Investigating the practice of classroom assessment*. Albany, NY: SUNY Press.

2 Align Assessments to Learning Objectives

What Is a Learning Objective?

A learning objective describes the knowledge, skills, abilities, and behaviors you want students to gain from an activity, unit of instruction, or course. Well-written learning objectives are:

* Centered on students, rather than instructors (Students will be able to . . .).
* Focused on the specific learning that results from an activity.
* Worded in clear, concise, and concrete language about learning.
* Focused on learning that can be measured and assessed.

Here is an example of a well-written learning objective: Given a diagram of an animal cell, students will be able to identify the various parts of the cell.

Why Should I Align My Assessments to Learning Objectives?

Developing assessments aligned to learning objectives ensures that you are giving students the opportunity to practice and meet the learning objective. Every assessment should be created with a specific learning objective in mind, and learning objectives can vary in learning level.

How Do I Align My Assessments to Learning Objectives?

Most learning objectives, regardless of the learning level, can be assessed by either selected-response or constructed-response assessments (see **selected- and constructed-response questions***). In some cases, however, only one of these formats is appropriate.

Given the learning objective above regarding the parts of a cell, an assessment that is well-aligned might be written as (see Figure 2.1):

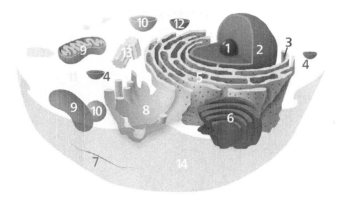

Given the diagram of an animal cell, match the various parts to its corresponding part on the diagram.

Cell Part	Number on Diagram
Cell membrane	
Centriole	
Cytoskeleton	
Cytosol	
Golgi apparatus (or Golgi body)	
Lysosome	
Mitochondrion	
Nucleolus	
Nucleus	
Ribosomes	
Rough endoplasmic reticulum	
Smooth endoplasmic reticulum	
Vacuole	
Vesicle	

Figure 2.1 Example of an Assessment Aligned to a Learning Objective

Source: https://commons.wikimedia.org/wiki/File:Animal_Cell.svg
CC0 public domain

A similar assessment question administered online might ask students to drag the various part labels to the corresponding part on the image (sometimes referred to as a drag-and-drop question).

A slightly modified version of the learning objective would necessitate a change to the assessment format: Given a list of the various parts of an animal cell, students will be able to construct a cell diagram with labeled parts.

For this learning objective, the matching or drag-and-drop question formats would not align well since the critical behavior you are trying to assess is students' ability to "construct" a cell diagram. In this case, the assessment question should be a constructed-response format where students sketch a cell diagram and label the various parts.

When aligning your assessments to your learning objectives, the critical component is to ensure that the behavior, or action verb, in your learning objective (identify, construct, explain, list, etc.) is appropriately reflected in how you frame your assessment question.

When you are writing your own assessments, begin with the learning objectives and construct assessments which best exemplify those objectives. If you are using items from a test bank, you should still confirm that you agree with the publisher's alignment of the item with the objective. Especially with new assessments, it would be useful to have a colleague look at your items and objectives to see if they agree with your alignment. One of the enduring lessons from the research on formal alignment in large-scale testing is that alignment is a tricky thing to get agreement on. So if you're having someone else look at yours, be ready for there to be disagreement, but the conversation should be valuable.

Summary

A learning objective describes the knowledge, skills, abilities, and behaviors you want students to gain from an activity, unit of instruction, or course. Your assessments, then, should demonstrate student mastery of the learning objective. Both the description and the demonstration need to be present and connected or aligned for learning to happen best.

See Also

Design Assessments First
Selected- and Constructed-Response Questions

Resources

Fink, L. D. (2005). A self-directed guide to designing courses for significant learning. Retrieved April 19, 2017 from www.deefinkandassociates.com/GuidetoCourse DesignAug05.pdf

Georgia State University. (1999). Mager's tips on instructional objectives. Adapted from R. F. Mager. (1984). *Preparing instructional objectives* (2nd ed.). Belmont, CA: David S. Lake.

3 Assessment Philosophy

What Is My Assessment Philosophy?

We all have a teaching philosophy—a framework of understandings and beliefs about what, why, and how we do what we do that we label "teaching." A subset of our teaching philosophy addresses assessment-related issues. For some of us, our teaching and assessment philosophies are well-formed, articulate, explicit, and coherent. For some of us, they are more nascent, less coherent, and implicit. Many of us have a written teaching philosophy statement, which likely also addresses assessment-related issues (cf. Kearns & Sullivan, 2011; Owens, Miller, & Grise-Owens, 2014; Schönwetter, Sokal, Friesen, & Taylor, 2002). If your written teaching philosophy statement doesn't have an assessment section, you should consider adding one.

Regardless of the state of your teaching and assessment philosophy, we encourage you to continually refine and articulate it. We want to make a clear distinction here between your teaching and assessment philosophy and your teaching and assessment philosophy *statement*. The latter is a document; the former is part of who you are that influences the choices you make moment by moment, day by day, semester by semester. Much of the guidance we've seen on preparing the document recommends that you discuss the methods you use to assess students. That is definitely important. This entry, though, is focused more on the philosophy itself, not the statement, and casts a broader view of the kinds of assessment thinking which should be a component of your philosophy. Advice on writing teaching philosophy statements often suggests you discuss the kinds of assessments you use (e.g. portfolios with rubrics) but doesn't usually suggest that you've considered issues such as whether it is possible for a student to fail a portfolio in your class.

As we stated in the **introduction***, reading and thinking about the entries in this book can certainly help you develop the assessment aspects of your teaching philosophy. These are the entries which have the greatest philosophical "load" and which, if you're working on your philosophy statement, may help you articulate it. In addition to specific entries, here are some other points for you to ponder:

- Why do you assess students? Why give grades at all?
- How are assessment and learning and teaching (inter-)related?

- Is assessing and grading solely your purview as instructor, a shared responsibility with the student(s), or solely the student's purview?
- Who are the audiences for your assessments and in what order of priority are they?
- How structured is your assessment environment? Is it highly structured and prescribed, or is it open, porous, organic?
- Does "failure" exist in your class? If so, what is it, and how will you and your students know when it has occurred?

(Frisbie & Waltman, 1992)

- What does an "A" mean in your class? A "B," etc.?

(Frisbie & Waltman, 1992)

Summary

Your assessment philosophy is a subset of your teaching philosophy and goes deeper and further than what assessment methods you use. Assessment should be an explicit, well-developed part of your teaching philosophy and of your teaching philosophy statement.

See Also

Introduction

Resources

Frisbie, D. A., & Waltman, K. K. (1992). Developing a personal grading plan. *Educational Measurement: Issues and Practice, 11*(3), 35–42.

Leach, L., Neutze, G., & Zepke, N. (2000). Learners' perceptions of assessment: Tensions between philosophy and practice. *Studies in the Education of Adults, 32*(1), 107–119.

References

Kearns, K. D., & Sullivan, C. S. (2011). Resources and practices to help graduate students and postdoctoral fellows write statements of teaching philosophy. *Advances in Physiology Education, 35*(2), 136–145.

Owens, L. W., Miller, J. J., & Grise-Owens, E. (2014). Activating a teaching philosophy in social work education: Articulation, implementation, and evaluation. *Journal of Teaching in Social Work, 34*(3), 332–345.

Schönwetter, D. J., Sokal, L., Friesen, M., & Taylor, K. L. (2002). Teaching philosophies reconsidered: A conceptual model for the development and evaluation of teaching philosophy statements. *International Journal for Academic Development, 7*(1), 83–97.

4   Assessment Plan

What Is an Assessment Plan?

An assessment plan is a map of the low- and high-stakes assessments your students will complete throughout the course. Your assessment plan, when included on or as a supplement to your course syllabus, communicates to students what you think is important for them to learn.

As you are thinking about your course assessment plan, there are several factors you will want to consider:

- How many assessments should you include?
- Why is it important to include both **formative and summative assessments*** in your assessment plan?
- What are the best formats to incorporate in your assessments?
- How much should you weight each of the various assessments?

How Many Assessments Should You Include?

Imagine your department chair informs you that your entire annual teaching evaluation will be based solely on two 15-minute classroom observations from a class you are teaching this semester. You protest to your chair and ask her to consider your entire teaching portfolio: syllabi from all classes you've taught this past year, example assessments and activities you give the students, student survey results, and your teaching philosophy statement. Evaluating your teaching based on two brief observations isn't representative of the breadth and depth of your teaching abilities. Similarly, giving students a mid-term and final exam as the only assessments by which their learning will be evaluated most likely doesn't adequately measure their learning.

There is no magic number of assessments you should include in your assessment plan. The guiding factor should be ensuring that your assignments, exams, projects, and other assessments help facilitate and evaluate the learning objectives you most want your students to learn. We suggest you map your assessments and the learning objectives evaluated by those assessments (see

align assessments to learning objectives*). Are there any learning objectives that aren't evaluated in some way? If not, why not? That gap pinpoints areas where you may want to add an assessment.

In addition to ensuring that you have a sufficient number of assessments to effectively measure your learning objectives, research also suggests that frequent testing helps improve student learning (see **quizzing frequency***). Retrieval practice is the cognitive process students engage in when accessing knowledge. When students retrieve knowledge from memory, the mental representation of that knowledge changes and becomes stronger and easier to access for students. Frequent retrieval opportunities have also been shown to improve not only recall of facts but deeper learning that includes making connections and transferring knowledge to new contexts. In this paradigm, tests are opportunities *for* learning rather than simply measures *of* learning (Paul, 2015). These tests do not have to be formal exams but rather can be more formative opportunities for students to engage in retrieval practice. Frequent assessment opportunities, particularly when combined with immediate and frequent **feedback***, are particularly effective at supporting student learning (see **feedback timing***). Additionally, Kuo and Simon (2009) found that more frequent exams are related to more positive student attitudes toward the instructor and class, lead to better attendance, and decrease student anxiety.

Why Is It Important to Include Both Formative and Summative Assessments in Your Assessment Plan?

Formative assessments allow students to practice with concepts as they are learning them in a low-stakes situation. Using the retrieval practice theory described above, frequent formative assessments force students to engage with the material in a way that helps deepen their learning. The low-stakes nature of formative assessments allow students to make mistakes, receive feedback about those mistakes, and address misconceptions without having to focus on a grade associated with their performance. Additionally, if students are only given high-stakes assessments, it is conceivable (if not likely) that many students will attempt to cram beforehand and retain little information after taking the assessment.

How you implement **formative and summative assessments*** depends on several factors, such as the content difficulty, what **prior knowledge*** your students bring into your course, and the resources you have to create, administer, and score the assessments. In general, you should give students frequent opportunities to practice applying their knowledge through ungraded formative assessments. These assessments should be complemented with multiple, low-stakes summative assessments, such as weekly quizzes. This strategy forces students to review material frequently as they prepare for each summative exam and helps them make stronger connections in their knowledge structure.

What Are the Best Formats to Incorporate in Your Assessments?

In addition to creating a plan for blending formative and summative assessments, you should also consider the best format(s) for your assessments. See **selected- and constructed-response questions*** for a thorough discussion of when it is best to use closed-ended (selected-response) or open-ended (constructed-response) questions. As with providing multiple assessment opportunities, you also should vary your assessment formats when possible. Students who perform poorly on multiple-choice exams may be able to better represent their learning when given the opportunity to complete a performance assessment. In all cases, the format of your assessment should align with your learning objectives.

How Much Should You Weight Each of the Various Assessments?

We discuss various grading strategies throughout this book (see **not everything that matters must be graded***). Overall, the weight you assign to your various assessments should correspond with their relative importance to the course. A given weight for an assessment should align with the significance of the learning objective(s) it measures.

Summary

Your assessment plan communicates to students what you think is important for them to learn. There should be a sufficient number of both formative and summative assessments to provide students ample opportunities to engage with the material. These assessments should also vary in their format, giving students multiple ways in which to demonstrate their learning. Lastly, the relative weight of each assessment should align to the importance of the learning objectives they measure.

See Also

Align Assessments to Learning Objectives
Formative and Summative Assessments
Selected- and Constructed-Response Questions

References

Kuo, T., & Simon, A. (2009). How many tests do we really need? *College Teaching, 57*(3), 156–160.

Paul, A. M. (2015, August 1). Researchers find that frequent tests can boost learning. *Scientific American*. Retrieved July 8, 2017 from www.scientificamerican.com/article/researchers-find-that-frequent-tests-can-boost-learning/

5   Attendance

Recommendation: Strongly encourage, but do not grade, attendance.

Attendance is a very important learning behavior (Credé, Roch, & Kieszc-zynka, 2010). You should encourage it (Moore, 2003). You can even require it as a non-negotiable (like wearing clothing to class). *But don't pay for it with points or grades.* Not everything that is important is graded, and what is graded are not the only important things (see **assessment plan*** and **not everything that matters must be graded***).

Instructors' experience and "common sense" are often at odds with the empirical research findings or with relevant theoretical frameworks regarding attendance. Just because others grade attendance doesn't mean you should. (A study of syllabi showed that class attendance was graded on 15.7% of syllabi studied, accounting for an average of 15% of the course grade (Parkes, Fix, & Harris, 2003)). Student attendance strongly correlates with academic achievement but mandatory attendance policies "appear to have a small positive impact on average grades" (Credé, Roch, & Kieszc-zynka, 2010, p. 272).

Attendance is a means to an end but not the end. Mastering learning objectives and contributing to the learning environment are the ends. Attendance is at best a proxy for other issues like **participation***. If you want participation, grade participation. Attendance does not align to any of your learning objectives in your courses, so why does it contribute to a student's grade?

While many of the reasons why students skip class are beyond the instructor's control, do what you *can* do. Make your classes worth attending. Have them be valuable learning experiences with activities and formative assessments (see **formative and summative assessments***) which engage students in the learning process. Make slides and presentation materials available before class (Babb & Ross, 2009). Make sure your assessments are aligned with what happens in class—meaningfully! (Do *not* put the "What color shirt did I wear to class last Tuesday?" question on a quiz or test!!!) Make sure students understand (Moore, 2005) that decades (e.g. Harris, 1940) of research show that attendance correlates with higher course grades (Credé, Roch, & Kieszczynka, 2010). Save yourself and your students all the logistical hassle of taking, recording, and haggling over attendance.

See Also

Assessment Plan
Not Everything That Matters Must Be Graded
Participation

Resources

Credé, M., Roch, S. G., & Kieszczynka, U. M. (2010). Class attendance in college: A meta-analytic review of the relationship of class attendance with grades and student characteristics. *Review of Educational Research, 80*(2), 272–295.

Moore, R. (2003). Helping students succeed in introductory biology classes: Does improving students' attendance also improve their grades? *Bioscene, 29*(3), 17–25.

Moore, R. (2005). Attendance: Are penalties more effective than rewards? *Journal of Developmental Education, 29*(2), 26–32.

References

Babb, K. A., & Ross, C. (2009). The timing of online lecture slide availability and its effect on attendance, participation, and exam performance. *Computers and Education, 52,* 868–881.

Credé, M., Roch, S. G., & Kieszczynka, U. M. (2010). Class attendance in college: A meta-analytic review of the relationship of class attendance with grades and student characteristics. *Review of Educational Research, 80*(2), 272–295.

Harris, D. (1940). Factors affecting college grades: A review of the literature 1930–1937. *Psychological Bulletin, 37*(3), 125–166.

Moore, R. (2003). Helping students succeed in introductory biology classes: Does improving students' attendance also improve their grades? *Bioscene, 29*(3), 17–25.

Moore, R. (2005). Attendance: Are penalties more effective than rewards? *Journal of Developmental Education, 29*(2), 26–32.

Parkes, J., Fix, T. K., & Harris, M. B. (2003). What syllabi communicate about assessment in college classrooms. *Journal on Excellence in College Teaching, 14*(1), 61–83.

6 Beneficence

What Is Beneficence?

Beneficence is not the latest Disney princess, rather, it is the concept that anything we do as educators should be done for the good and the welfare of students. This is a particularly important ethical principle in assessment because assessment situations often bring the ethical weighing and balancing into stark relief. It is also important to understand where the boundaries of beneficence are and what beneficence is not.

In differentiating "good" from "harm," we must further distinguish between what students like and enjoy and what promotes their learning. Your students do not enjoy studying for and taking quizzes, but they might acknowledge that doing so aids their learning. For us, promoting learning is the sine qua non of academic good or welfare. A close second for us is that scores and grades represent mastery of the course learning objectives and little else. The American Association of University Professors' (2009) *Statement of Professional Ethics* reads, in part, "Professors make every reasonable effort to . . . ensure that their evaluations of students reflect each student's true merit."

Academic Beneficence

We are also focused here on academic beneficence, that is, actions which promote the students' academic good and academic welfare. We are instructors, not our students' parents, friends, or therapists. Our job is to see that their education is maximized. We must at times acknowledge that a student's academic welfare and her general welfare are at odds. A student's diagnosis of mononucleosis mid-semester is something that an individual course instructor does not have good tools to address. The institution likely has medical leave or withdrawal policies which would suit that need better. It is not beneficent of us to try to address a several-weeks' absence within our course, even with an incomplete (see **incomplete grades***), though we could point the student to those at the school who could advise on those other mechanisms. It is critical that we are able to articulate explicitly for ourselves and for our students that, although we clearly recognize that general welfare takes precedence over academic welfare, we are responsible to them, to ourselves, and to our institution to make academic welfare decisions only.

Beneficence as a Continuum

The welfare of the student is a continuum. At one end of the continuum is maleficence, doing something with the intention of doing harm to a student. The punitive pop quiz (see **pop quizzes***) or mean-spirited comments on student work likely fall here. So do clearly unethical actions like deliberately falsifying students' grades or assigning a lower score because you don't like a student.

In the middle of the continuum is non-maleficence: "do no harm." This isn't really appropriate in teaching either. None of our students should leave our tutelage having gained nothing. The morality of teaching demands that they be better for having studied with us.

Beyond these on the continuum is beneficence, improving the good and welfare of our students. Being treated beneficently is a right of each and every student and not a privilege. It is not something that can be lost by the student or withdrawn by you.

What Is Beneficent Assessment?

So what constitutes beneficent assessment? Promoting student learning is a principle we often use. Are you assessing and grading in such a way as to promote student learning? Many of the other topics in this book expand on assessment and grading that promotes student learning, e.g. **mastery opportunities***, **learning-oriented assessment***, and **feedback***, and which we would judge as beneficent assessment practice.

Beneficent assessment also includes striving to have scores and grades represent only mastery of course learning objectives (see **align assessments to learning objectives***). It is ethically wrong to score a student down because of an off-hand comment they made about your wardrobe. It is equally ethically wrong to score them better than their performance deserved because they complimented you on your wardrobe. Giving a student credit for a response on a test because, even though their answer was lousy, you "know they know it" is not beneficent. Similarly, sometimes we assess because we need to certify competence to students, ourselves, and others, like the public at large. The public expects civil engineering programs to graduate only students who can design a bridge that won't fall down.

What Is NOT Beneficent Assessment?

It is not beneficent to do something purely because the students will like it or think better of you for it. There must (also) be some good imparted to students thereby. You are not the Candy Man or a Fairy Godmother dispensing treats and gifts. It is not doing a student good to artificially inflate a grade, provide additional testing time without rationale, or dispense **extra credit***.

That is ultimately a harm because their transcript indicates that they have mastered material which they have not. Their bridge could fall down.

Here is a less extreme example which by its ordinariness demonstrates how often college teachers need to navigate these ethical waters.

On the first paper of the semester, Maria did not get as high a grade as she wanted. She comes to your office hours to explain that she had planned plenty of time to work on the paper the week before it was due, but her toddler nephew got really sick, and she had to assist her brother and sister-in-law with caring for him. It was really scary; he visited the emergency room twice in three days. Is there anything she can do?

Not one of us fails to see the humanity in Maria's situation. She seems like a wonderful aunt and sister. This is just college, after all, not "real life." Could I just deploy my professional judgment, be understanding, and change her grade?

We also see the humanity here and agree that Maria seems like a wonderful aunt and sister. But changing her grade is not beneficent, it is not for her *academic* good. It does not promote her learning. It makes her and you feel good about the situation but it is not beneficent.

If this situation, or one a lot like it, hasn't already happened to you, it will. We suggest that prevention here is worth much. What if you provided mastery opportunities to all of your students so that, after your initial grade, they could rewrite the work? There are lots of ways to structure this (see **mastery opportunities***), but such a policy would not only promote learning but it would also provide a place for life to happen to students and their learning not to suffer. Such a policy would be beneficent and fair (see **fairness***).

Summary

In conclusion, beneficence is working for students' academic good and welfare, and is something we should always do. It does not mean dispensing treats or gifts, however. Doing what students like is not always the same as doing what promotes their welfare. Sometimes we also have to distinguish between academic welfare and general welfare and act from the former.

See Also

Effort
Fairness
Learning-Oriented Assessment

Resource

Knapp, C. (2007). Assessing grading. *Public Affairs Quarterly*, *21*(3), 275–294.

Reference

The American Association of University Professors. (2009). Statement of professional ethics. Retrieved January 4, 2017 from www.aaup.org/report/statement-professional-ethics

7   Borderline Grade Cases

Recommendation: Have a rule or policy for determining borderline cases and stick to it consistently. Determine an error threshold for your grading scale for which you will award the next highest course grade (this could be none at all!) and clearly state your borderline case policy in your syllabus.

How Do You Handle Awarding Grades to Students Just Below the Borderline?

One of the elements you most likely include in your syllabus is your grading policies. Depending on the grading guidelines at your institution, you use either an unfractionated (A, B, C, D, F) or fractionated (A, A−, B+, B, etc.) approach. Suppose your institution uses the unfractionated grading scale (A–F). Your course has 1,000 possible points that students can earn with the following grading scale:

    900–1,000 = A
    800–899 = B
    700–799 = C
    600–699 = D
    599 or less = F

You use a criterion-referenced grading approach (see **criterion-referenced grading approaches***) in that your grades represent how well students have mastered the course learning objectives (see **align assessments to learning objectives***) and any number of students can earn an A, B, etc. Invariably, you will encounter a borderline case when a student is right on the edge of receiving the next highest letter grade in the course. What do you do with the student who earns 898 points and should be given a B? Is she qualitatively different than the student who earns 901 points and receives an A?

You can certainly stick consistently to your stated cutoffs. If you are providing lots of support to students through study guides, study sessions, office hours, **mastery opportunities*** or offering comments on drafts of papers, you can argue that students have already had lots of opportunities to maximize their grades and so further adjustment is unwarranted.

No assessment is perfect, and no assessment score is completely free of error, so a relatively small distance between a student's score and the grade cutoff could be due to measurement error. This effect is magnified if you are using only a few assessments in a course. Conversely, with relatively many assessments contributing to the course grade, the measurement error, though cumulative, likely has less of an overall impact on the accuracy of the course grade.

Despite those considerations, you may still decide you want to review students who are within some number of points, say 5 points, of the next highest grade (895–899, 795–799, etc.). But what additional information will you examine to help make decisions about these borderline cases? We recommend in the **effort*** and **participation*** entries that you should *not* include these as part of a student's grade, especially on an ad hoc, case-by-case basis. We also recommend that you do not use **extra credit***. So what elements can you consider for borderline cases that still maintain **fairness*** to all the students in the course? Considering fairness issues, the most defensible course of action is not to review these cases. Either decide that you will not bump up the grade for borderline students or decide on some threshold (for example, 5 points from the cutoff). While you certainly strive to ensure that your assessments are well-constructed and that you have clear and well-articulated criteria in your scoring **rubrics***, we know that there will be some error in measuring your students' learning. If you allow for an error threshold (5 points out of 1,000 is 0.5%!) and award the higher grade to students within that threshold students will see this as beneficent (see **beneficence***), if not fair and equitable, treatment. Whatever decision you make about borderline cases you should have a clear policy in your syllabus about how these cases will be handled.

Summary

Each term, many instructors have to deal with borderline cases where a student is just below the cutoff for the next highest grade. The most defensible and fairest way to handle borderline cases is to determine an error threshold below each grade cutoff for which you will award the higher grade. Clearly state that policy in your syllabus and do not agree to review borderline cases on an ad hoc basis or outside of your stated policy.

See Also

Assessment Philosophy
Criterion-Referenced Grading Approaches
Fairness

Resource

Svinicki, M., & McKeachie, W. J. (2011). The ABCs of assigning grades. In *McKeachie's teaching tips: Strategies, research, and theory for college and university teachers* (13th ed. pp. 125–128). Belmont, CA: Wadsworth, Cengage.

8   Cheat Sheets or Crib Sheets

Recommendation: While the empirical evidence is inconclusive, as educational psychologists we'll side with the learning theories which suggest that having students (re)process course material into a cheat sheet should have some benefits for student learning. Feel free to use them as appropriate to your learning objectives (see **align assessments to learning objectives***).

A "cheat sheet" or "crib sheet" is material constructed by the student specifically to be used during an in-class examination. It shares some similarities and overlapping issues with **open-book exams*** and **take-home exams***.

Aren't Cheat Sheets a Crutch?

Larwin, Gorman, and Larwin (2013) conducted a meta-analysis of 15 effect sizes comparing "student-prepared testing aids" to closed-book exam conditions. They found that, indeed, students do better with a cheat sheet than a closed-book condition across the studies they examined (mean effect size, d, of +0.402). That's not really the issue. The issue is *why* do students do better with cheat sheets? Do they bring answers into the testing room, or does it aid their reasoning during the test? Is it the learning accrued through the process of constructing the cheat sheet? Is it the anxiety reduction that comes from the "security blanket" of the cheat sheet? Most of those effects are actually good.

Another important consideration is the learning objectives you're trying to assess. Does the cheat sheet hinder your ability to know whether students have mastered the learning objectives, does it heighten your ability, or is their impact neutral? You have to work that through carefully with your students and your learning objectives.

In Favor of Cheat Sheets

The literature reviewed by Larwin, Gorman, and Larwin (2013) suggests several potential benefits of cheat sheets, including increased student engagement with the content and reduced test anxiety (see **evaluation anxiety***). Whether cheat sheets encourage or discourage good studying behavior is contended, according to Larwin, Gorman, and Larwin (2013).

Students do seem to like the cheat sheets; however, student perception of how they will do with or without a cheat sheet is unrelated to their actual performance (Matthew, 2012).

Considerations in Cheat Sheets

While the empirical evidence is inconclusive, as educational psychologists we'll side with the learning theories which suggest that having students (re)process course material into a cheat sheet should have some benefits for student learning. The degree to which it heightens learning versus giving away answers depends to some extent on the kinds of questions you're asking on your examination.

If you use cheat sheets, give your students guidance about how you expect them to use them on the exam and what kinds of things should be on their cheat sheet. When Jay teaches statistics, he tells students that they need not bother writing formulae on their cheat sheets since, if they need a formula, he will provide it to them. This is because he's more interested in whether they know how to use the formulae and how to interpret the results than he is in them memorizing them.

Summary

Cheat sheets probably provide learning and test anxiety benefits to students on exams. The kinds of questions you ask on the test matter in terms of whether cheat sheets are ultimately appropriate or not in your classes. How you talk with your students about them may also impact their effects.

See Also

Open-Book Exams
Take-Home Exams

Resource

Erbe, B. (2007). Reducing test anxiety while increasing learning: The cheat sheet. *College Teaching, 55*(3), 96–98.

References

Larwin, K. H., Gorman, J., & Larwin, D. A. (2013). Assessing the impact of testing aids on post-secondary student performance: A meta-analytic investigation. *Educational Psychology Review, 25*(3), 429–443.
Matthew, N. (2012, March). Student preferences and performance: A comparison of open-book, closed book, and cheat sheet exam types. *Proceedings of the National Conference on Undergraduate Research*, Ogden, UT.

9 Cheating and Plagiarism

Let's begin with some fundamentals: students cheat. They cheat in your class. Cheating and plagiarism are voluminous and multifaceted topics well beyond the scope of this book. In fact, there are book-length treatments of each (e.g. Carroll, 2013; Cizek, 1999; Lang, 2013; McCabe, Butterfield, & Trevino, 2012; Velliaris, 2016). We wish to address just a few aspects about cheating: what is cheating, the conceptual frameworks you might adopt when thinking about cheating, prevention strategies, and responses to cheating.

What Is Cheating?

You need to have your own definitions of what cheating and plagiarism are in your classes, and you need to be explicit with yourself and your students what those definitions are. For our purposes, cheating is a student's unauthorized departure from the rules and expectations for completing an assessment. Plagiarism is a particular form of cheating. At its heart, plagiarism is representing the work of another as one's own, which is a deceptively simple definition. Plagiarism can be everything from buying a paper for a course from an online "paper mill," to copying from a classmate, to patchwriting (e.g. Jamieson, 2016). Note that our definitions do not presume motive or even awareness that they have departed from the rules and expectations.

Instructors and students in and from varying cultures, disciplines, geographies, etc., will come to a class with different inherent and learned rules and expectations and definitions of what constitutes violations of rules, expectations, and definitions. Words like *collaboration, plagiarism,* and *peer learning* mean different things to different people. See Simpson (2016) as an example.

The social construction of cheating (and plagiarism) is a fascinating topic, but we will cut to the chase. In your class, you are responsible for having, or co-constructing with your students, definitions of what the rules and expectations are in your class. As you (and your students) establish those expectations you must consult your institution's policies and guidelines. Your institution has an honor code or a student conduct policy; it probably has definitions of academic dishonesty, cheating, plagiarism, etc.; and it likely spells out procedures for addressing violations.

Conceptual Frameworks for Thinking About Cheating

In our work with college instructors, we see two predominant approaches to cheating. There's the "crime and punishment" approach and the "educator" approach. That is perhaps oversimplifying but we find these classifications useful. We need to be clear—cheating is wrong. It harms the individual student, the other students in your class, you, the institution, and society. These approaches completely agree on that point.

> *Crime-and-Punishment Approach*—This approach views cheating as a moral, ethical, and quasi-legal infraction. Cheating students are criminals who knowingly violated the rules to gain an academic advantage. The instructor's role is to be a detective (Scanlon, 2003), that is, to patrol, to detect cheating, to apprehend the perpetrator and the evidence, to impose a sentence, and to record the infraction with the authorities. See Fendler and Godbey (2016).
>
> *Educator Approach*—This approach views cheating as confusion about socially constructed norms and expectations. The cheating students are learners in need of further learning about the expectations. The instructor's role is to be an educator (Scanlon, 2003), that is, to watch for opportunities to reteach the expectations.

McCabe, Butterfield, and Trevino (2012) prefer a "culture of integrity," which acknowledges that some aspects of both are necessary. There is to be an aspiration of integrity backed up by accountability for students who engage in unethical behavior.

Preventing Cheating

Perhaps the most important way you can prevent cheating incidents in your courses is to communicate very explicitly and frequently with your students what your expectations are. If you want to go so far as to have them co-construct those expectations, that's a fine thing to do. Make sure you talk about important issues like collaboration—should students work together on homework or not?—and when and how to cite sources, etc. Jay explicitly tells students, and includes it in the syllabus and on the assignment sheets, that students may work together on homework assignments but they must individually construct their final responses. No group-constructed or group-submitted assignments will be accepted.

Have clear, written statements in your syllabus regarding definitions and penalties. Point to the broader institutional policies.

The more, and more varied, assessments you can include in the final course grade (see **assessment plan***), the less pressure there is for the student to cheat on any given one (McKeachie & Svinicki, 2013).

Design sound, engaging assessments (Cizek, 1999). Obviously, it's harder to cheat on an essay exam than a multiple-choice test—in class anyway. Require connections between students' personal experiences and the learning objectives in writing assignments when it makes sense to do so. This makes it harder for students to appropriate others' writing and still have completed the assignment.

Take common-sense precautions during an examination or with an assignment (Cizek, 1999). Actively proctor; move around the room. Spread students out, or turn their seats, so they have a harder time seeing each other's exams (McKeachie & Svinicki, 2013). Have multiple forms of the exam so that students are unaided by seeing a neighbor's test (see **test security***). Use, and teach students to use, plagiarism checker software. Online assessments present different challenges related to cheating. For a further discussion of these issues see the **online assessment and authentication*** and **online test security*** entries.

Responding to Cheating

Know ahead of time how you will respond during an examination if you suspect a student is cheating. What institutional policies bear on your response and what do they say? Do you interrupt the student's work or not? Do you speak to them at their seat, or ask them into the hallway? What will you say? What will you ask them? Thinking through these questions before an incident will help you manage your emotions during an incident (Lang, 2013).

How aggressively will you seek to detect cheating or plagiarism above and beyond the "common-sense" minimums above? For example, will you use some cheating detection software or application (Cizek & Wollack, 2016) or plagiarism detection software?

Be consistent in your application of consequences with different students, and think carefully about **beneficence***; that is, "letting a student off" may not be the best way to serve their academic welfare. What consequences will you use? Will you be progressive—warning the first time, loss of points the second time, etc.? These should be stated on your syllabus.

Some institutions have clerical central structures in which instructors can report infractions, and the central structure's main purpose is to address repeat offenses across multiple instructors. McCabe, Butterfield, and Trevino (2012) make it clear that, after you've addressed an incidence of cheating with the student, regardless of how you've addressed it, you should report it to the appropriate central university authority. Doing so is seldom a punishment in and of itself, so don't make it one (e.g. "If you accept an F on this assignment, I won't further turn you in to the Dean of Students"), something McCabe, Butterfield, and Trevino find unethical.

Other institutions have judicial central structures in which the accusation of cheating is to be adjudicated with the instructor bearing the burden of proof. Instructors inside judicial systems can feel that the efforts to pursue a cheating occurrence are not worth the trouble.

We advise that you know which kind of system your institution has, and that you consider when and how you'll engage that system well before you have an issue. We certainly understand the viewpoint that pursuing cheating centrally is a burden on you. We also know that research suggests that making an impression on first offenders is an important deterrent (Lang, 2013), and we think McCabe, Butterfield, and Trevino's argument is well worth your consideration.

Lang (2013, pp. 213–215) presents four objectives that any response to cheating should meet: 1) the response should be commensurate with the severity of the infraction; 2) the response should provide flexibility to differentiate between first-time and repeat offenders; 3) the response should contribute to a student's learning; and 4) the response should reduce bureaucracy.

Summary

As the instructor, you have the obligation to define cheating and plagiarism specifically in your courses and in a way that is consistent with your institution's policies. You also need to do most of your thinking about cheating prior to students' having an opportunity to cheat in your course so that you can engage prevention and communication strategies and predetermine responses and consequences. There's little as unpleasant in college teaching as being caught off guard by students cheating.

See Also

Equity
Online Assessment and Authentication
Online Test Security
Test Security

Resources

Carroll, J. (2013). *Handbook for deterring plagiarism in higher education* (2nd ed.). Oxford Brookes University, UK: Oxford Center for Staff and Learning Development.

Lang, J. M. (2013). *Cheating lessons: Learning from academic dishonesty.* Cambridge, MA: Harvard University Press.

McCabe, D. L., Butterfield, K. D., & Trevino, L. K. (2012). *Cheating in college: Why students do it and what educators can do about it.* Baltimore, MD: Johns Hopkins University Press.

Nath, L., & Lovaglia, M. (2009). Cheating on multiple choice exams: Monitoring, assessment, and an optional assignment. *College Teaching, 57*(1), 3–8.

Shon, P. C. H. (2006). *How college students cheat on in-class examinations: Creativity, strain, and techniques of innovation.* Ann Arbor, MI: Publishing, University of Michigan Library. Retrieved from http://hdl.handle.net/2027/spo.5240451.0001.010

References

Carroll, J. (2013). *Handbook for deterring plagiarism in higher education* (2nd ed.). Oxford Brookes University, UK: Oxford Center for Staff and Learning Development.

Cizek, G. J. (1999). *Cheating on tests: How to do it, detect it, and prevent it.* New York, NY: Routledge.

Cizek, G. J., & Wollack, J. A. (Eds.). (2016). *Handbook of quantitative methods for detecting cheating on tests.* New York, NY: Taylor & Francis.

Fendler, R. J., & Godbey, J. M. (2016). Cheaters should never win: Eliminating the benefits of cheating. *Journal of Academic Ethics, 14*(1), 71–85.

Jamieson, S. (2016). Is it plagiarism or patchwriting? Toward a nuanced definition. In T. A. Bretag (Ed.), *Handbook of academic integrity* (pp. 503–518). Singapore: Springer.

Lang, J. M. (2013). *Cheating lessons: Learning from academic dishonesty.* Cambridge, MA: Harvard University Press.

McCabe, D. L., Butterfield, K. D., & Trevino, L. K. (2012). *Cheating in college: Why students do it and what educators can do about it.* Baltimore, MD: Johns Hopkins University Press.

McKeachie, W., & Svinicki, M. (2013). *McKeachie's teaching tips.* Boston, MA: Cengage Learning.

Scanlon, P. M. (2003). Student online plagiarism: How do we respond? *College Teaching, 51*(4), 161–165.

Simpson, D. (2016). Academic dishonesty: An international student perspective. *Academic Perspectives in Higher Education, 2*(1), 5.

Velliaris, D. M. (Ed.). (2016). *Handbook of research on academic misconduct in higher education.* Hershey, PA: IGI Global.

10 Collaborative Testing

It is possible to have students work together on part or all of an exam. There are several considerations and practices in doing so.

Considerations in Collaborative Testing

The major concern with collaborative testing is to what extent does working together mask what an individual student knows about the content. There have been a number of well-designed studies and some good thinking about exam logistics which should adequately address this concern.

What Are the Learning Benefits?

Those students who collaborated not only had higher test scores, but retained the knowledge better (Bloom, 2009). There are also some indirect effects worth considering, such as lower test anxiety (see **evaluation anxiety***) (LoGiudice, Pachai, & Kim, 2015; Pandey & Kapitanoff, 2011; Zimbardo, Butler, & Wolfe, 2003), elimination or reduction in cheating (see **cheating and plagiarism***) (Zimbardo, Butler, & Wolfe, 2003), higher student confidence (Zimbardo, Butler, & Wolfe, 2003), higher completion rate of assigned readings in the class (Slusser & Erickson, 2006), and better attitudes about the course (Slusser & Erickson, 2006; Zimbardo, Butler, & Wolfe, 2003).

Does This Inflate Grades?

It first depends on what you mean by "inflate." Do students receive a higher score when working collaboratively than they would working by themselves? Yes, they do, but the issue is why. "**Grade inflation***" implies an artificiality or invalidity to the higher scores. But if the scores are higher because students have better mastered the content, that's a good thing. And that seems to be what's happening (e.g. Bloom, 2009; Jensen, Johnson, & Johnson, 2002; LoGiudice, Pachai, & Kim, 2015).

Ways to Do Collaborative Testing

For collaborative testing, sometimes students work in pairs, sometimes in ad hoc groups defined for the test itself, and sometimes in pre-existing groups. Collaborative testing is a special circumstance of **groupwork***, so we incorporate all we said there here by reference.

A type of collaborative testing is called team-based learning which originated with Larry Michaelsen in the 1970s. In this approach, students are assigned to permanent small groups. Students individually take quizzes on reading assignments and then take the same quiz in their groups. Both the individual and team quizzes count as part of the course grade (Fink, 2002).

Having individual time as well as group time has direct benefits to student learning (LoGiudice, Pachai, & Kim, 2015) as well as providing a way to weight the individual and collaborative portions differentially to account for concerns over grade inflation and knowing what each student knows (e.g. Bloom, 2009). There are also means to do this in an electronic environment (e.g. Byrd, Coleman, & Werneth, 2004; Jensen, Moore, & Hatch, 2002).

Summary

There are ways to structure group testing to make it beneficial for students and still get you information about individual students' mastery.

See Also

Groupwork

Resources

LoGiudice, A. B., Pachai, A. A., & Kim, J. A. (2015). Testing together: When do students learn more through collaborative tests? *Scholarship of Teaching and Learning in Psychology*, *1*(4), 377.

Sandahl, S. S. (2009). Collaborative testing as a learning strategy in nursing education: A review of the literature. *Nursing Education Perspectives*, *30*(3), 171–175.

References

Bloom, D. (2009). Collaborative test-taking: Benefits for learning and retention. *College Teaching*, *57*(4), 216–220. DOI: 10.1080/87567550903218646

Byrd, G. G., Coleman, S., & Werneth, C. (2004). Exploring the universe together: Cooperative quizzes with and without a classroom performance system in astronomy 101. *Astronomy Education Review*, *3*(1), 26–30.

Fink, L. D. (2002). Beyond small groups: Harnessing the extraordinary power of learning teams. In L. K. Michaelsen, A. B. Knight, & L. D. Fink (Eds.), *Team-based learning: A transformative use of small groups*. Westport, CT: Praeger Publishers.

Jensen, M., Johnson, D. W., & Johnson, R. T. (2002). Impact of positive interdependence during electronic quizzes on discourse and achievement. *The Journal of Educational Research, 95*(3), 161–166.

Jensen, M., Moore, R., & Hatch, J. (2002). Cooperative learning—Part 3: Electronic cooperative quizzes. *The American Biology Teacher, 64*(3), 169–174.

LoGiudice, A. B., Pachai, A. A., & Kim, J. A. (2015). Testing together: When do students learn more through collaborative tests? *Scholarship of Teaching and Learning in Psychology, 1*(4), 377.

Pandey, C., & Kapitanoff, S. (2011). The influence of anxiety and quality of interaction on collaborative test performance. *Active Learning in Higher Education, 12*(3), 163–174.

Slusser, S. R., & Erickson, R. J. (2006). Group quizzes: An extension of the collaborative learning process. *Teaching Sociology, 34*(3), 249–262.

Zimbardo, P. G., Butler, L. D., & Wolfe, V. A. (2003). Cooperative college examinations: More gain, less pain when students share information and grades. *The Journal of Experimental Education, 71*(2), 101–125.

11 Compensatory and Conjunctive Grading

Examine carefully the gradebook entry below (Table 11.1). There are three different students in the same class, each of whom earns 425 (85%) of the points available in the course.

These grades were arrived at using an extremely common approach where each assessment has a total number of points. The points an individual student earns on each assessment are then summed and divided by the total number of points possible and multiplied by 100 to arrive at a percentage of total possible points earned by each student in the entire course. All three women earned 425 out of 500 possible points, which is 85%. Using a fairly standard scale for assigning course grades (F < 60%; D = 60–69%; C = 70–79%; B = 80–89%; A = 90–100%), all three would earn a B.

Presuming that the assessments align largely to different learning objectives (see **align assessments to learning objectives***) (with some overlap, of course), would you say that all three women equally mastered every learning objective? No, they didn't. Juanita seems to do much better on papers than Sandra does, although Sandra seems to be the best test-taker of the three. Astrid shows steady improvement throughout the semester. So should they have the same final grade?

Table 11.1 Example Gradebook Entry

Assessments	Points Allotted	Juanita	Sandra	Astrid
Quiz 1	33	27	29	20
Paper 1	100	95	75	80
Quiz 2	33	26	30	23
Quiz 3	33	30	32	28
Paper 2	100	97	77	90
Final Exam	200	150	182	184
Total	500	425	425	425
Percent		85	85	85
Course Grade		B	B	B

This method of grading is called *compensatory grading*. It is so labeled because performance in one area can compensate for performance in other areas. Sandra's test-taking skills have compensated for her poorer writing ability and vice versa for Juanita. And Astrid's mastery of learning objectives which occurred later in the course has compensated for her lack of equal mastery on the early learning objectives. Compensatory grading also lets students who are doing very well on early assessments perhaps back off on their efforts late in the semester (Lluka & Chunduri, 2015).

But what if those early learning objectives were really critical; mastery of them is essential. What if the instructor here concluded that students simply could not pass this course unless they mastered those early learning objectives? Similarly, what if this is a freshman-level course at an institution with a strong emphasis on writing so that a student could not pass a class without passing the writing assignments in the class? Then this compensatory approach would not meet those goals. But a *conjunctive grading* system would.

In a conjunctive grading system, students must achieve a certain score on *each graded activity*, not across graded activities as with a compensatory system. In a conjunctive system, the overall course grade would be determined through a more complex metric. One possibility would be to assign letter grades to each piece of graded work based on the scale above and then articulate some decision rules:

A = 90% or better on each assessment
B = 80% or better on each assessment
C = 70% or better on each assessment
D = 60% or better on each assessment
F = less than 60% or better on each assessment

Refer to Table 11.2 for an example of how conjunctive grading might look in a gradebook entry.

Whereas the compensatory system overemphasized the better performances, this conjunctive system overemphasizes the poorer performances.

Table 11.2 Gradebook Entry Illustrating Conjunctive Grading

Assessments	Points Allotted	Juanita	Sandra	Astrid
Quiz 1	33	27 (82% B)	29 (88% B)	20 (61% D)
Paper 1	100	95 (95% A)	75 (75% C)	80 (80% B)
Quiz 2	33	26 (79% C)	30 (91% A)	23 (70% C)
Quiz 3	33	30 (91% A)	32 (97% A)	28 (85% B)
Paper 2	100	97 (97% A)	77 (77% C)	90 (90%) A
Final Exam	200	150 (75% C)	182 (91% A)	184 (92% A)
Total		425	425	425
Course Grade		C	C	D

The compensatory system doesn't hold Astrid accountable for mastery of the early learning objectives nor does it encourage Sandra to work on her writing. But the conjunctive system seems to overly penalize them for those faults, too.

One approach to balance these two approaches would be a blend of the two. Suppose the grading rule was that a student had to have an average across all assessments of 90% or better AND to have a 90% or better on each assessment to earn an A. If a student had an average of 90% or better but did not have an A on each assessment, they would earn a B+.

Another variation on the blend would be to combine some assessments, for example, the papers for the situation where the department is focusing on writing. So the rule might be in order to earn an A, students must have an average total of 90% or above AND an average of 90% or above on the two papers.

A third option is not to make every letter grade conjunctive, but make passing the course conjunctive. For example, letter grades A through D would be based on the overall average AND the condition that on none of the assessments could a student have earned less than 60%. In other words, in order to pass the class, a student must pass each assessment.

A conjunctive system strongly communicates to students—and anyone else—that each assessment matters and each learning objective matters. If that is so, another way to lessen the contingencies would be to permit **mastery opportunities*** for students on the assessments. For example, perhaps the quizzes are administered through an online course management system, and you permit students to take them multiple times. Or perhaps students are able to do rewrites on papers to show additional mastery. These kinds of procedures in combination with conjunctive grading send a very strong message to students about how important mastery is.

Neither approach is inherently right or wrong, better or worse. Both represent different philosophies and realities (Hofstee, 1983). We've been touting conjunctive mainly because we suspect you've not heard of it before. But compensatory systems do work and work well.

Using Conjunctive Scoring on Individual Assessments

Even if you don't adopt conjunctive grading for arriving at your final course grades, you might still find it useful for certain individual assignments. Imagine that you require students to complete a paper for your course, and that you use a rubric (see **rubrics***) that looks like this to score them (see Table 11.3).

These are *very* common. Usually, the total score is derived as a sum of the different categories. When scored this way, though, strong style conventions could compensate for poor subject knowledge. If scored conjunctively, however, in order to earn an "Acceptable" on this paper, all categories must be scored "Acceptable." Or the blended approach could be used to emphasize

Table 11.3 Example Conjunctive Scoring Rubric

	Expert	Acceptable	Needs Improvement	Points
Subject Knowledge	5	3	1	
Organization	5	3	1	
Style Conventions	5	3	1	
Total				/15

style conventions, for example. In order to receive an "Acceptable" on this paper, subject knowledge and organization must be at least "Acceptable" and style conventions must be "Expert."

Incorporating a Conjunctive System Into Your Classes

Putting a conjunctive system in place will take a great deal of thinking, planning, and communicating on your part (Lluka & Chunduri, 2015). You will need to make sure you know why you're doing it, what advantages it has for your students, and that you're committed to it. No changing your mind half-way through the semester!

Work out your grading system in detail before the semester starts. Where will the minimums be? How will you handle situations where all but one minimum has been met? What supports, mastery opportunities, and drafting options will you provide?

Make sure your syllabus (for a grading system) and the rubrics and assignments (for a scoring system) are very clear for students. Communicate early and often with students so they clearly understand how to strategize for this system.

Lluka and Chunduri (2015) describe in detail how they have implemented a conjunctive approach they call the Grading Matrix Assessment Approach in a biology class.

Summary

Compensatory systems are definitely the norm and what most faculty and students expect as the default. You may have good, sound rationale for considering conjunctive scoring and/or grading in your courses, though.

See Also

Assessment Philosophy
Mastery Opportunities

Resource

Chester, M. D. (2003). Multiple measures and high-stakes decisions: A framework for combining measures. *Educational Measurement: Issues and Practice, 22*(2), 33–41.

References

Hofstee, W. K. (1983). The case for compromise in educational selection and grading. In S. B. Anderson & J. S. Helmick (Eds.), *On educational testing.* San Francisco, CA: Jossey-Bass.

Lluka, L., & Chunduri, P. (2015). A grading matrix assessment approach to align student performance to Threshold Learning Outcomes (TLOs) in a large first year biology class. *The International Journal of the First Year in Higher Education, 6*(1), 49–60. DOI: 10.5204/intjfyhe.v6i1.262

12 Contract Grading and Learning Contracts

Recommendation: Do not use contract grading. Learning contracts, however, can be done appropriately and well. Treating your syllabus as a contract also has some merit.

There is some ambiguity in the literature regarding the terms "contract learning," "learning contract," and "contract grading." They are at times used interchangeably. We will strive to be clear about what we see as the critical distinctions for you and your students. As you engage this literature yourself, look carefully not at the label applied but at the structure of the contract.

Contract Grading

Contract grading usually refers to the practice of determining at the outset of a course what a student will need to do in order to attain each course grade (A, B, C, etc.) and then the student naming which grade they will attempt to achieve (Ware, 2011). The contract also articulates what the student and the instructor will each do toward that goal. Once each has fulfilled the contract, the student is assigned the grade.

While not universal, these components are often part of a contract grading system. Students may select from among a range of assignments to earn their grade (Lindemann & Harbke, 2011). The grade for each assessment in the contract is recorded as pass/fail with some standard (e.g. 85% on a quiz) set as the passing criterion (Lindemann & Harbke, 2011). There is usually a mastery component to each assessment in the contract so that a student has a certain number of attempts at the assessment (LeJeune, 2010; Lindemann & Harbke, 2011). Students can "recontract" throughout the semester as their goals or performance change (Polczynski & Shirland, 1977).

Instructors are drawn to contract grading because it acknowledges and makes explicit what we all know: not every student is striving for an A in the class, and not every student is going to participate (see **participation***) and engage equally. Why not declare that explicitly up front and let the student who really isn't all that interested but needs at least a C in the class know exactly how to fulfill those goals?

Contract grading has been shown to promote student effort (Polczynski & Shirland, 1977), to reduce dropping out, to increase academic performance, and to increase student ownership of their learning (Lindemann & Harbke, 2011). Be prepared, however, for student reluctance and resistance (Spidell & Thelin, 2006). There's also some evidence that contracts work differently with students of different ethnicities (Inoue, 2012).

Our main concern is that the distinction between grade levels (i.e. what it takes to earn an A versus a B) is usually quantitative not qualitative (despite Hassencahl's (1979) advice), and thus it is really a proxy measure of **effort*** or engagement, not of mastery of the learning objectives (see **align assessments to learning objectives***). Ware (2011) provides an example where, among other activities, a student contracting for an A is to write three or four reflective journal entries per week; a student contracting for a B is to write at least two per week; and a student contracting for a C is to write at least one per week. To us, the distinction between an A and a B should rest on the degree to which the reflections represent mastery of the learning objective and not how much text each student produced. The four entries per week may actually be less evidence of mastery than one really good entry would be. Setting expectations for the number of reflections per week a student should write is something that we argue should be done separately from the grading plan (see **not everything that matters must be graded***).

Contract grading can be used for a single assignment or for an entire course. We recommend against its use for an entire course, but it might meet your needs for particular assignments.

Learning Contracts

A learning contract is a broader document which often has grading elements addressed in it (cf. Anderson, Boud, & Sampson, 1996). These can be applied to independent studies, theses hours, etc. We think there is a time and an appropriate use for learning contracts.

Learning contracts fall on a continuum from completely instructor-defined to completely student-defined (Hassencahl, 1979). Somewhere in between is the opportunity for an instructor–student negotiation, which can be a way of not only sharing responsibility for the learning with students but also of encouraging students to take the responsibility and learn how to use it (Anderson, Boud, & Sampson, 1998; Andrews, 2004). Students express what it is they want to or need to master in the domain. They identify resources and activities that will help them gain that mastery. They then express the performance criteria and the evaluation system that will be used to demonstrate they've reached mastery (Andrew, 2004). Students often appreciate the autonomy (Chyung, 2007; Ware, 2011) and feel more motivated and self-directed (Chyung, 2007).

Summary

Adopting either contract grading or learning contracts is not simply changing your model of grading. It is a total upending of much of your **assessment philosophy*** and of your students' expectations. You need to work through all of the implications of adopting either and be ready to buy them lock, stock, and barrel for them to work well. Your students will balk, so be ready to work them through it (Litterio, 2016; Spidell & Thelin, 2006).

In an even broader sense, there's a degree to which your syllabus serves as a "contract" (Parkes & Harris, 2002) which articulates how grades in the course will be determined, etc. We also think including your **assessment plan*** and other assessment-related policies in your syllabus is a great idea.

Resources

LeJeune, N. (2010). Contract grading with mastery learning in CS 1. *Journal of Computing Sciences in Colleges*, *26*(2), 149–156.

Ware, M. C. (2011). Insuring self-direction and flexibility in distance learning for adults: Using contracts. In *Encyclopedia of information communication technologies and adult education integration* (pp. 322–336). IGI Global.

References

Anderson, G., Boud, D., & Sampson, J. (1996). *Learning contracts*. New York, NY: Psychology Press.

Anderson, G., Boud, D., & Sampson, J. (1998). Qualities of learning contracts. In J. Stephenson & M. Yorke (Eds.), *Capability and quality in higher education* (pp. 162–173). New York, NY: Routledge.

Andrews, B. W. (2004). Musical contracts: Fostering student participation in the instructional process. *International Journal of Music Education*, *22*(3), 219–229.

Chyung, S. Y. (2007). Invisible motivation of online adult learners during contract learning. *Journal of Educators Online*, *4*(1), n1.

Hassencahl, F. (1979). Contract grading in the classroom. *Improving College and University Teaching*, *27*(1), 30–33.

Inoue, A. B. (2012). Grading contracts: Assessing their effectiveness on different racial formations. In A. B. Inoue & M. Poe (Eds.), *Race and writing assessment* (pp. 78–94). New York, NY: Peter Lang.

LeJeune, N. (2010). Contract grading with mastery learning in CS 1. *Journal of Computing Sciences in Colleges*, *26*(2), 149–156.

Lindemann, D. F., & Harbke, C. R. (2011). Use of contract grading to improve grades among college freshmen in introductory psychology. *Sage Open*, DOI: 10.1177/2158244011434103

Litterio, L. M. (2016). Contract grading in a technical writing classroom: A case study. *Journal of Writing Assessment*, *9*(2).

Parkes, J., & Harris, M. B. (2002). The purposes of a syllabus. *College Teaching*, *50*(2), 55–61.

Polczynski, J. J., & Shirland, L. E. (1977). Expectancy theory and contract grading combined as an effective motivational force for college students. *The Journal of Educational Research*, *70*(5), 238–241.

Spidell, C., & Thelin, W. H. (2006). Not ready to let go: A study of resistance to grading contracts. *Composition Studies, 34*(1), 35–68.

Ware, M. C. (2011). Insuring self-direction and flexibility in distance learning for adults: Using contracts. In *Encyclopedia of information communication technologies and adult education integration* (pp. 322–336). IGI Global.

13 Criterion-Referenced Grading Approaches

Recommendation: Criterion-referenced grading is preferred to **norm-referenced grading approaches*** in college courses because grades are awarded based on how well a student's performance compares to an established standard.

What Is Criterion-Referenced Grading?

In criterion-referenced grading, also known as mastery grading, students' grades are based on a fixed scale established by the instructor before the assessment is graded. Under this grading approach, graded assignments are linked to specific course learning objectives (see **align assessments to learning objectives***), typically outlined in the course syllabus. Students are made aware of the criteria and standards by which their performance will be graded. Criterion-referenced grades have three critical characteristics:

- Any number of students can earn A's and B's.
- The focus is on learning and mastery of material.
- Final grades demonstrate what students know compared to standards set by the instructor.

Advantages

A criterion-referenced grading system outlines criteria for various grades from the beginning of the course (Svinicki, 1999). This allows students to learn from mistakes and improve their understanding and performance. The criterion-referenced grading system provides specific information about student strengths and weaknesses. Current theories of learning support the notion that most, if not all, students can master most learning objectives under the right conditions. This approach allows all students to demonstrate mastery of the skills (i.e. all students have potential to pass or earn A's). An instructor can set standards for excellence in different skills/content areas (e.g. writing, oral presentations, conceptual understanding). Since this approach is based on a set of standards, grades always mean the same thing from year to year and do not vary depending on the students in a given class. Criteria for various grade standards are known ahead of time, reducing uncertainty for students. Finally, criterion-referenced grading approaches focus on individual reward structures that can foster motivation to learn to a greater extent than other grading approaches (Snowman & Biehler, 1997).

Disadvantages

In criterion-referenced grading, the rationale for the grade cutoffs can be unclear. Additionally, instructors can find it challenging to create valid, reliable exams and assignments that maintain the same level of difficulty throughout the course. This could lead to some students earning a high number of points simply by doing well on many small, less essential assignments (Center for Teaching and Learning—University of North Carolina, 1991). (See also **compensatory and conjunctive grading*.**) Using the criterion-referenced grading approach there is no way to rank students and it does not adjust for difficulty variations across sections or semesters. Many students may meet given criteria levels and therefore have the same grade. Finally, this system does not provide "selection" information about who the "best" students are, only that certain students have reached specified levels (Svinicki, 1999).

Developmental Method of Criterion-Referenced Grading

Developmental grading might be the most complex kind of criterion-referenced grading because the method attempts to equate grades with different *kinds* of performance. This approach focuses on the learning objectives inherent in the assessment by considering not only the amount of material students learn but also how cognitively complex the material is. To use developmental grading, the instructor must first identify the *implicit* knowledge and skills embedded in the course materials and assessments and make them *explicit* as learning objectives (Center for Teaching and Learning—University of North Carolina, 1991).

Summary

In criterion-referenced grading, instructors do not predetermine the distribution of student performance. The final grade distribution may contain many or very few A's and B's. Ultimately, grades are decided by comparing each student's performance to established criteria, not against their peers. In very large-enrollment courses, particularly those that are introductory courses, criterion-referenced grades may appear normally distributed. However, the criterion-referenced grading approach still allows for all students to attain A's should their performance demonstrate they have met those standards. Given that criterion-referenced grading compares student performance against the important learning objectives in the course, this is often the more appropriate grading option (Enerson & Plank, 1997).

See Also

Compensatory and Conjunctive Grading
Norm-Referenced Grading Approaches

References

Center for Teaching and Learning—University of North Carolina. (1991). Grading systems. Retrieved from http://ctl.unc.edu/fyc10.html

Enerson, D. M., & Plank, K. M. (1997). The Penn State teacher II, chapter IV: Measuring and evaluating student learning. Retrieved from www.psu.edu/idp_celt/PST/PSTchapter4.html

Snowman, J., & Biehler, R. (1997). *Psychology applied to teaching, chapter 12: Ways to evaluate student learning* (8th ed.). Retrieved from http://college.hmco.com/education/resources/res_project/students/tc/assess.html#5

Svinicki, M. S. (1999). Some pertinent questions about grading. Retrieved from www.utexas.edu/academic/cte/sourcebook/grading.html

14 Design Assessments First

When Designing Your Course, Why Should You Write Your Assessments First?

The Backward Design process as defined by Wiggins and McTighe (2005) has three stages:

Stage 1: Identify the desired results you would like your students to achieve. This includes defining the goals and learning objectives your students should be able to meet by the end of the course.

Stage 2: Determine what constitutes acceptable evidence that students have met the desired results. Essentially, this involves identifying the assessment evidence you need to collect for students to demonstrate their mastery of the learning objectives (see **align assessments to learning objectives***).

Stage 3: Design the instructional activities students will need to support the desired results and evidence.

Wiggins and McTighe (2005) point out that "it doesn't matter exactly where you start or how you proceed, *as long as you end up with a coherent design* reflecting the logic of the three stages" (p. 29). While course design is an iterative process that does not follow a linear path, we argue that you should consider writing your assessments first, at least the major summative assessments (see **formative and summative assessments***). These could be mid-term or final exams, final projects or performances, or other cumulative assessment activities.

We are asking you to "begin with the end in mind," to use a phrase from Stephen Covey (2004). What would you have students do at the end of your course to demonstrate they understood the course material? What kinds of questions would you ask? What grading criteria would you use in the corresponding rubric (see **rubrics***) for open-ended assessments? Even if you haven't fully articulated all of your learning goals and objectives, you have a sense of what you want your students to be able to do or know. Imagine writing the final cumulative exam or project as the first thing you do when developing your course. From that should stem the supporting assessments and instructional activities students need to be successful in the cumulative assessment. Out of those supporting assessments will come the instructional materials and activities students need in order to be able to complete those intermediary assessments. Embedded in each one of those assessments is the underlying learning objectives you are trying to measure.

Essentially, by developing your assessments first, you are designing your course to "teach to the test." We know that tests and other assessments focus students' attention and effort in terms of what they deem is important in the course. And assessments should help focus your attention as well. If a skill or concept is important and you are not measuring it in any way, then you need to revise your assessments so that it is included. If you are including questions on your assessments that are too detailed or not salient to the core objectives of the course, it should be removed from your assessments. As Robert Duke (2008) said,

> Teaching for the test is only a bad thing if the test is a dumb test. If the test really embodies what's most meaningful and important about the subject matter, then we ought to be practicing the test every day, because the test is what's most meaningful and important about the subject matter.
>
> (1:04:31)

If you design the assessments first, and then build your course around those assessments, you will be focusing your teaching, activities, and objectives in the course around the most meaningful aspects of the course.

Summary

Courses designed using the Backward Design approach include desired results, evidence that students have met those results, and activities to support achieving those results. While the design process is iterative and can start with any one of those three components, we suggest that you design your assessments first as the guiding element around which the rest of your course should be built.

See Also

Formative and Summative Assessments

Resources

Brookhart, S. M., & Nitko, A. J. (2014). *Educational assessment of students* (7th ed.). NJ: Pearson.

Wiggins, G., & McTighe, J. (2005). *Understanding by design, expanded* (2nd ed.). Alexandria, VA: Association for Supervision and Curriculum Development.

References

Covey, S. R. (2004). *The 7 habits of highly effective people.* New York, NY: Free Press.

Duke, R. (2008, April 18). Why students don't learn what we think we teach. Retrieved July 27, 2017 from www.cornell.edu/video/robert-duke-why-students-dont-learn-what-we-think-we-teach

Wiggins, G., & McTighe, J. (2005). *Understanding by design, expanded* (2nd ed.). Alexandria, VA: Association for Supervision and Curriculum Development.

15 Drop a Question

Can I Drop a Test Question?

Recommendation: Do not drop a test question. Give some, or all, students credit instead.

If you use multiple-choice questions, you no doubt have been in the situation after the test when you discover a flaw in one of the questions. Sometimes it's a simple mistake on your part such as indicating an incorrect key (right answer) during the scoring. More frequently, a student makes a good case that there is a second correct answer to the question.

There are two main issues in addressing these occurrences. First, the scores on the test really need to be correct and accurate. Getting it right is important. Second, there are consequences to anything you do (or don't do) about the issue. Choosing a solution with the best and most fair (see **fairness***) consequences is also important.

What You Should Do

Consider a four-option multiple-choice question where your answer key says A is the correct answer. The simplest kind of error is an incorrect key where the correct answer really is B. You should rescore that test question giving those who answered B credit and subtracting credit from those who answered A. "But they'll have a fit!" you say. They will understand, if you explain what happened, and they will see that your fix is the most correct and fairest thing. No, they won't like it, but they'll acknowledge it as correct.

Another common circumstance is discovering that B is just as correct as A is. In that instance, give credit to students who chose A and credit to students who chose B.

It is possible that you find a flaw in the question itself (not in the keying or in the options). It's also possible that it turns out none of the options is correct. We advocate for giving everyone credit for the item rather than deleting it. Giving "everyone" credit does not mean adding one question's worth of points to each student, however, because the students who answered

A already received credit for this question. So if you give "everyone" credit, that means students who answered B, C, or D.

So why do we advise against dropping an item?

Consequences of Dropping an Item

Let's assume you just gave a 25-question multiple-choice test. And, in order to detect the impact of different ways of addressing the problem question, let's further assume that every student missed one other question on the test other than the one we're focusing on. To make this all a little more concrete, let's look at several students' scores (see Table 15.1).

If you discard the item we're concerned about (Resolution #2 in the table), each question is now worth $1/(n-1)$, not $1/n$ points. On your 25-question test, each item would originally be worth 4 percentage points but is now worth 4.167 percentage points on your 24-question test. Juan, who answers A (what you originally thought was the right answer), loses those 0.167 points from a 96 to a 95.83. Jeanette, who answers B (what you now think is also correct), originally earns a 92 but now would receive a 95.83. So would Jordan, who answered C (which is still wrong).

Table 15.1 Illustration of Resolution Approaches for Handling a Bad Test Question

Resolution Approaches	Response to the Problematic Question	Juan	Jeanette	Jordan
		A	B	C
1. Problematic Question as Is (A Is the Key)	Total Number Right out of 25	24	23	23
	Percentage Correct	96	92	92
2. Drop the Problematic Question	Total Number Right out of 24	23	23	23
	Percentage Correct	95.83	95.83	95.83
3. Credit A and B	Total Number Right out of 25	24	24	23
	Percentage Correct	96	96	92
4. Add 1 Question to Each Student's Score ("Give Everybody Credit")	Total Number Right out of 25	25	24	24
	Percentage Correct	100	96	96
5. Give "Everyone" Credit, That Is, Those Who Answered B, C, or D	Total Number Right out of 25	24	24	24
	Percentage Correct	96	96	96

Assuming most instructors would round to the nearest whole percentage point, tossing the item would result in Juan receiving the same score most of the time (but not every time) on tests of 15 items or more. It also results in a score increase every time for Jeanette and Jordan, who answered B and C, respectively. The increase is more than 2 percentage points until there are more than 50 items on the test and never less than 1 percentage point.

If, instead of deleting the question, you give Jeanette, who answered B, credit in addition to Juan, then Juan receives a 96 on 25 items, as does Jeanette. Jordan, most correctly, stays at 92. This is Resolution #3 in the table.

So from a consequences perspective, throwing out an item does little (the rounding bobbles could be decided in the student's favor) or no harm directly to students who answered A in the first place (Juan). But it does add points to B and C students (Jeanette and Jordan) equally. Remember, you still think C is an incorrect answer. Most would view the latter specifically or the entire scenario as "unfair" to Juan and those who got the item correct in the first place. Most would also view "rewarding" C students for being wrong as a negative consequence of this approach.

This is why we advocate for a nuanced solution of keeping even a flawed item on the test but giving credit to those students who actually got the question right, Resolution #5. That has a better set of consequences for all students than getting rid of the item would. If the problem is with the question itself, or if some other issue—like you forgot to cover that content in class—means the entire question is suspect, then give everyone credit for the item; don't delete it. But giving everyone credit does not mean adding points to everyone's score (Resolution #4). Juan, who answered A already, received credit for this question so should not receive more. It means rescoring the test with any response to the item given credit. If someone failed to answer the question, they don't get credit either.

An Ounce of Prevention . . .

Heading off such scoring issues is much better than cleaning them up. Proofread your exams, or better yet, have someone else do it. Take the exam yourself, or better yet, have someone else do it.

We also strongly recommend that you conduct distractor analyses and perhaps other item analyses (e.g. Parkes & Zimmaro, 2016, chapter 6) after you've scored the exam but before you release scores to the students. This helps you detect problems and gives you time to address them before students are involved. This makes any resolutions a *fait accompli* when you share them and scores with students. This is much more palatable to students.

Summary

Take a nuanced approach to addressing a problematic test question. First, try to prevent problematic questions. But if a question proves problematic after the test, use an approach which is fair to everyone in dealing with it.

See Also

Beneficence
Fairness

Reference

Parkes, J., & Zimmaro, D. (2016). *Learning and assessing with multiple-choice questions in college classrooms.* New York, NY: Routledge.

16　Drop the Lowest Grade

Recommendation: Do not drop the lowest grade or let students choose one to drop.

Professor N. Valid gives six quizzes during the semester but only counts the highest five scores in computing the final course grade. Doing so rewards high-performing students by letting them skip a quiz. It removes all that squabbling with students over acceptable excuses for missing a quiz. If they're absent, they drop the zero. It reduces the grade grubbing of students complaining about a low quiz score. So what's wrong with any of that? Well, we think there are several things wrong with that.

It's a safe bet that Professor Valid's six quizzes cover different content and learning objectives (see **align assessments to learning objectives***). Therefore, when different students choose different quizzes to drop, their final course grades do not represent mastery of the same material. Their final course grades are not comparable; one student's B means something different than another student's B.

While dropping one quiz score alleviates a lot of student complaining and communication on Professor Valid, it probably doesn't operate fairly (see **fairness***). If one student was sick on a quiz day, she has to use her drop for that. But another student can do well on the first five and then just skip the last one. That's not really fair.

It's also a safe bet that the quizzes aren't of equal difficulty, so that one of the quizzes is likely to be the lowest score for many students. But, chances are when that happens, that material was also challenging because it was important. So the course grade represents the most important content least well.

Finally, it puts the focus on the course grades, not on the course learning. Dropping a score communicates that getting a higher grade is more important than learning *all* the material in the course.

Thus, we advise against a Drop the Lowest Grade policy in favor of reasonable make-up policies (see **make-up exams***), and retesting and rewriting opportunities (see **mastery opportunities***).

Summary

Dropping a grade has several negative consequences and few positive ones. We advise that you do not drop the lowest grade or let students choose one to drop.

See Also

Make-Up Exams
Mastery Opportunities

17 Effort

Recommendation: Student effort is very important. Do not grade effort directly either by itself or as part of a grade on an assignment. Do not take effort into account when calculating course grades.

Student effort is very important. There is a large literature base on the effects of students' efforts on their achievements in class. That's not the focus of this entry, however. The focus here is on whether you should consider or include effort in calculating a grade. Consider Jeanine and Arturo.

Jeanine started her final paper right after Spring Break, has come to your office hours regularly, and e-mails you in between with really good questions. On the other hand, as students are gathering for the class period before the paper is due, you overhear Arturo say to another student that he hasn't started the paper yet. When you eventually are scoring each paper, they are about the same in quality. Should they receive the same grade?

What Does the Grade Mean?

We argue that they should receive the same grade because marks on papers and grades in courses should represent the degree to which students have mastered the learning objectives (e.g. Close, 2009) (see **align assessments to learning objectives***), not the journey they have taken to attain that mastery.

To do otherwise, to assign Jeanine a higher mark on the paper because she obviously put in more effort than Arturo did, means that their scores mean different things. This is what Cross and Frary (1999) called "hodgepodge grading." It also implies that you can perfectly and consistently divine effort. Did you hear Arturo correctly? Was he posturing for classmates but really had been working on it?

Suppose that Jeanine's paper, after all of her work, wasn't actually very good? Would you give her the same grade as Arturo? We advise against it.

Effort *Does* Matter

We're not saying effort doesn't matter. Of course effort matters! Arturo is actually a rare student. Much of the time, students' efforts and investments in their studies do pay off. Jeanine has written a much better paper—and learned so much more—than she would have without those efforts. This means that, for most students, their effort *is* reflected in their grades.

This can be torturous for instructors when a student is on a borderline (see **borderline grade cases***). It's tempting to reward the hard worker by tipping them up over the border (something that more than 70% of faculty reported they would do in one study (Cross, Frary, & Weber, 1993)) and to punish the "slacker" by leaving them where they are. We believe that scores at the borderline do not change the underlying issue: effort has contributed to where the student is, and it is really difficult for you to assess effort consistently and accurately.

Ways to Address Effort

You really are not as interested in students "working hard" as you think you are. What you're really interested in, if you interrogate it a bit, is that students work hard *effectively*. As the old saw goes, there's no point in climbing briskly up the ladder of success if it's leaning against the wrong wall. What you want is students to be diligent at doing effective work and employing strategies that are successful in the field. If that really is very important to you, then write learning objectives about it. Have learning objectives about using solution strategies, or management techniques, or drafting processes, and then assess those (see McCrickerd, 2012).

A similar approach is to grade effort explicitly but separately (e.g. Swinton, 2010). The advantage of these two approaches is that articulating separate learning objectives or at least separate grading criteria for effort makes the role of effort explicit to you and to students. This can help curtail the inadvertent, and therefore more likely biased, stereotyped, or capricious, influence of effort on your assigned grade. However, quantifying effort into specific criteria or some sort of grade is challenging and may still be viewed by students as unfair or biased.

There's also an argument that grading on completion of assignments (like journal entries) or on **participation*** or **attendance*** (like answering a clicker question) without scoring the quality of the response is a way to have effort affect students' grades (see Immerwahr, 2011). We disagree, but the argument exists.

Expect effort from students as fundamental just as you expect lots of things from students that you don't grade, like civility. Effort is, to some extent, about values, not about course content (e.g. Sabini & Monterosso, 2003). **Not everything that matters must be graded***. You've got many ways to promote effort.

Acknowledging the Debate

We need to acknowledge that ours is one end of a continuum of possibilities that you can find in these discussions, even in the professional literature on grading. Hodgepodge grading is theoretically ill-advised but often very pragmatic. Hodgepodge grading in general and including effort in grades in particular have been long-standing practices and routinely appear in studies of grading (Brookhart et al., 2016). They are popular with students and with instructors (e.g. Adams, 2005; Cross & Frary, 1999; Sabini & Monterosso, 2003). One aspect of the pragmatism is that instructors know that students' perceptions of them include how they take effort into account (Tippin, Lafreniere, & Page, 2012).

There are arguments that grading effort is justified on moral grounds (Sabini & Monterosso, 2003). So you will see and read lots of differing opinions. We still believe our recommendation is the most defensible.

Summary

Effort is critical to student success. Do all you can to promote students' investing effort in their mastery of learning objectives. Then grade only for mastery of learning objectives.

See Also

Align Assessments to Learning Objectives
Late Work
Not Everything That Matters Must Be Graded
Participation

Resource

Close, D. (2009). Fair grades. *Teaching Philosophy*, *32*(4), 361–398.

References

Adams, J. B. (2005). What makes the grade? Faculty and student perceptions. *Teaching of Psychology*, *32*(1), 21–24.
Brookhart, S. M., Guskey, T. R., Bowers, A. J., McMillan, J. H., Smith, J. K., Smith, L. F., Stevens, M. T., & Welsh, M. E. (2016). A century of grading research: Meaning and value in the most common educational measure. *Review of Educational Research*, *86*(4), 803–848.
Close, D. (2009). Fair grades. *Teaching Philosophy*, *32*(4), 361–398.
Cross, L. H., & Frary, R. B. (1999). Hodgepodge grading: Endorsed by students and teachers alike. *Applied Measurement in Education*, *12*(1), 53–72.
Cross, L. H., Frary, R. B., & Weber, L. J. (1993). College grading: Achievement, attitudes, and effort. *College Teaching*, *41*(4), 143–148.
Immerwahr, J. (2011). The case for motivational grading. *Teaching Philosophy*, *34*(4), 335–346.
McCrickerd, J. (2012). What can be fairly factored in to final grades? *Teaching Philosophy*, *35*(3), 275–291.

Sabini, J., & Monterosso, J. (2003). Moralization of college grading: Performance, effort, and moral worth. *Basic and Applied Social Psychology, 25*(3), 189–203.

Swinton, O. H. (2010). The effect of effort grading on learning. *Economics of Education Review, 29*(6), 1176–1182.

Tippin, G. K., Lafreniere, K. D., & Page, S. (2012). Student perception of academic grading: Personality, academic orientation, and effort. *Active Learning in Higher Education, 13*(1), 51–61.

18 Equity

Equity in classroom assessment implies that every student has sufficient access to learning, that every student is able to demonstrate what they have learned, and that every student's outcomes (scores and grades) are not unduly influenced by who they are but rest solely on what they have learned in the class.

Classically, in educational measurement, equity has been about how testing and test results were different for subgroups of examinees defined by gender, ethnicity, race, class, socioeconomic status, and culture. Those may yet be important ways for you to think about your students. We encourage you to think about *any meaningful way* your students may differ, not only those more traditional categories. It might be important for you to attend to differences due to which "feeder school" your students came from, due to which set of prerequisite courses they have had (see **prior knowledge***), or due to their introverted or extroverted personality. Tanner (2013) discusses students who engage easily during in-class discussions versus those who don't.

Equitable does not always mean equal. *Standardization*, as in standardized test, is often used to "level the playing field." Students are allotted the same amount of time, see the same questions, receive the same exam preparation materials, etc. However, sometimes equity demands that standardization be broken—different students are provided with different testing conditions—in order to level that playing field. When you give your mid-term, you give students two hours during which to take the exam. Keeping the exam time equal for all students is a strategy for achieving equity. If you have a student with a learning disability in the course, the Accessibility Services staff may suggest you provide three hours for that student. Three hours isn't equal to the other students, but it is equitable given this student's learning disability.

Equity Through Access

Access—providing various ways for students to approach your course content—is an important part of equity. As you are designing assessment experiences and assessment-related policies, be aware that different students will understand and access them in different ways. If you are grading class

participation*, for example, then you need to have mechanisms to ensure that every single student has similar opportunities to participate.

Dealing with plagiarism (see **cheating and plagiarism***) is a case where understanding your students may prove useful (Hayes & Introna, 2005). Students from different cultural backgrounds have different ethics regarding how and when it is appropriate to use someone else's work. Equity, here, demands that you provide your students access to what your (and/or your institution's) ethics are on the matter. You have lots of ways to provide access to your students to this issue. You can give them your definition. You can show them examples. You can have them do a brief tutorial on the topic. You can provide "shots across the bow" where you call a potential instance to a student's attention and seek to understand why they did what they did before imposing a sanction.

As another example, consider your course learning objectives. Are they written in such a way that students will know what they mean even before they've mastered them? Do you give examples of what successfully meeting the learning objectives looks like? If you're routinely and explicitly displaying and discussing learning objectives in class, that aids students in accessing them, in building their own understanding of what the learning objectives mean and the evaluation criteria related to each objective (see **align assessments to learning objectives***).

Equity Through Opportunity

Equity in practice also means that your students have various opportunities to show what they know, to demonstrate their learning in the course (see **assessment plan***). Sometimes this can be achieved through giving students choices in assessment (see **student choice***). Sometimes, especially for large overarching learning objectives, they might be assessed multiple times throughout the course. Using sources appropriately in scientific writing is an example.

Opportunity can also encompass "second chances" like **mastery opportunities*** or when you offer students **feedback*** on a draft of an assignment before it is due.

Equity in Outcomes

Aligned with the classical testing definition of equity is subgroup differences in outcomes. Do men tend to earn higher grades on particular assignments or in final course grades in your course, for example? Do you ever check?

There are also psychological effects such as **evaluation anxiety*** and stereotype threat which you could inadvertently be triggering among your students that differentially impact them. Knowing more about how those work will lessen the likelihood that they are at work within your course.

Designed for Some; Offered to All

While it is imperative that you understand how your students differ and to attend to those differences *vis-à-vis* whether they affect students' ability to learn in your courses and to demonstrate that learning, it is equally imperative that you not make assumptions and presumptions about those effects and insist on certain solutions. The individual differences among your students provide probabilistic information to you and to them, not deterministic information. Just because a student is a woman, or Hispanic, or speaks a language other than English at home, or came from the "bad" high school, does not dictate how she will perform in your class. The strategy, then, is to design your policies, instruction, and assessment with those differences in mind, but then make the availability of them open to all students. Let the students make the final decision of whether to invoke a choice.

To suggest that students who have not taken a certain class prior to yours really should do more practice problems is patronizing. To suggest that doing more practice problems would promote deeper learning in the course is not only not patronizing but also is a suggestion that may benefit students whom you didn't expect to need it.

Abedi and Lord (2001) designed a study to see if linguistically simplified mathematics problems would help the test performance of 8th grade English Language Learners (ELL). They took 8th grade mathematics problems, left the mathematics alone, but simplified the language so that the reading level was lower than 8th grade. They administered the questions to ELLs and non-ELLs alike. Guess what happened? Everyone did better! While the linguistic simplification was designed for the ELL students, it benefited all students. Thus we encourage you to design your assessments and assessment policies with specific kinds of students in mind, but provide those options to all your students.

Summary

Equity is a very important value in education and in your teaching. Equity does not necessarily come through equivalence, however. Look at equity in your teaching with respect to access, opportunity, and outcomes. Finally, design to be equitable to subgroups of students but offer those options to all students.

See Also

Evaluation Anxiety
Fairness
Participation
Student Choice

Resources

Astin, A. W. (1990). Educational assessment and educational equity. *American Journal of Education, 98*(4), 458–478.

Elwood, J. (2006). Gender issues in testing and assessment. In C. Skelton, B. Francis, & L. Smulyan (Eds.), *The Sage handbook of gender and education.* Thousand Oaks, CA: Sage.

Leathwood, C. (2005). Assessment policy and practice in higher education: Purpose, standards and equity. *Assessment and Evaluation in Higher Education, 30*(3), 307–324.

Spencer, S. J., Logel, C., & Davies, P. G. (2016). Stereotype threat. *Annual Review of Psychology, 67,* 415–437.

Tanner, K. D. (2013). Structure matters: Twenty-one teaching strategies to promote student engagement and cultivate classroom equity. *CBE-Life Sciences Education, 12,* 322–331.

von der Embse, N., Barterian, J., & Segool, N. (2012). Test anxiety interventions for children and adolescents: A systematic review of treatment studies from 2000–2010. *Psychology in the Schools, 50*(1), 57–71.

References

Abedi, J., & Lord, C. (2001). The language factor in mathematics tests. *Applied Measurement in Education, 14*(3), 219–234.

Hayes, N., & Introna, L. D. (2005). Cultural values, plagiarism, and fairness: When plagiarism gets in the way of learning. *Ethics & Behavior, 15*(3), 213–231.

Tanner, K. D. (2013). Structure matters: Twenty-one teaching strategies to promote student engagement and cultivate classroom equity. *CBE-Life Sciences Education, 12,* 322–331.

19 Evaluation Anxiety

Being judged by someone else often elevates stress levels. Reflect back on the last time a colleague observed your teaching. Stress responses are common, natural, and adaptive. But stress can reach uncomfortable, even unhealthy, levels based on a variety of factors. In assessing students, we may encounter evaluation anxiety, performance anxiety, stage fright, or test anxiety. There's debate regarding whether each is distinct or whether they are the same thing but occur under different sets of conditions. That debate is well beyond the scope of this book. For the purposes of this entry, we're going to refer to evaluation anxiety. Evaluation anxiety can also mix with other kinds of anxieties, like math anxiety, language anxiety, or writing anxiety, in your specific domain.

We're proposing that whether you give exams, assign presentations, or have students write papers, you should give some thought to how those assessments might provoke stress in students and what you might choose to do about that.

What Is Evaluation Anxiety?

Evaluation anxiety is stress experienced by a student in a situation in which her academic performance is being judged. Symptoms of mild evaluation anxiety, which may actually be eustress, which enhances performance, include sweaty palms, dry mouth, increased heart rate, increased respiration rate, fidgeting, and verbal expressions of concern (Cizek & Burg, 2006). Symptoms of moderate evaluation anxiety, which are probably no longer eustress, include poorer performance on the assessment, crying, eating disturbances, sleep disturbances, illness, high blood pressure, and acting out (Cizek & Burg, 2006). Moderate evaluation anxiety, particularly if it is chronic and not just occasional, can affect academic performance, attitudes toward school, and even dropping out.

Severe evaluation anxiety is likely indicative of some major, chronic illness such as Generalized Anxiety Disorder or Major Depressive Disorder. These symptoms can include major life disruptions up to suicidal thoughts or suicide attempts.

Cizek and Burg (2006) summarized the literature for K–12 students, which indicates that females are more likely than males to be test-anxious; Hispanics and African Americans are more likely than Whites; low-performing students are more likely than middle-performing students, who are more likely than high-performing students; and at-risk students more likely than not-at-risk students.

Factors That Contribute to Evaluation Anxiety

There are several factors which can influence the degree of evaluation anxiety a student experiences, many of which are at least partially within your control.

The *stakes* of the evaluation, that is how much it is worth or how large the consequences are for it, impact the anxiety. Anxiety will be higher around a mid-term exam if it constitutes 40% of the course grade than if it constitutes 10% of the course grade. This is another reason to have several assessments and a variety of assessments in your course (see **assessment plan***). Allowing students to turn in drafts of papers as they're working on them, or providing **mastery opportunities*** or other ways for students to show mastery after an exam, are other ways of drawing down the stakes on this one performance.

One factor that may not be as obvious as it should be is the degree to which students have actually mastered the content. The better they know the material, the less anxious they should be. Thus how well students study and prepare for exams will influence their anxiety. That's actually a very cognitively complex relationship (e.g. Sung, Chao, & Tseng, 2016), but studying well and knowing the material helps.

Whether the evaluation will occur publicly or privately influences the anxiety. We would advise that, unless your learning objectives require public evaluation, evaluate in private (see **align assessments to learning objectives***). Even for a class presentation, for example, you can choose to provide your **feedback*** and the grade privately rather than publicly.

The environment during the exam can influence students' anxiety. Is the environment distraction-free? Do students have sufficient space to work? Is the lighting conducive to concentrating?

Finally, we note that a significant portion of test anxiety is driven by the social processes and pressures around an evaluation. You know the students who choose to come to the exam at 1:59 p.m. for a 2:00 p.m. start because they find the student chit-chat prior to the exam worrisome. You are part of that social pressure.

How You Can Mitigate Evaluation Anxiety

A large component of addressing evaluation anxiety does rest with the students themselves. Depending on each student's own experiences with evaluation anxiety, they might find techniques like positive self-talk, relaxation and mindfulness exercises (Quinn & Peters, 2017), and general test-taking strategies (Cizek & Burg, 2006) helpful. Relatedly, they may benefit from general study skills instruction, time management, etc. Encourage your students to know themselves and learn strategies for dealing with evaluation anxiety. You can decide how much of this you wish to help them with (Bledsoe & Baskin, 2014). For example, you might find if you're teaching freshman and sophomore level courses you may wish to do more explicit work with these strategies than in upperclass courses. You can definitely communicate with your students about workshops and resources on campus.

There are many ways in which you can mitigate your students' experience of evaluation anxiety with your assessments. It is important that you communicate your expectations to students clearly and often so that they are not surprised during the exam.

On the exam or assignment sheet itself, make sure directions are clear so that students are worrying neither about the content of the assessment nor the process of the assessment, the "what does she want" kind of thinking. Assure students that they're welcome to ask you clarifying questions during the exam. For online assessments, take extra time to craft the expectations and directions since students won't be able to ask for clarification during the assessment.

Do all you can to help students prepare for the exam. There's some evidence to suggest that **cheat sheets or crib sheets*** reduce test anxiety (Erbe, 2007).

Consider the testing environment. As we've mentioned, make it as conducive to the purposes of the assessment as you can. There's even a bit of evidence to suggest that calming sensory activities such as a lemon scent diffuser or playing classical music during the exam may reduce student test anxiety (Quinn & Peters, 2017). There's also some suggestion that humor may help reduce test anxiety (Berk, 2000), though we've elaborated on that in the **humor*** entry (we're very skeptical that the risks and rewards of using humor balance properly).

Be aware that everything you say and do, especially about assessments, contributes to the social milieu around those assessments (Bledsoe & Baskin, 2014). If you are reassuring your students that they are ready to do well on the test, that will aid them in thinking so, too. If you make comments about how half the students usually fail this first exam, that too can influence their anxiety (and perhaps their performance, too, through something called stereotype threat (e.g. Spencer, Logel, & Davies, 2016)). It doesn't take much to have an impact on anxiety and performance (e.g. McCarthy et al., 2017).

Summary

Stress is a natural, sometimes even helpful, component of being evaluated. You and your students can both contribute to that stress staying adaptive and not becoming debilitating.

Resources

The American Test Anxieties Association—http://amtaa.org/
The Stress and Anxiety Research Society—www.star-society.org/

References

Berk, R. A. (2000). Does humor in course tests reduce anxiety and improve performance? *College Teaching, 48*(4), 151–158.

Bledsoe, T. S., & Baskin, J. J. (2014). Recognizing student fear: The elephant in the classroom. *College Teaching, 62*(1), 32–41.

Cizek, G. J., & Burg, S. S. (2006). *Addressing test anxiety in a high-stakes environment.* Thousand Oaks, CA: Corwin Press.

Erbe, B. (2007). Reducing test anxiety while increasing learning: The cheat sheet. *College Teaching, 55*(3), 96–98.

McCarthy, J. M., Bauer, T. N., Truxillo, D. M., Campion, M. C., Van Iddekinge, C. H., & Campion, M. A. (2017). Using pre-test explanations to improve test-taker reactions: Testing a set of "wise" interventions. *Organizational Behavior and Human Decision Processes, 141,* 43–56.

Quinn, B. L., & Peters, A. (2017). Strategies to reduce nursing student test anxiety: A literature review. *Journal of Nursing Education, 56*(3), 145–151.

Spencer, S. J., Logel, C., & Davies, P. G. (2016). Stereotype threat. *Annual Review of Psychology, 67,* 415–437.

Sung, Y. T., Chao, T. Y., & Tseng, F. L. (2016). Reexamining the relationship between test anxiety and learning achievement: An individual-differences perspective. *Contemporary Educational Psychology, 46,* 241–252.

20 Extra Credit

Recommendation: Do not use extra credit.

We agree with Pynes (2014), who is unequivocal: "there are no good arguments for the use of extra credit assignments in the college classroom" (p. 191). There are other mechanisms to address some of the reasons why you might employ extra credit.

What Is Extra Credit?

Extra credit refers to 1) the points accrued to students above and beyond the points defined in the syllabus and connected directly to the course learning objectives as constituting the final course grade, and 2) whatever activity students must complete in order to earn those points. Pynes (2014) adds that the purpose of extra credit is "to provide an opportunity for a student to increase a grade by performing additional work" (p. 192).

For us, the pivotal element in this discussion is "extra." If you provide all students an opportunity to respond to **feedback*** on a paper in your course, to revise the paper and resubmit it for some specified number of points, that isn't "extra credit" by our definition. We would label that a mastery exercise if the initial feedback came with graded work, and draft writing if it did not (see **mastery opportunities***). These definitions, and some of the rhetorical posturing that goes with them, will, we hope, become clearer as we go.

Arguments in Favor of Extra Credit

Students love extra credit because it represents a second chance, and we're all in favor of second chances, right? In one study, 62% of students expected instructors to provide extra credit opportunities (Hassel & Lourey, 2005). (Five percent of students actually reported interpreting an F in a course not that they failed but that they required extra credit.) Extra credit provides a safety net or relief valve for them. It provides them with an additional chance, when they've fallen "just short" to gain a proper reward for their efforts (their "blood and sweat" as Hill, Paladino, and Eison (1993) call it).

(See **effort***.) It forms a bit of grease on the academic wheels to compensate for the vagaries of the student experience. The student argument almost always boils down to: "I need a better grade than I'm earning through the regular assignments."

There is a line of argument in the literature about extra credit assignments being a way to scaffold self-regulatory and motivational aptitude among developmental (Staats, 2007) or "marginal" (Junn, 1995) students. We are highly skeptical of this argument, because why should that be "extra"? Why isn't that something you're duty-bound to build into your courses?

Chances are you use extra credit. Hill, Paladino, and Eison (1993), for example, surveyed instructors and found that only 18% said they never used extra credit. Instructors use extra credit to incentivize student engagement and involvement in the topic of the course (Norcross, Horrocks, & Stevenson, 1989). Pynes (2014) calls this the "relevance" argument (and he totally demolishes it). Instructors use extra credit also, if we're honest, as our own safety valve to diffuse and defuse grading complaints.

Some instructors argue that, inevitably, scores on exams and papers contain some unreliability of measurement. Providing extra credit compensates for that unreliability. The problem with that claim is that there is unreliability in your scoring of the extra credit, too. Why not hit the unreliability head-on instead of patching over it? Are you doing good quality control on your exams to check for scoring errors and bad questions? Are you using a well-designed rubric (see **rubrics***) for scoring papers and using best practices for how to score student work (see **scoring essay tests, papers, or assignments***)? Do you have an appeals procedure in your syllabus that students can deploy if they think their grades are inaccurate? Do you have a policy for dealing with borderline grade cases (see **borderline grade cases***)? Start with these things rather than extra credit.

Arguments Against Extra Credit

Extra credit is often hugely diverting for students. It communicates that there is knowledge above and beyond that represented by the learning objectives and that it is important enough to contribute to the grade but not important enough to actually be in the course (see **align assessments to learning objectives***). That sounds backwards to us (see **assessment plan***). If an activity is important enough for you to reward with points, why isn't it part of the course directly?

If you have articulated your learning objectives, developed a comprehensive set of assessments to address those objectives, and thought through how they'll be graded and how they'll contribute to a course grade, why is there anything "extra"? Isn't there enough "credit" in the course already—why should there be "extra"? Burke writes,

> As a graduate of a staunch liberal arts background, it was anathema to me that anyone would think that deficient course performance could be "made up". The conventional student attitude seems to be that extra

credit is something one does to salvage one's grade after a disastrous performance on an exam or other assignment.

(Burke, 1991, p. 220)

From a grading perspective, extra credit enhances hodgepodge grading (Cross & Frary, 1999), in which two students who each earn a B− may have achieved a B− for very different reasons. It can also contribute to inadvertent compensatory grading (see **compensatory and conjunctive grading***). Compensatory grading means that points earned through one activity can compensate for points not earned in a different activity. For example, if a student earns 60 of 75 points on an exam but then they earn 15 points of extra credit by attending an on-campus evening speaker, the speaking event compensates for the exam questions the student missed. If the speaker was addressing the same learning objectives as the missed questions on the exam (highly unlikely!), that's acceptable. If the speaker isn't addressing those learning objectives, that's problematic.

From a measurement perspective, compensatory grading like extra credit brings the validity of the course grades into question. If those two students with the B− each got a B− through doing different work, then the B− has a different meaning for each student. But on a transcript, a B− is a B−, so how is an employer or scholarship-giver supposed to make that distinction? The meaning of the course grades is thus called into question with extra credit. Another aspect of invalidity is that, since extra credit almost never hurts a student's course grade but almost always helps it, it contributes to **grade inflation*** (Pynes, 2014).

Providing extra credit puts an emphasis on grading rather than learning (see **learning-oriented assessment***). It encourages students to focus on winning points (and arguments with you) rather than on what knowledge they need to yet master. It can invite the "Moral Hazard" (Wilson (2002) and discussed in Pynes (2014)) of encouraging students not to study as hard or to do their best on assessed work because of the safety net of extra credit.

Extra credit creates an "unnecessary burden" (Pynes, 2014, p. 201) on instructors, for whom there is now extra grading, and on students, for whom there is now extra work. For students who are already struggling with their academic workload, extra credit is a bit like tossing a drowning person a glass of water (what Pynes (2014) calls the "Assigned Work Paradox" (p. 205)). (We hasten to add that not all "struggling students" are struggling only with or because of workload.) Research also suggests that the students who need extra credit the most, that is students with the poorer grades, are the least likely to engage in extra credit (Harrison, Meister, & LeFevre, 2011).

Alternatives to Extra Credit

We are not arguing that additional ways for students to show their mastery of course learning objectives are inappropriate or that you cannot, in any way, incentivize student engagement in the topic you're teaching. We do not believe, however, that those objectives should be "extra."

Let's return for a moment to the regular credit (not the "extra" credit). You are already assessing your students in multiple ways; you're teaching them, guiding them, and supporting them to do well on those assessments. You provide lots of lead time; study guides; example papers; teaching assistants; tutors; a writing center; other support staff; your office hours. Do you believe, in your instructional heart of hearts, that all of those efforts and resources are *insufficient* for students to master everything they need to master in your course? Perhaps you're thinking you can always do more or provide more resources. Sure! But that's not what we just asked you. When a student asks you for extra credit, are you completely convinced that they have used every opportunity you have already provided? If you are not, and they're not attending office hours, for example, why should you take it upon yourself to provide yet more supports?

So one alternative to extra credit is regular credit. Help students to understand all the resources which are available to them. Remind them to be using them. Show them positive examples of how using those supports results in better student performance. Communicate clearly and often with your students about all of the credit that is already in the course. Help them focus on learning the content, "grade capture," rather than on "grade recovery."

If you are learning-oriented and not grade-oriented in your courses, you will have procedures in place to promote student learning. You will have methods for downplaying grades and playing up learning opportunities. This also shifts not only your attention and your students' attention to mastering course content but it also shifts the goals of the course from point-earning to learning.

Elsewhere in this book we describe some additional alternatives to extra credit in detail. Quickly here:

Mastery opportunities*—The opportunity after work has been graded to return to that same performance and demonstrate mastery at a second point in time.

Not everything that matters must be graded*—Not everything that is important in a course is graded. You have plenty of other incentives to offer students: their own learning; your pride in their work; basic expectations.

If You Are Going to Use Extra Credit Despite Our Injunction

Whether you call it "extra credit" or something else, **fairness*** is a critical consideration (Hill, Paladino, & Eison, 1993). Sometimes, faculty offer mastery opportunities or extra credit to subsets of students (Hill, Paladino, & Eison report 26% of the faculty they surveyed did this). For example, if students earn less than an 85% on an examination, they are offered some extra credit opportunity. But why shouldn't the student who earned an 86 or 87—or even a 98—have the same opportunity? Junn (1995) reports pulling certain students aside, whom she deems "marginal," to offer them extra credit. Worse yet is when a "squeaky wheel student" wears you down and negotiates some opportunity to earn points which no other student in the class even knows about (sometimes called off-book grading). These points then represent the student's negotiating skills, not mastery of the course learning objective. Do not do these things, no matter what! If mastering the course content is the goal, then all students can improve their mastery.

Make the opportunities relevant to the course learning objectives (Alley, 2011). Hill, Paladino, and Eison (1993) report instructors who offered students extra credit in psychology courses for donating blood, donating food to a food bank, and for attending class on the day the professor wore a certain color! A little less outrageous but still inappropriate extra credit included points for finding typos on exams or for answering trivia questions. (See Hill, Paladino, & Eison's Table 1 for all of their examples.)

Plan—and announce—extra credit opportunities ahead of time (Alley, 2011). Alley further recommends that part of that planning be multiple entry points throughout the semester, that is, your extra credit opportunities should be activities that, at any point in the semester, a student could decide to do.

We'll say one more time, however: If good extra credit is available to everyone, premeditated, and aligned with course learning objectives, why is it extra? Why isn't that something which all students should have to do?

The Special Case of Research Participation

Students receiving extra course credit for participating in research studies as participants is a special case of extra credit because there are some additional layers. By and large, this kind of extra credit must follow all of the recommendations we have made so far, namely, don't do it. If you're going to do it, follow all of our guidance above. Then know that the additional ethical considerations of research participants make this even shakier ground.

First, research participants must be volunteers, which means you cannot require research participation. In some kinds of courses—like undergraduate psychology, for example—the department forms a research pool in which multiple studies per semester are available. Requiring students to pick among a set of studies mitigates, but does not eliminate, participants' rights to be volunteers. Often, then, a written assignment, like reviewing research papers, is also included as an alternate choice to participating in a research study. In research participant pools, though, this is a requirement; it's not extra credit.

Second, that voluntary choice must not be coerced, and a grade contingency for participating is a form of coercion. So is asking your own students to participate in your own research projects. There are methods and mechanisms for being able to handle the ethics of studying your own students, but those are beyond the scope of this book. When in doubt, or even if you're not in doubt and feel quite sure of what you're doing, talk to a research compliance official at your school before you provide any course credit for research participation, especially if you're studying your own students.

Third, paying for research participants with course credit may induce self-selection biases into the study being conducted (Padilla-Walker, Zamboanga, Thompson, & Schmersal, 2005).

Summary

Do not use extra credit. It puts the focus on grades, not on learning. There are much better alternatives for you to use.

See Also

Assessment Plan
Attendance
Pop Quizzes

Resources

Alley, D. (2011). The role of extra-credit assignments in the teaching of world languages. *Hispania, 94*(3), 529–536.
Pynes, C. A. (2014). Seven arguments against extra credit. *Teaching Philosophy, 37*(2), 191–214.

References

Alley, D. (2011). The role of extra-credit assignments in the teaching of world languages. *Hispania, 94*(3), 529–536.
Burke, J. F. (1991). The extra credit project: Turning a bane into a blessing. *Political Science and Politics, 24*(2), 220–222.
Cross, L. H., & Frary, R. B. (1999). Hodgepodge grading: Endorsed by students and teachers alike. *Applied Measurement in Education, 12*(1), 53–72.
Harrison, M. A., Meister, D. G., & LeFevre, A. J. (2011). Which students complete extra-credit work? *College Student Journal, 45*(3), 550–555.
Hassel, H., & Lourey, J. (2005). The dea(r)th of student responsibility. *College Teaching, 53*(1), 2–13.
Hill, G. W., Paladino, J. J., & Eison, J. A. (1993). Blood, sweat, and trivia: Faculty ratings of extra-credit opportunities. *Teaching of Psychology, 20*(3), 209–213.
Junn, E. N. (1995). Empowering the marginal student: An innovative skills-based extra credit assignment. *Office of the Provost Scholarship.* Paper 11. Retrieved February 1, 2016 from http://scholarworks.sjsu.edu/provost_schol/11
Norcross, J. C., Horrocks, L. J., & Stevenson, J. F. (1989). Of barfights and gadflies: Attitudes and practices concerning extra credit in college courses. *Teaching of Psychology, 16,* 199–203.
Padilla-Walker, L. M., Zamboanga, L., Thompson, R. A., & Schmersal, L. A. (2005). Extra credit as incentive for voluntary research participation. *Teaching of Psychology, 32*(3), 150–153.

Pynes, C. A. (2014). Seven arguments against extra credit. *Teaching Philosophy*, *37*(2), 191–214.

Staats, S. K. (2007). An intensive option for developmental algebra: Student achievement on extra credit test problems. *Research and Teaching in Developmental Education*, *23*(2), 49–61.

Wilson, M. L. (2002). Evidence that extra credit assignments induce moral hazard. *Atlantic Economic Journal*, *30*(1), 97.

21 Fairness

Fairness means different things to different people, which makes it a moving target for you and your students. Here, we'll address some of the more common meanings and/or the meanings which we believe are actionable for you and your students. We'll also explore some strategies you can employ to promote fairness. We have two goals for this entry: 1) to spark your own explicit articulation of what fairness means to you and to your students, and 2) to leaven your thinking about how you promote fairness in your own teaching. We have relied heavily on Robin Tierney's (2012) chapter, "Fairness in Classroom Assessment," and we encourage you to read it, too, as a much more thorough and comprehensive treatment of fairness as it relates to classroom assessment.

"Fair"ly Straightforward? The Meanings of Fairness

While there are lots of different ways we use the word "fair" in the English language (read Tierney (2012, pp. 126–127) for a playful and breathless catalog of them), there are some underlying themes in that usage: neutrality, balance, even-handedness, consistency, openness, self-determination.

We need to make a couple of broader notes before delving into some of these aspects. First, fairness is a continuum not a dichotomy. We and our students tend to talk about it as a dichotomy ("That was unfair!"); however, in planning for and working with fairness, it is a continuum. No matter what we do, we could always do something to make a practice even more fair. Relatedly, different people are going to draw that fair/unfair line in different places.

Second, fairness is a matter of perception. Of course there are objective practices in which you can engage that will imbue fairness into a situation and yet, given other factors, students may yet perceive a decision as unfair. You and your relationship with your students are critical contextual factors. Tierney (2012) is clear that a relationship of respect and trust between instructors and students (and among students) is a critical foundation for fairness. Jerome Groopman (2007), in his book *How Doctors Think*, describes studies done about which doctors get sued for malpractice. One of the key factors in a patient's decision to sue is whether the doctor was a boor or not. Don't be a boor.

Third, in this compendium we have made a distinction which is not always made between fairness and **equity***, so you would do well to read that entry, too. There's a point to equity that needs also to be considered here with fairness: equivalence does not always serve fairness. One of the most commonly cited strategies by teachers for promoting fairness is to follow the same procedures for everyone (Tierney, 2012), to treat every student equally. But there are times when not treating everyone the same is the fairer option.

With those preliminary points in view, here are some ways you might think about fairness:

> *Opportunity to Learn*—Students perceive your support of their studying as important in fairness (Gordon & Fay, 2010). So have you given them plenty of opportunities to learn the material that is being assessed? Has the material been covered in multiple ways such as in class, in text, through other resources?
>
> *Alignment*—What is the connection between the assignment or the exam and what's been happening in class? Did you spend 10% of your instructional time with the concepts in chapter 12, but that content was 30% of the exam? Students won't think that's fair. Did you focus in class on applying that chapter 12 content to real-world problems but the exam required only memorization?
>
> *Communication*—There are several key aspects of your communication with students that are part of fairness. Are you communicating early and often enough about assessments? How much notice and time do students have to prepare for exams or other assignments? Do they have sufficient time to do the work or to prepare for an assessment? Is your communication transparent, that is, are you clear about deadlines, due dates, expectations, learning objectives (see **align assessments to learning objectives***), etc.
>
> *Consistency*—Are you grading everyone using the same criteria? Are you applying those criteria in the same way to everyone? (See **scoring essay tests, papers, or assignments*** for concrete procedures you can employ.)
>
> *Validity*—Do scores and grades mean the same thing for different students? That is, do you engage in hodgepodge grading (Cross & Frary, 1999) where, for some students, you gave them the benefit of the doubt, for other students you considered **effort***, for other students you considered their personal situations right now, etc., so that students got a B− in your class for very different reasons?
>
> *Bias*—Do you intentionally or unintentionally let something about a student other than her performance influence her grade? (See **equity*** for more on this issue.) Tierney (2012) notes, "being fair in classroom

assessment requires more than being unbiased, it also involves being receptive to diversity" (p. 132). (See **scoring essay tests, papers, or assignments*** for concrete procedures you can employ.)

Power Dynamics—There are more and less powerful—influential, knowledgeable, intimidating—people in your classroom, including you. When those power dynamics are used to promote learning, that can be really good. You are more expert in your field than your students are, so placing yourself in that expert role can be a good thing. Having a destructive racial dynamic amongst a student team trying to complete a project is not a good thing.

360° Fairness—Fairness needs to be weighed with everyone in mind, not just the student who is presenting you with an issue. If a student turns an assignment in late claiming illness, the remedy you select needs to be crafted in a way that is not only fair to that student but also fair to every other student in the class. It's easy to forget about them in these situations. We suspect that for each one of the ill students asking you to accept **late work*** because they have a "good excuse," there were two other students who were also ill but, because your syllabus says, "No late work will be accepted," didn't even turn work in or ask you for a dispensation. It's thus important when faced with a request from a single student to look completely around the situation, attending to implications of your decisions on others. This also includes you. You should also weigh what is fair to you. Does accepting the work late impose an inordinate burden on you, too?

With those themes in mind, let's turn to concrete suggestions for what you and your students can do to promote fairness in your assessment policies and practices.

Strategies for Promoting Fairness

You want to be fair. Everyone wants to be fair. Most people think they're fair and even would say they work at being fair. But, absent an explicit definition of fairness and some core practices, it is very difficult to achieve fairness or even the perception thereof. It can be really frustrating to have a student claim you weren't fair—especially when they show up in your department chair's office!—when you thought you were being fair. Below are some concrete strategies you can employ that will mitigate concerns about whether or not you are being fair.

Everyday Opportunities

There are a number of actions you can be taking routinely, daily, that promote fairness in all aspects of your course. Start with your syllabus. Does it communicate your views about fairness? Does it clearly communicate learning objectives, due dates and deadlines, major policies that will impact how students work?

Work toward making learning objectives explicit, visible, transparent, and tractable for students. Is the learning objective for the day visible on your PowerPoint slides, on the classroom wall? Are they included on handouts; are your assignment sheets linked to them; do they appear on your study guides?

Do you hold high expectations for all students, even if you permit multiple avenues for them to demonstrate that they've met those expectations (see **student choice***)? Are you designing groups and **groupwork*** assignments to make them more fair?

Planning and Preparing for Assessment

While you are preparing for assessments and while you are preparing your students, you can be promoting fairness. Students perceive attempts to aid their learning and studying as promoting fairness more so than after-the-test scoring artifices like curving (Gordon & Fay, 2010). There are many activities to choose from that provide students with information about what to expect on an exam or during a project.

Do you provide students with a test blueprint at the beginning of units (Parkes & Zimmaro, 2016)? Do they receive study guides? Do you show them example questions for exams, especially early in the semester? Do you show students examples of what successful assignments look like so they know what they're aiming for?

Do you have review sessions, office hours, discussion boards in your learning management system (LMS), specifically designated for test prep or for working on papers or projects? Do you show them how to study?

Make sure you are communicating the place, time, equipment needs (e.g. blue book, stethoscope), permitted and not permitted items (e.g. calculators), exam format, etc., to students *in multiple media, multiple times.* There's a classroom application of Horstman's Law of Organizational Communications (Manager Tools, 2012): "Say something seven times and half of your people will say they've heard it once."

While you are preparing for an assessment, we encourage you to dedicate some of that time for "what if" thinking about potential scenarios. Fairness is easier to ensure if it is planned for rather than dealt with in the heat of an event. What will you do if a student comes late to an exam or gets ill during the exam? What will you do if a student turns a paper in late? What will you do if you suspect a student of plagiarizing (see **cheating and plagiarism***)? What will you do if you see a student with his phone on his desk during the exam when you told them that wasn't allowed? What will you do if you think students are inappropriately collaborating on an online assignment (see **online assessment and authentication***)? In-the-moment decision-making about these scenarios is less likely to produce fair results than decisions built on some thinking ahead.

While You Are Assessing

Inevitably, while students are working on an assignment or a project, one of them will e-mail you with a clarifying question. Much of the time, all your students' work would benefit from receiving that clarification, too. Sharing your clarification with the entire class would be the fair thing to do. You can streamline some of that by using a discussion board for such questions in your learning management system (LMS), or dedicating (and announcing!) the last five minutes of class time for questions about the project. (Not only is this fair, but may cut down on the number of e-mails you receive.)

In an exam setting, (re)state your rules and expectations for what resources students may or may not access, the directions for completing the examination successfully, the time limit(s), what students should do if they have a question or if they need to use the restroom. Post the most salient reminders visually in the room so students can access them at any time. If using online assessments, these rules and expectations needs to be explicitly stated as a part of the assessment since students won't be able ask clarifying questions like they can in a classroom setting.

Proactively avoid triggering stereotype threat or heightening test anxiety (see **evaluation anxiety***) during the exam session.

While You Are Grading or Giving Feedback

Once students have handed in a project or paper or exam, you need to derive a score and promote student learning through feedback. Fairness is a critical issue in those processes. Simple procedures like scoring papers anonymously, using a rubric or scoring guide, and shuffling a stack of essay exams after your score each question, can make a large impact on the fairness of your procedures. We make lots of concrete suggestions in the entries on **feedback***, **feedback timing***, **rubrics***, **scoring essay tests, papers, or assignments*** and in entries like **drop the lowest grade***, **grade explanation***, and **low test scores***. If you are using **peer assessment*** you need to ensure that peers are adequately trained to provide feedback, particularly if their review will influence a classmate's grade in any way.

After You Have Handed Back Papers or Exams

Now that you have announced scores to the class and distributed feedback to students, threats to fairness can still arise. Using techniques like **mastery opportunities*** provide a remedy for addressing unfair consequences. Communication remains important. Encouraging students to visit office hours with questions or to let you know if they think you have scored their work inappropriately (which is different from **grade feeding frenzy***) are important post-assessment mechanisms.

Summary

We are unable to be comprehensive or even thorough here, but we have tried to seed ideas and practices with you that will grow. We encourage you check the cross-references in this compendium for other dimensions of fairness. You might also choose to consult more comprehensive treatments.

Our final suggestion for you, though, comes from Tierney. Perhaps one of the most intriguing issues she discusses is the centrality of teacher critical reflection in addressing fairness. That is, one of the best ways of being more fair is for you to be conscious of fairness in your teaching and for you to critically think about how fairness is or isn't operating in your classroom.

See Also

Assessment Philosophy
Equity

Resources

Gordon, M. E., & Fay, C. H. (2010). The effects of grading and teaching practices on students' perceptions of grading fairness. *College Teaching, 58*(3), 93–98.

Tierney, R. D. (2012). Fairness in classroom assessment. In J. McMillan (Ed.), *Sage handbook of research on classroom assessment* (pp. 125–144). Thousand Oaks, CA: Sage.

References

Cross, L. H., & Frary, R. B. (1999). Hodgepodge grading: Endorsed by students and teachers alike. *Applied Measurement in Education, 12*(1), 53–72.

Gordon, M. E., & Fay, C. H. (2010). The effects of grading and teaching practices on students' perceptions of grading fairness. *College Teaching, 58*(3), 93–98.

Groopman, J. (2007). *How doctors think.* Boston, MA: Houghton Mifflin.

Manager Tools. (2012, January 8). Routine town hall meetings—Part 1. *Manager Tools.* Retrieved from www.manager-tools.com/2012/01/routine-town-hall-meetings-part-1

Parkes, J., & Zimmaro, D. (2016). *Learning and assessing with multiple-choice questions in college classrooms.* New York, NY: Routledge.

Tierney, R. D. (2012). Fairness in classroom assessment. In J. McMillan (Ed.), *Sage handbook of research on classroom assessment* (pp. 125–144). Thousand Oaks, CA: Sage.

22 Feedback

Why Should I Give Students Feedback Other Than the Assignment Grade?

Recommendation: From informal, formative assessments to more formal, summative assessments like tests (see **formative and summative assessments***), create opportunities to provide students timely, targeted feedback focused on addressing misconceptions and how students can improve.

What Is Feedback?

Feedback refers to information given to students about a performance, response, or action that they can use to guide their learning and/or improve their next performance (Hattie & Timperley, 2007). It should be specific and inform the learner what she did well or what may still need improvement and why. Feedback should also be timely and follow the student's response as soon as possible. For more information on immediate versus delayed feedback see **feedback timing***.

What Feedback Is NOT

While some instructors use praise (e.g. "Good Job!," "Well Done!," "Excellent!") as a form of feedback, research shows that praise is ineffective in enhancing achievement (Hattie, 1999). Additionally, feedback is not generic statements about deficiencies (e.g. "Needs improvement," "Not enough detail," "Poorly worded"), but rather specific comments about where and how to improve. Feedback helps support students' learning most when it helps students address misconceptions and provides cues to the appropriate strategies to use to answer a question (Hattie & Timperley, 2007). Unspecific comments used as "feedback" may cause students to view it as useless, or even worse, become frustrated (Shute, 2008).

Why Is Feedback Important?

While feedback in terms of correctness on a selected-response question or a total score on an open-ended assessment (see **selected- and constructed-response questions***) are informative, to improve student learning feedback needs to provide more than a simple measure of performance.

Research shows that timely and targeted feedback can significantly enhance student performance by addressing misconceptions as students have them (Butler & Winne, 1995; Corbett & Anderson, 2001; Hattie & Timperley, 2007; National Research Council, 2000; Wiggins, 1998). Hattie and Timperley (2007) proposed a model of feedback that suggests effective feedback answers three questions: Where am I going (what is the goal)? How am I going (what is the student's progress toward the goal)? Where to next (what activities does the student need to engage in to make better progress toward the goal)?

When Is Feedback Counterproductive?

Deci and Ryan (2000) have identified several factors that can contribute to negative outcomes related to feedback. If students feel they are being strictly monitored they might not fully engage in learning. Additionally, when students believe that feedback is focused on telling them how to do something rather than providing guidance they may not view feedback as a means to improve learning. Lastly, if students feel feedback is being given to create a sense of competition among their peers they may also disengaged from learning. To avoid this, Deci and Ryan (2000) suggest explaining how feedback is meant to help students answer the three questions outlined above in pursuit of making progress toward their learning goals.

Feedback During Class

Angelo and Cross (1993) developed several classroom activities designed to give instructors and their students feedback as it is happening, called Classroom Assessment Techniques (CATs). These simple, non-graded, anonymous activities can help uncover **prior knowledge***, misconceptions, and knowledge gained from a classroom lesson. For example, the *Background Knowledge Probe* is a short, simple assessment asking students what they know about the course, unit, or lesson to uncover what they already know and don't know about a topic and/or identify any misconceptions. Another example, the *Muddiest Point*, is used to help assess where students are having difficulties (Angelo & Cross, 1993). Instructors can use these techniques to guide instruction and/or classroom dialogue about where students are most struggling and provide collective feedback to the class about those misconceptions. Feedback to the whole class is appropriate when most of the class is missing a concept or needs reinforcement.

Feedback on Tests

For classroom tests that are administered via paper-and-pencil, the sooner results can be returned the better. For selected-response questions scored correct/incorrect, it is advisable to review questions and the answer choices, including the misconceptions addressed in each choice, which a majority of the class got incorrect. For constructed-response questions, written comments should focus on identifying exactly what the student did well, and what may still need improvement, providing as much specificity as possible. (See **grade feeding frenzy*** and **grade explanation***.)

Feedback on Written Assignments

Giving feedback for papers, projects, or other performance assessments can be laborious and time-consuming (see **scoring essays tests, papers, or assignments***). There are several strategies you can use to make giving feedback easier on you. Dawn worked with an English professor who would audio record herself reading and commenting on students' written papers. Then she would e-mail the students the audio file. She found that she could provide more feedback and in greater depth in less time using this approach than she could when giving written feedback. Using this approach, or even writing comments on hard copies, needs to be done with some focus and discipline. Students will benefit more from less but more targeted and detailed feedback than from tons of small corrections and stream-of-consciousness comments.

One strategy that provides some focus as well as efficiency is to construct and use a master list of feedback comments. These feedback comments could be based on common mistakes you repeatedly encounter across papers or projects. **Rubrics*** are effective for scoring open-ended products and could contain not only guides for awarding a score or set of scores but space for you to comment on why students received a given score. Another strategy is to use **peer assessment*** as a means to engage students in the class in giving feedback. Having peers give feedback using a rubric with written comments is especially helpful for giving students feedback on early drafts of a paper or project.

Feedback and Technology

Online technologies can provide immediate feedback as students work through an assessment or after they complete one. This assessment can be done during or outside of class for either low-stakes or high-stakes situations. This feedback can range from a focus on misconceptions targeted at specific answer choices to overall performance for individual students or the entire class (Parkes & Zimmaro, 2016).

Summary

Feedback is information given to students about a performance, response, or action that they can use to guide their learning and/or improve their next performance. Whether you give feedback during class, after tests, or on written assignments, your feedback should address these three questions for the student (Hattie & Timperley, 2007): Where am I going (what is the goal)? How am I going (what is the student's progress toward the goal)? Where to next (what activities does the student need to engage in to make better progress toward the goal)?

See Also

Feedback Timing
Grade Explanation
Peer Assessment

References

Angelo, T., & Cross, P. (1993). *Classroom assessment techniques: A handbook for college teachers.* San Francisco: Jossey-Bass.
Butler, D. L., & Winne, P. H. (1995). Feedback and self-regulated learning: A theoretical synthesis. *Review of Educational Research, 65*(3), 245–281.
Corbett, A. T., & Anderson, J. R. (2001). Locus of feedback control in computer-based tutoring: Impact on learning rate, achievement and attitudes. *Proceedings of ACM CHI 2001 Conference on Human Factors in Computing Systems,* 245–252.
Deci, E. L., & Ryan, R. M. (2000). The "what" and "why" of goal pursuits: Human needs and the self-determination of behavior. *Psychological Inquiry, 11,* 227–268.
Hattie, J. A. (1999, August). Influences on student learning (Inaugural Lecture, University of Auckland, New Zealand). Retrieved April 22, 2015 from http://growthmindseteaz.org/files/Influencesonstudent2C683_1_.pdf
Hattie, J. A., & Timperley, H. (2007). The power of feedback. *Review of Educational Research, 77*(1), 81–112.
National Research Council. (2000). *How people learn: Brain, mind, experience, and school, expanded edition.* Washington, DC: National Academies Press.
Parkes, J., & Zimmaro, D. (2016). *Learning and assessing with multiple-choice questions in college classrooms.* New York, NY: Routledge.
Shute, V. J. (2008). Focus on formative feedback. *Review of Educational Research, 78*(1), 153–189.
Wiggins, G. (1998). *Educative assessment: Designing assessments to inform and improve student performance.* San Francisco: Jossey-Bass.

23 Feedback Timing

When Should Students Receive Feedback?

Recommendation: Provide task feedback to students immediately after a response is given or as soon as is practical.

What Is Timely Feedback?

If you are using selected-response questions for formative assessment purposes (see **formative and summative assessments***), try to provide **feedback*** aimed at correcting errors and misconceptions immediately after a response is given. In this instance, the immediate feedback supports students' subsequent practice on a particular concept or learning objective. Research shows that timely and targeted feedback can significantly enhance student performance by addressing misconceptions as students have them (Butler & Winne, 1995; Corbett & Anderson, 2001; Hattie & Timperley, 2007; National Research Council, 2000; Wiggins, 1998). The timing and frequency of feedback should align with your learning objectives for the activity or assessment.

For constructed-response questions (see **selected- and constructed-response questions***), it is not always possible to provide feedback immediately after a student responds. One strategy to mitigate this is to use **peer assessment*** whereby other students can review and provide input on a student's responses, particularly as a part of formative assessments. However, it is critical that peers be trained in how to provide constructive and informative feedback to their classmates.

When Should Feedback Be Delayed?

In a meta-analysis by Kulik and Kulik (1988) the authors found that delayed feedback, ranging from a few seconds to several days, appears to help learning only in special experimental situations. Hattie and Timperley (2007) report that feedback which points to how effectively a task was completed is most beneficial when provided immediately after a response. This can include indicating incorrect answers. However, feedback about the processes underlying the task, such as cues for providing information on how to search and/or strategize related to the task, is best when delayed (Hattie & Timperley, 2007). Additionally, Clariana, Wagner, and Roher Murphy (2000) discovered that delayed feedback has higher effect sizes when test items are difficult, surmising that, on more difficult items, students need more processing and more processing time, which the delay facilitates. In contrast, providing time for processing isn't as critical with easy items (Clariana, Wagner, & Roher Murphy, 2000).

How Can Technology Help Support Giving Feedback?

Online assessments, either completed during or outside of class, afford instructors the ability to provide immediate feedback to students, particularly for selected-response questions. This feedback can be tailored to the student's particular answer choice addressing the misunderstanding designed into that option. Additionally, advances in technology and artificial intelligence algorithms are now providing instructors the opportunity to do some machine-scoring and feedback for constructed-response questions. These include not only numeric input and short-answer responses but also longer text-based responses. For both the selected-response and constructed-response questions, this feedback can be delivered immediately and be personalized to the student's particular response or input.

Summary

It is not only the quality but also the timing of feedback that influences how well students learn. Whenever possible, instructors should provide immediate feedback on student responses to assessments, leveraging the power of technology to do so. Delayed feedback works best when instructors want students to reflect on the learning processes they used when responding to a task.

See Also

Feedback
Peer Assessment

Resource

Shute, V. J. (2008). Focus on formative feedback. *Review of Educational Research, 78*(1), 153–189.

References

Butler, D. L., & Winne, P. H. (1995). Feedback and self-regulated learning: A theoretical synthesis. *Review of Educational Research, 65*(3), 245–281.

Clariana, R. B., Wagner, D., & Roher Murphy, L. C. (2000). Appling a connectionist description of feedback timing. *Educational Technology Research and Development, 48*(3), 5–22.

Corbett, A. T., & Anderson, J. R. (2001). Locus of feedback control in computer-based tutoring: Impact on learning rate, achievement and attitudes. *Proceedings of ACM CHI 2001 Conference on Human Factors in Computing Systems*, 245–252.

Hattie, J., & Timperley, H. (2007). The power of feedback. *Review of Educational Research, 77*(1), 81–112.

Kulik, J. A., & Kulik, C. C. (1988). Timing of feedback and verbal learning. *Review of Educational Research, 58*(1), 79–97.

National Research Council. (2000). *How people learn: Brain, mind, experience, and school, expanded edition.* Washington, DC: National Academies Press.

Wiggins, G. (1998). *Educative assessment: Designing assessments to inform and improve student performance.* San Francisco: Jossey-Bass.

24 FERPA (Family Educational Rights and Privacy Act)

The federal Family Educational Rights and Privacy Act has several implications for how you communicate with your students about their grades in your courses and how, or whether, you communicate with anyone else about student performance.

The initial federal legislation was meant to provide students and their families with access to educational records (Weeks, 2001). Schools cannot have secret files which students and their families cannot see. But, in the other direction, the legislation also provides boundaries on who does have the right to see a student's educational record. This legislation has several implications for you *daily* as you communicate with your students about their performance in class. Let's have a look at several of them.

What Are These Rights?

Students (or legal guardians) have the right to inspect (though not necessarily to receive free copies of) any educational record about them being maintained by an educator or educational institution. They also have the right to have those educational records stay confidential. There are other rights under FERPA, but these are the ones that pertain to you as an instructor.

Directory information (e.g. e-mail addresses, phone numbers, mailing addresses, and dates of attendance) are not protected information under FERPA. Most institutions have policies through which students can opt to have that information not be publicly available. But such information does not have FERPA protection.

Educational records include but are not limited to:

• Graded work—papers, exams, posters—anything which bears evaluative comments or other marks which contribute to a grade in the course.
• Information about a student's academics—letters of recommendation, grade books, written progress reports.

FERPA exempts "sole possession records" from these requirements. These are any documents you create yourself to aid you with your work but that you do not share with others or place in a student's official file. They remain in your sole possession. For example, perhaps as a dissertation advisor, you keep notes or even a journal about your work with a particular student. As long as you are making them for yourself and not sharing them with others, students do not have a right to inspect them under FERPA. If, while you are reviewing applications for your undergraduate program, you take notes which you then use when the admissions committee meets, they are no longer sole possession records because you shared them.

Whose Rights Are They?

FERPA rights belong to the parents or legal guardians of minors (those less than 18 years old) or to the students directly once they are 18. FERPA makes an exception for college students of any age; the rights are directly their own. If a college student, of any age, is a dependent for tax purposes, then those of whom they are a dependent still retain these rights. Your institution may or may not have provisions for documenting dependence and for providing those parents access (Weeks, 2001). You should probably see how your institution handles this particular issue before you wade in yourself.

With Whom Can I Discuss a Student's Class Performance?

You are legally able to discuss a student's performance with only three categories of people:

- The student herself—simple enough.
- Anyone for whom the student has granted written permission—your institution might have a form or other procedures for students to grant this permission. Minimally, such permission must be in writing with a date, signature, what is to be released, to whom it is to be released, and why it is to be released.
- Anyone with a *Legitimate Educational Interest* in that student's progress. Legitimate Educational Interest is specified in the Act itself as anyone who, by virtue of the position they hold, needs to know how a student is doing. For example, employees in your institution's financial aid office need to know whether the student is on probation or not in order to make financial aid decisions. That person has a legitimate educational interest.

Notice who is NOT on that list:

- A student's mom, dad, or step-uncle on her mother's side who is footing the bill for her education. You'll hear that on the phone: "I'm paying for this class! I want to know how she's doing!" If the student is their dependent for tax purposes, they have a right to the information. If not, they do not. Check to see how your institution addresses permissions regarding dependents.

- A student's spouse, partner, or child.
- You, under certain circumstances. If your niece is attending your institution, and you're curious about how she did last semester, you would actually be violating FERPA to pull up her transcript. Even though you have access to transcripts because you are a faculty member, that position does not give you a legitimate educational interest in your niece's progress. When looking at her transcript, you are an aunt or an uncle, not a faculty member, so you may not look at her transcript.

Examples of FERPA Violations:

- Posting a gradebook with identifiable student information (names, student IDs) in a public place, like on your office door, or on a website.
- Posting a gradebook sorted by identifiable student information (like last names) even if the names are obscured or absent.
- Handing a graded paper to a classmate to give to another student without that other student's written permission.
- Letting students sort through a stack of graded papers to find theirs if evaluative information is visible.
- Telling a faculty colleague how a student is doing in your class unless they have a legitimate educational interest with respect to that particular student.
- Including FERPA-protected information in a letter of recommendation without the student's written consent for you to write that letter.

(Rainsberger, 2007)

Under FERPA, It Is Still OK To:

- Have students grade each other's work in class when that grading is also a learning experience. (Believe it or not, this clarification is a Supreme Court ruling! (*Owasso Independent School District v. Falvo*, 2002.)
- Post grades on your door or bulletin board or public website as long as the list is not ordered in any meaningful way from which students could discern other student's identities. Use a student ID system of your own devising which students cannot hack.

Examples of FERPA Best Practices:

- Make students aware of what you will and won't do because of FERPA. If you and your institution are OK with a student e-mailing you to say, "Please give my paper to Jenna in class today; I have a cold," then make that your policy.

- E-mailing FERPA-protected information to students is a gray area. Jay still asks students to provide him with an e-mail address which he can use to communicate with them about their course performance. Right on that form, Jay mentions that, if students provide a family e-mail address which other members of the family have access, they are granting him that permission. Many institutions have course management systems some of which allow you to post secure messages to students that could be used in lieu of e-mail.
- Ask students to make requests for letters of recommendation from you in writing. They need to include date, signature, person to whom the letter is to be addressed, and the reason for the recommendation (e.g. a job, internship, scholarship).

(Rainsberger, 2007)

Please Learn More About This Topic, Particularly If You Are Wondering About a Current Practice

We suspect your institution actually has training available for you about FERPA issues on campus. You may even be required to take this training. If you're not sure if you're required, ask your department chair. We suggest you take the training at your institution or refresh it if it's been a while.

We also should mention that our discussion of FERPA here is confined to its implications to you as an individual instructor working with academic records. FERPA has broader implications for your institution regarding health/medical, disciplinary, financial, and legal records, too.

Summary

The federal Family Educational Rights and Privacy Act has several implications for how you communicate with your students about their grades in your courses and how, or whether, you communicate with anyone else about student performance. Understand that what you do with graded materials is regulated by this federal law. Learn about your institution's approaches to FERPA and craft practices which are in compliance. Communicate clearly with your students about your FERPA-driven practices.

Resource

Ramirez, C. A. (2009). *FERPA: Clear and simple.* San Francisco, CA: Jossey-Bass.

References

Family Educational Rights and Privacy Act (FERPA) (20 U.S.C. § 1232g; 34 CFR Part 99).

Owasso Independent School District v. Falvo, 534 US 426 (2002).

Rainsberger, R. (2007). Ensure that letters of recommendation don't violate FERPA. *Successful Registrar, 7*(1), 3.

Weeks, K. M. (2001). Family-friendly FERPA policies: Affirming parental partnerships. *New Directions for Student Services, 94,* 39–50.

25 Formative and Summative Assessments

What Are Formative Assessments?

Formative assessments are assessments *for* learning administered during instruction with the goal to support learning (Oosterhof, Conrad, & Ely, 2008; Vonderwell, Liang, & Alderman, 2007). They are designed to provide students **feedback*** about their learning and instructors feedback about their teaching in a low-stakes format. Specifically, formative assessments can help answer the following questions:

- How well are my students learning?
- How effectively am I teaching?
- How can I improve my teaching?
- Is the course on track? If not, how far is it off and how can I get it back on the right track?

Formative assessments can include student feedback about what question(s) they have from that day's class to a short quiz embedded in a video that require students to check their understanding before proceeding. Other examples include journals, concept maps, drafts of a project or paper, **self-assessment***, and peer feedback (see **peer assessment***). Angelo and Cross (1993) created a collection of Classroom Assessment Techniques (CATs) that are formative assessments to measure student knowledge and skills, attitudes and values, and reactions to instruction.

While there is general agreement that formative assessments should be low-stakes, there is some debate about whether they should be ungraded or given low point values. Those that argue for ungraded formative assessments suggest that the goal of formative assessments is to help reveal student misconceptions and areas for improvement and grading can hinder students' willingness to make "mistakes." Advocates for including some weight, even minimal, to formative assessments suggest that students will not take the activity seriously if no grades are attached to it. (We discuss these issues in **not everything that matters must be graded***.) The latter is an issue of motivation and engagement and is not an inherent issue with formative assessments. We recommend not grading formative assessments and explicitly informing your students about the purpose they serve: to help identify areas for improvement in their learning (see **learning-oriented assessment***). Additionally, student engagement with frequent low-stakes formative assessments is shown to be positively related to their performance on high-stakes summative assessments (Angus & Watson, 2009; Black & Wiliam, 1998; Smith, 2007). Let your students know that the formative assessments are practice and feedback opportunities to help prepare them to be more successful on summative assessments.

What Are Summative Assessments?

Summative assessments are used to evaluate student learning typically at the end of some instructional unit, such as at the end of a project, set of modules, program, or course. They are usually high-stakes in that they are graded with a relatively large weight and influence decisions such as passing a course, achieving a certificate, or meeting outcomes standards. Common examples include tests, projects, papers, and portfolios. Although primarily focused on evaluating learning and contributing to course grades, summative assessments also can be used to identify learning gaps and suggest areas for additional intervention.

Why Should You Care About the Difference?

Whereas formative assessments are viewed as measures *for* learning, summative assessments are used as measures *of* learning. However, what makes a given assessment formative is not the specific assessment itself, but how the information is used. An ungraded quiz can be used formatively in that its purpose is to identify where students have gaps in their understanding based on a reading assignment or online module. You can then use that information to guide your in-class discussion on that topic. A graded quiz might then follow the lesson to gauge what students have learned at its conclusion. Formative and summative assessments should not be seen as a dichotomy but rather parts of a continuum of practice, feedback, diagnostics, and improvement. A well-constructed **assessment plan*** will contain assessments for both formative and summative purposes.

Summary

Formative assessments are typically ungraded practice activities that focus on providing feedback to the learner and the instructor about gaps in understanding. Students engage in formative assessment during the course of instruction. Summative assessments are typically graded activities that occur at the end of some unit of instruction and are used to evaluate how well students have learned a set of concepts. The same assessment tool can be used for formative or summative purposes. A well-designed course will blend both formative and summative assessments to provide feedback to your students about their learning as well as to you about the effectiveness of your instructional approaches.

See Also

Assessment Plan

Resource

Angelo, T., & Cross, P. (1993). *Classroom assessment techniques: A handbook for college teachers.* San Francisco: Jossey-Bass.

References

Angelo, T., & Cross, P. (1993). *Classroom assessment techniques: A handbook for college teachers.* San Francisco: Jossey-Bass.

Angus, S. D., & Watson, J. (2009). Does regular online testing enhance student learning in the numerical sense? Robust evidence from a large data set. *British Journal of Educational Technology, 40*(2), 255–272.

Black, P., & Wiliam, D. (1998). Assessment and classroom learning. *Assessment in Education, 5*(1), 70–73.

Oosterhof, A., Conrad, R. M., & Ely, D. P. (2008). *Assessing learners online.* NJ: Pearson.

Smith, G. (2007). How does student performance on formative assessments relate to learning assessed by exams? *Journal of College Science Teaching, 36*(7), 28–34.

Vonderwell, S., Liang, X., & Alderman, K. (2007). Asynchronous discussions and assessment in online learning. *Journal of Research on Technology in Education, 39*(3), 309–328.

26 Gatekeeping

Assessment Issues in Gatekeeper Courses

Gatekeeper courses, sometimes referred to as killer courses, present a warren of complex issues at the student, instructor, departmental, institutional, and even societal levels. Here, we wish to focus on an extremely discrete set of those issues which impact your daily assessment life with your students. We begin with a discussion of your philosophy and mindset about gatekeeping. We'll point to a broader classroom assessment picture, the constellation of issues discussed elsewhere in this book which bear on gatekeeper courses. Finally, we'll discuss some of the nuts and bolts: course alignment, pre-testing, and grading.

The Philosophy and Mindset of Gatekeeping

Even to call your course a "gatekeeper course" drapes a mantel of preconceptions and expectations on it. We like Smith's (1997) expression of this: "Even the term 'gatekeeping' itself expresses distaste, suggesting as it does both barriers ('gates') and selectivity ('keeping')—not to mention the barbarians said to be just outside" (p. 301). Regardless of what you call it, there is a very legitimate function in some (all?) courses to make sure students know what they need to know to succeed in their next course(s) and ultimately in the profession for which you are preparing them. You are your "profession's advocate" (Cairney, Hodgdon, & Sewon, 2008, p. 132). The issue for us is *how* you gate-keep.

There's a philosophy which says that the job of teaching such courses is to weed out those who aren't good enough, which has a negative valence and focus compared to a philosophy which says that the job is to make sure that students are prepared for what lies ahead. The former leads to a focus on failure and to instructors who make the course hard—in any way they can—to preserve a certain failure rate. (Some researchers of gatekeeping use a failure rate of 25–30% as definitional.) This is a "sink or swim" mentality resulting in many disadvantageous teaching and learning behaviors. In **beneficence*** we discuss more fully why we believe this stance is inconsistent with education.

What if the focus is on passing, not failing? What if the emphasis is on doing all you can to promote student success rather than "weeding them out"? What if being the profession's advocate and being the student's advocate are congruent, not in conflict? Then, a different set of practices comes to the fore. Interestingly, students notice the difference: students who persisted in engineering courses but who struggled academically were more willing to believe that faculty deliberately made the courses hard in order to weed out weak students than students who did well academically (Suresh, 2006–2007). Further, Suresh found that "students did not utilize professors' office hours for help, or approach them when they encountered difficulties" (p. 225).

Seeing the Whole Picture

With a mindset of successfully shepherding students into the profession, you now share your students' goals and are working with them towards those goals rather than standing athwart their paths. In another study, students who believed the faculty were open to questions and that faculty felt they were there to help students succeed were more academically engaged in class (Gasiewski, Eagan, Garcia, Hurtado, & Chang, 2012). What a difference!

It also changes how you view the content of these courses. Prerequisite knowledge to enter the profession is more than just content and facts; it's also dispositions and ways of thinking. Teach it all! What are the good behaviors that make an effective professional in your field? Is punctuality important? Expect them to be in class, ready to go, at the scheduled start time. Is formatting critical, or are certain annotation conventions in programming critical? Then require them on assignments (see **not everything that matters must be graded***). Such requirements, however, do not serve an exclusionary role with this mindset; rather they are part of preparing students for the profession. It helps immensely also if you are explaining those aspects to students.

Once you are beside your students on this journey, not blocking their route, lots of other issues we discuss in the book become relevant, for example: **learning-oriented assessment***, **formative and summative assessments***, **criterion-referenced grading approaches***.

Alignment Practices

If your goal is preparing students for subsequent courses, it is critical that your course be aligned with those next courses. That sounds commonsensical to say, but course alignment doesn't just happen. It needs to be consciously built and assiduously maintained. This is largely an issue of planning which happens prior to teaching the course.

It begins with your learning objectives. Are they derived from explicit knowledge of those subsequent courses? Using a given textbook is helpful but confirm that it does, indeed, align.

Talk regularly to those who teach the next courses. Get their feedback about how your students do in those courses. Ask them to review your learning objectives, your assignments, and your assessments on a routine basis (see **align assessments to learning objectives***).

Gatekeeper courses tend to be the very first ones (after remedial or developmental ones) that students take, which means you may not see the need to align them strongly to the profession beyond the upper division courses. But you might think about that. Why lose the opportunity? How can you tie your intro course to the profession itself? More importantly, how can you immediately help students see those connections? It's important that students understand how this intro course includes knowledge and dispositions that are required on the job.

There are more formal mechanisms in some disciplines. You would know if this is you: national accreditation standards defining content; departmental committees overseeing courses; outcomes assessment sequences; local advisory boards.

Establishing a Terminus a Quo

Jay had an educational psychology professor as an undergraduate who had some Latin training in his background, and he was fond of saying that the teacher's job is to take students from the "terminus a quo" to the "terminus ad quem." That's a very learned-sounding way of saying you've got to get students from where they *are*, regardless of where that is or why (it may not be your fault but it is now your problem), to where they *need to be* by the end of your class. Knowing where each student's terminus a quo stands is an important consideration. We have an entire entry on assessing **prior knowledge***. Note also that, if your colleagues teaching the subsequent courses to yours do a prior knowledge assessment, getting those results from them would be extremely useful alignment information for you as well as serving as another measure of your students' terminus ad quem.

Criteria for Passing

How will you know that your students have reached the terminus ad quem, that is, how will you define passing? **Norm-referenced grading approaches*** and curving are common choices in gatekeeping courses, although we were heartened to discover the empirical finding of Barnes, Bull, Campbell, and Perry (2001) that there is only a modest correlation between use of norm-referenced grading and a sense of a gatekeeping role. That is, even faculty with a strong sense of a gatekeeping role often use criterion-referenced grading.

One of our overarching philosophies is that, in any learning setting, norm-referenced grading is seldom appropriate because a high grade should result anytime a student masters a learning objective without respect to who else in the class has done so.

This also means that you should not be thinking before the class or during the class about what percentage of your students may or will fail. Considering that percentage afterwards may have some value, but proactive consideration of it does not. You and your colleagues can carefully weigh what you deem to be unacceptably high failure rate. (The concept of an "unacceptably low failure rate" is antithetical to any educational endeavor, in our view.) We would actually consider it unethical to engineer assessments and grades in order to achieve a certain failure rate, and we have the support of the *Standards for Educational and Psychological Testing* (American Educational Research Association, American Psychological Association, & National Council on Measurement in Education, 2014).

Summary

In a gatekeeping course, you should position yourself beside your students, helping them to achieve their goal of being a well-prepared member of a profession or a discipline rather than positioning yourself athwart that path. Focus on doing all you can, and equipping them to do all they can, to help them pass and to excel in your course. Make sure your course is well-aligned with subsequent courses and with the profession. Know what knowledge they come into your course with. Then assess and grade in ways that document whether students have met those expectations or not.

Gatekeeper courses constitute a warren of complex issues at the student, instructor, departmental, institutional, and even societal levels. Here, we have focused on an extremely discrete set of those issues which impact your daily assessment life with your students.

Resource

Bloom, L. Z. (2004). The seven deadly virtues. *The Journal of the Assembly for Expanded Perspectives on Learning, 10*(1), 3.

References

American Educational Research Association, American Psychological Association, & National Council on Measurement in Education. (2014). *The standards for educational and psychological testing.* Washington, DC: AERA.

Barnes, L. L., Bull, K. S., Campbell, N. J., & Perry, K. M. (2001). Effects of academic discipline and teaching goals in predicting grading beliefs among undergraduate teaching faculty. *Research in Higher Education, 42*(4), 455–467.

Cairney, T., Hodgdon, C., & Sewon, O. (2008). The effects of individual, institutional, and market factors on business school faculty beliefs about grades. *Review of Business Research, 8*(3), 131–138.

Gasiewski, J. A., Eagan, M. K., Garcia, G. A., Hurtado, S., & Chang, M. J. (2012). From gatekeeping to engagement: A multicontextual, mixed method study of student academic engagement in introductory STEM courses. *Research in Higher Education, 53*(2), 229–261.

Smith, J. (1997). Students' goals, gatekeeping, and some questions of ethics. *College English, 59*(3), 299–320.

Suresh, R. (2006–2007). The relationship between barrier courses and persistence in engineering. *Journal of College Student Retention, 8*(2), 215–239.

27 Grade Explanation

Grade explanation can actually refer to two different things. First, there's a usage that means, in a multiple-choice question, for example, explaining why A is the right answer. In the literature, this is labeled "corrective feedback," or "knowledge of results" (Hattie & Timperley, 2007). Second, there's what you were probably thinking, which is why did a student receive the score she did.

Corrective Feedback: Why Is A the Right Answer?

Providing students knowledge of results, the cue that they are right or wrong, is something we do almost constantly. When a student makes a comment in class, and you say, "Yes!," that's corrective feedback. When your students take an online quiz, click submit, and receive right/wrong information on each item, that's corrective feedback. For very discrete knowledge, like a sum or a fact, right/wrong by itself is useful, and should occur as quickly as possible (see Hattie & Timperley, 2007; Shute, 2008). For most learning objectives, knowledge of right/wrong does almost nothing to further the student's learning. "OK, I got the question wrong. Why!?!?!?!?" So some explanation beyond corrective feedback is more beneficial (see **feedback***).

Grade Explanation: Why Did I Get a B?

There are several levels at which the student may be asking the "Why did I get a B?" question. First is the knowledge of results level. Here we let students know how many items on the test they got wrong, or where on the rubric their work corresponded (see **rubrics***). Second is a calculation question: "How did you arrive at my score?" Third would be more substantive feedback where you explain why the student's response was inadequate.

Students have a right to understand why they've received the grade they did. How the grade was determined should never be mysterious to a student. (See **beneficence***, **grade feeding frenzy***, and also our discussion in **make-up exams*** about the Good Faith Contract if the previous sentences don't ring true for you.)

Methods of Providing Grade Explanation

Here, briefly, are some strategies you can employ in making grade explanations.

Knowledge of Results

- Release the test and the scoring guide to the students.
- Provide the test and scoring guide for review during class or office hours if you are concerned about test security.
- Provide the scoring guide, the rubric, or definitions of a good response before the test and again afterward.

Calculations

- Let students know ahead of time how their score will be calculated. For semester grades, this should be on the syllabus as a part of the **assessment plan***. For assignments, it should be on the assignment sheet. For exams, it can be part of the study guide and written right in the test's directions.
- Repeatedly encourage students to contact you immediately if they believe your gradebook is inaccurate or if they believe you have mis-scored their work. Imagine for a moment that A is the right answer to multiple-choice question #17 on your mid-term exam. There's a difference between a student who answered A but you marked it wrong and a student who answered B who thinks B should also be correct. We should do all we can to encourage the former student to voice her question about how her grade was calculated. We have a range of options for how to address the second issue, which is a different kind of grade explanation (see **drop a question***). Do not confuse the two!
- Communicate with students about their progress to date in the course. With a gradebook in a learning management system (LMS), you only need to remind them to check. Otherwise, you'll need to devise a way to let them know not only their score on the current exam but where that puts them in the semester.

Substantive Feedback

- There is an entire entry on **feedback***, so we encourage you to check that out.

Summary

Grade explanations can mean "why was A the right answer" on a multiple-choice question. It can also mean "why did I get a B" on that test. The former is best addressed as feedback. The latter is a broader communication matter with your students.

See Also

Feedback
Feedback Timing
Grade Feeding Frenzy
Learning-Oriented Assessment

References

Hattie, J., & Timperley, H. (2007). The power of feedback. *Review of Educational Research,* 77(1), 81–112.

Shute, V. J. (2008). Focus on formative feedback. *Review of Educational Research,* 78(1), 153–189.

28 Grade Feeding Frenzy

How Do I Avoid the Feeding Frenzy When Giving Out Grades?

"So why is the answer to number 14 C and not B?"

"Why did he get more points on his paper than I did on mine? We worked together!"

"Will you give us some points back because they were mowing the lawn outside the room when we took this test?"

These are the first ominous sounds preceding a classroom feeding frenzy. Can you hear those first few low pitches of the *Jaws* theme sounding? (Really, you feel them before you hear them.) A question like, "So why is the answer to number 14 C and not B?" are the first two low notes of the *Jaws* theme. What you say next will set you on a course toward safety or total disaster.

We're using some melodramatic humor here, but this is actually a serious topic. Jay has observed instructors who navigated this situation poorly and it really was a total disaster. How you give back tests or papers can become a wretched personal experience for you and your students.

If, in response to questions like these, you cede control of the decision-making and the agenda, the students will notice. They will take control of the decision-making and the agenda. And you will struggle mightily to get it back, if you ever get it back. Once you start entertaining arguments about question #14, they'll ask you about #22. And then #5. And then how could #27 possibly be OK? The longer this goes on, the more defensive, frustrated, and vulnerable you become and the more emboldened and mean-spirited they can become. It's a nasty downward spiral for everyone involved and it will change the entire term for you. A shark feeding frenzy is not a terribly hyperbolic analogy.

For your own sake, but more importantly, for the learning environment during this class period and the relationship you'll have with these students for the rest of the term, be ready for this moment. Do not fumble into this unprepared. As with most dangerous situations, there are steps you should be taking to prevent them from developing and there are steps you can take when you find yourself there.

Who Is in Control?

First, some basic classroom management theory. The college is paying *you* to teach this class. You are responsible. You are in control. No matter how democratic you are or think you are, you are in control and ultimately responsible. Matters of grading and decision-making about grades are your ultimate responsibility. You can cede some of that to students (like with peer grading), but it is yours to cede. If there is a feeding frenzy, it is of your own doing.

Manipulate Time and Timing

Students need time to think about feedback and to digest the grade they just received. When you return tests or papers, students will have an immediate reaction. It will be emotional. Sometimes it's elation. Sometimes it's relief. Sometimes it's frustration. Sometimes it's anger. "Self-expression often trumps self-control" (Hampton, 2002, p. 62). Give students time to have those reactions, to get past those reactions, and to reflect on the score and the feedback. Handing back tests at the beginning of the next class period does not provide them with any time to process.

Preventively, do what you can to insert time between when they receive their scores and when they have an opportunity to discuss them with you. You can leave this loose by handing papers back at the end of class. Or you can make it more structured by having some formal process for a mastery opportunity (see **mastery opportunities***) or an appeals procedure. You can tell students that you will hear appeals regarding the test but not until 48 hours have elapsed after the exam. This can be critical with online or otherwise technologically delivered tests. They can see their score immediately after finishing and then e-mail you directly. By imposing a minimum wait period, you give them time to react and then to reflect.

You also want to attend to the timing. Again, don't give evaluative information back at the beginning of a class period. Students at a minimum will be thinking about the grade and not about class. And they're likely to want to talk about their grades.

Those are all preventative ideas. Suppose you find yourself faced with those ominous low notes? Buy time. Tell them that your office hours would be more conducive to addressing their questions or concerns. Or that after class would be fine. Unless you know—and you're sure—that you can quickly and decisively address the inquiry, defer it. Put off answering. Move on to other topics. If they persist, be a broken record: "As I said, this discussion is more appropriate during my office hours." This doesn't mean you can't be accommodating and even gracious: "I want to make sure I give myself the time to fully consider your question as it deserves. I'll come back with an answer next class."

Manipulate Space

Not only do you want to insert time between the test and their ability to communicate with you about it, you want also to insert some space. Handing exams out at the end of class provides you with the ability to leave the classroom and to let them leave the classroom. If you hand them out at the beginning, you are both, essentially, trapped there together. Even if you hand them out at the end, you could end up with ten students clamoring around you. Hopefully, many of your assignments are electronically handled these days, so space isn't much of an issue.

A classroom full of students is a daunting place to be on the defensive. Change the venue. By insisting that these discussions occur in your office, you limit the number of students who can question you at one time. It also introduces time, as we've discussed.

Students are much more likely to treat you with the dignity due an individual if they are with you one on one in your office than if there are 75 of them in a lecture hall. Use that to establish and maintain control.

Provide Feedback

Providing feedback about the test as a whole or about individual questions on a test can help alleviate some of the feeding frenzy behaviors. If the class as a whole did poorly on a test, it may be worthwhile to discuss the questions that seemed most problematic after you return the test. You can still use the strategies above to manipulate time and space after providing students this feedback. See **feedback*** for a more detailed discussion about how to use this strategy to focus students on the learning processes embedded in your assessment rather than their grades.

Message

Proactively communicate with students about their grades. Make sure students know before they take the test when and how they should expect to receive scores back. Let them know ahead of time if you will provide mastery opportunities, or if there is an appeals process.

If you find yourself with a feeding frenzy about to start, buy time by telling them you need time to think about the issues they've raised. Tell them you want the assessment to be as fair as possible, so you're willing to hear from them if they think it was not. But they need time to think about it and so do you. Make sure you communicate to them that their learning is the truly important thing.

Summary

Prevent feeding frenzies by introducing time between when they receive grades and when they can talk with you about them. Defer questions out of the classroom both in terms of time and in terms of space. Communicate well with your students about the pre-eminence of their learning.

See Also

Feedback
Mastery Opportunities

Reference

Hampton, D. R. (2002). Making complaining appealing. *College Teaching, 50*(2), 62. DOI: 10.1080/87567550209595876

29 Grade Inflation

What Is Grade Inflation?

Grade inflation refers to the increase in average course grades given to students at colleges and universities. Rojstaczer and Healy (2012) analyzed historical data from 200 four-year colleges and universities from 1940–2009 and found that A's represent 43% of all letter grades, which is a 28% increase since 1960 and a 12% increase since 1988. Additionally, D's and F's collectively account for less than 10% of grades awarded. However, this trend is not as prevalent in community colleges where about 36% of grades awarded are A's, but that percentage has declined in recent years (Jaschik, 2016).

Grade Inflation vs. Grade Compression

Grade compression refers to the narrowing of the grading scale, for example, when instructors award mostly A's and B's, and grade inflation is the increase in average course grade over time. In economic terms, inflation is an increase in the price level of goods and services over time. However, there is no cap or limit to the cost of these goods and services. Since grades have a ceiling of A or A+, when a greater number of higher grades are awarded, a concentration of students occurs at the top end of the grading scale. Grade compression may be a result of a movement toward mastery learning where students must meet a certain level of performance, or reach mastery, before moving on to the next unit. Under this instructional paradigm, more students will receive higher grades thereby compressing the grading scale.

Why Does Grade Inflation Happen?

Instructors awarding higher grades may be due to higher quality students at an institution or possibly due to lowering standards making it easier for students to earn an A. Rojstaczer and Healy (2012) believe that institutional shifts in viewing students as "consumers" has led to pressure on faculty and instructors to lower standards and award higher grades. Using student course evaluations as a measure of satisfaction with instructors and courses may increase this pressure. Additionally, institutions report average GPA to help recruit future students (Rojstaczer & Healy, 2012).

Why Is Grade Inflation a Problem?

The biggest issue with grade inflation is that it makes grades a poor differentiator of student abilities and performance. Rojstaczer and Healy (2012) conclude,

> It is likely that at many selective and highly selective schools, undergraduate GPAs are now so saturated at the high end that they have little use as a motivator of students and as an evaluation tool for graduate and professional schools and employers.
>
> (p. 2)

Additionally, a study by Babcock (2010) reported a relationship between student effort and anticipated expected grade. Students in courses where the expected average course grade was an A had an average self-reported study time 50% lower than students in courses where the expected average course grade was a C.

However, Pattison, Groadsky, and Muller (2013) argue that while average course grades are indeed increasing, the ability of grades to act as a "signaling" power, or the ability to provide information to and about students, for employment after graduation has not changed (i.e. in the quality of jobs and salaries earned). They argue that since the signaling power of grades has not changed, the value of grades, despite grade inflation trends, has remained steady.

What Are Some Ways Institutions Have Tried to Combat Grade Inflation?

One approach some institutions have adopted is to provide recommendations on the percentage of grades that can be awarded A's. For example, in 2004 Princeton issued a guideline that no more than 35% of grades given in undergraduate courses should be A's. However, Princeton abandoned that strategy in 2014 as the practice led to stress for students and may have affected applicants to the school (Kohil, 2014).

Setting caps on the percentage of students who can earn a particular grade essentially employs a norm-referenced grading approach (see **norm-referenced grading approaches***). Kamber and Biggs (2003) proposed a return to norm-referenced, or normal curve, grading or a new system that takes advantages of norm-referenced grading approaches. They propose a ranking system whereby all students who receive a passing grade are ranked. Instead of grade point average, students would receive a class rank average (CRA) on their transcript (Kamber & Biggs, 2003).

For institutions that find capping the percentage of A's, adopting a true norm-reference grading strategy, or using and reporting ranks unpalatable, a possible compromise approach is to report the mean or median course grade on a student's transcript (Kamber & Biggs, 2003). This would allow employers and others making decisions based on student transcripts to see where a student stands relative to her peers.

Another strategy is to address grade compression by uncapping the highest grade. Institutions could give grades such as A+++ instead of capping them as A or A+ (Slavov, 2013). This strategy most likely doesn't address the grade inflation issue, but rather shifts the compressed grading scale so that over time grades range from A+ to A+++ rather than C to A.

How Can You Prevent Grade Inflation?

While institutions have several strategies at their disposal to systematically address grade inflation, there are some steps you can take as well. First and foremost, ensure that you are clearly articulating your learning objectives and demonstrate how your assessments align to those learning objectives (see **align assessments to learning objectives***) as part of your **assessment plan***. Additionally, if you use open-ended assessments make sure that you use **rubrics*** with well-defined criteria to score those assessments. Avoid including things like **participation*** or **effort*** in your grades as these can artificially and unnecessarily increase students' grades. These approaches will ensure that you have precise and transparent standards by which students are being evaluated in order to earn a certain grade in your course. As an individual instructor the concern is that you are lowering those standards in order to appeal to students who expect certain grades. By communicating those standards to your students and administrators and the evidence you are collecting to determine if students have met those standards, you can avoid the perceived leniency that has crept into college grading. In addition, if the standards you set are reasonable, then students who meet those standards and receive high grades demonstrated their competency in meeting the learning objectives for the course.

Summary

Grade inflation is generally seen as an issue on college campuses, particularly at more selective four-year universities. The primary concern with rising average course grades is that they no longer help to differentiate students, a particular concern for employers and graduate school admissions offices. Strategies to combat grade inflation often focus on using some sort of norm-referenced grading approach, either by limiting the percentage of students who can earn a certain grade or by ranking students. Regardless of which grading strategy you use, you should clearly articulate the learning objectives students need to master in your course, align your assessments to those learning objectives, and create graded activities and assessments that provide evidence students have met those learning objectives. This approach will make your grading strategies transparent to students, administrators, and employers.

See Also

Align Assessments to Learning Objectives
Criterion-Reference Grading Approaches
Norm-Referenced Grading Approaches

Resource

Hunt, L. H. (Ed.). (2008). *Grade inflation: Academic standards in higher education.* Albany, NY: State University of New York Press.

References

Babcock, P. (2010). Real costs of nominal grade inflation? New evidence from student course evaluations. *Economic Inquiry, 48*(4), 983–996.

Jaschik, S. (2016, March 29). Grade inflation, higher and higher. *Inside Higher Education.* Retrieved May 19, 217 from www.insidehighered.com/news/2016/03/29/survey-finds-grade-inflation-continues-rise-four-year-colleges-not-community-college

Kamber, R., & Biggs, M. (2003). Grade inflation: Metaphor and reality. *The Journal of Education, 184*(1), 31–37.

Kohil, S. (2014, October 7). Princeton is giving up ground in its fight against grade inflation. *Quartz.* Retrieved from https://qz.com/277288/princeton-is-giving-up-ground-in-its-fight-against-grade-inflation/

Pattison, E., Groadsky, E., & Muller, C. (2013). Is the sky falling? Grade inflation and the signaling power of grades. *Educational Research, 42*(5), 259–265.

Rojstaczer, S., & Healy, C. (2012). Where A is ordinary: The evolution of American college and university grading, 1940–2009. *Teachers College Record, 114*(7), 1–23.

Slavov, S. (2013, December 6). How to fix grade inflation. *U.S. News & World Report.* Retrieved from www.usnews.com/opinion/blogs/economic-intelligence/2013/12/26/why-college-grade-inflation-is-a-real-problem-and-how-to-fix-it

30 Groupwork

Groupwork is one of the most complained about educational techniques ever known. Everyone has a "group-project-gone-wrong" story from some part of their educational experience. We don't have to tell you the complaints: one member carries the group and is highly resentful; everyone gets the same grade, *no matter what*; no one's contributions are equivalent, and I always think yours were less than mine; groups are not actually synergistic or actual teamwork but rather an amalgam of individual projects.

Your students will not make these complaints, however, because you will have a set of understandings and strategies to mitigate, if not eliminate, the problems with groupwork and group grading. We want to begin with some key principles for better groupwork and then follow on with some specific strategies for groups in general and for assessment in particular.

Principles for Better Groupwork

No one, to our knowledge, does a better, more comprehensive job of discussing these issues than David and Roger Johnson in their book, *Assessing Students in Groups: Promoting Group Responsibility and Individual Accountability*. We will draw on it heavily here, and, though it's pitched at K–12 teachers, most of it is very relevant to college classrooms. We encourage you to check it out.

The first thing for you to know is that some of the complaints are about the groups themselves and some of the complaints are about overlaying grading on top of groups. Johnson and Johnson (2004) articulate the distinction between using groups for individual assessment (chapter 4) and assessing groups as a whole (chapter 5).

As with most assessment decisions, knowing what learning objectives you are assessing is critical for forming, guiding, and assessing groups (see **align assessments to learning objectives***). If your learning objectives are purely course content (e.g. "students will construct a design plan for a smartphone app which exhibits iOS and/or Android UX/UI best practices") that will call on different decisions from you than learning objectives around processes like teamwork (e.g. "students will be able to work effectively in teams").

A related issue is whether groups are a tool by which you will assess student mastery or whether groupwork constitutes some aspect of the student mastery. In other words, are groups like a magnifying glass that you're using to look at something, or are groups part of the something you're trying to see. Perhaps it would prove helpful here also to ask, "Must I use groups, or would other strategies allow me to meet my assessment goals?"

Groups—whether used in assessment or for instruction without grades—work best when they are constructed using five basic elements (Johnson & Johnson, 2004, pp. 31–33). We want to mention two of them here: positive interdependence and accountability.

Positive interdependence means that students in a group *must* work together to accomplish their individual and collective goal(s). It also means that they see that, know that, and feel that. They must be invested in each other's learning as well as their own. They must be invested in each individual's grade as well as their own.

Accountability, here, means that each member must be held responsible for her own learning, her own grade, *as well as* being held responsible for each other group member's learning and grade. So there must be individual and collective responsibility.

Perhaps you are already understanding why most students hate groupwork. In most group assignments, one or both of those basic elements are missing. They must be structurally provided for by you as you define and manage the group assignment.

The three other basic elements that Johnson and Johnson (2004) outline are about how you get the students sufficiently skilled and refocused to work in groups this way. So they must interact in ways that drive true collaboration and support ("promotive interaction," p. 32), they must have or learn the necessary skills to make this work, and the group needs to explicitly examine how it is working.

There's SO MUCH more to the conceptual and theoretical bases here, so if you're intrigued, follow up with the resources at the end of this entry. Here are some techniques you can use to put these elements into practice.

Strategies for Better Groups

Specific methods and strategies that you can use for better groups break down into several categories. We'll take each in turn:

> *Group Composition*—Who is in the group and how did they get there? Research is clear that mixed-ability groups promote learning better than same-ability groups. That probably means you need to make group assignments rather than letting students self-select. This will also permit you to attend to racial, gender, age, cultural, linguistic, etc., issues, which are critical ones to attend to (see Popov et al., 2012; Rosser, 1998). Students don't self-select well to ensure that no

one is isolated. The decisions whether to keep groups intact (and for how long) or whether to reconstitute them (and how frequently) depends on your goals and uses of the groups (e.g. Walker, Bush, Sanchagrin, & Holland, 2017). Groups should usually have an odd number of members (or they split into subgroups) and, for most purposes, should not be larger than five students.

Group Structure—One of the keys to successful groupwork is to have differentiated roles. You need to actively define roles for students and explain how those roles work. One often overlooked element here, however, is whether every role permits students to practice and demonstrate knowledge of the learning objectives. So when someone is assigned the role of scribe or copy-editor, do they get to use their own knowledge of the objectives in checking the grammar of the final paper?

The Task—The tasks which you give to the groups must require inter-dependence and must include accountability or those two elements will not materialize. One group member must need something from another group member in order to complete her part of the task. There must be internal and external accountability measures to determine whether that exchange happened effectively and on time. You can choose to pitch groups a total task all at once or to break it down into subtasks that unfold over time.

The Products—What deliverables you require from individuals in the group and from the group in total also form part of the invitation for positive interdependence and accountability.

Technology—There's at least some indication that technology may also provide a way to improve group experiences for students. For example, introverted students reported more involvement in groups using technology than face-to-face (Voorm & Kommers, 2013). The information in this entry is relevant also to groups online, although the online environment presents particular challenges through asyn-chronicity and curtailing the modes and potential richness of inter-personal interactions (Smith et al., 2011).

Strategies for Assessment in or of Groups

Student complaints about groupwork get sharper when the stakes rise, that is, when grades are attached. The foundation of the complaints here is one stu-dent's ability to control her grade. If all members of the group will be assigned the same grade, any individual member has lost control over much of what will contribute to her grade unless particular contingencies are set in place. Here are some ideas to do group grading or grading through groups better.

Grading Through Groups means that each member of a group will receive an individual grade, although intermediate steps will be done as a group. The classic study group is a good example. Here, each student takes a test herself, but she studies with other students. One way to ramp up the power of the study group is to employ positive interdependence and accountability by allocating a small portion of the total points to the group performance. For example, allocate a small bonus (e.g. 5%) to each group member if every group member meets a minimum standard (e.g. 90%) on the individual test (Johnson & Johnson, 2004, p. 59). Now the focus of the study group isn't the material, but everyone's mastery of the material. If Juan and Susan are in the same group, Susan now has a defined stake in assisting Juan to master the material so he can earn at least a 90%.

Groups can be employed not only before a test but also during and/or after a test. Here's a quick list of such strategies (see also **collaborative testing***):

> *The Academic Tournament*—Here, groups compete against each other, which drives the group members to make sure each group member has mastered the material. Each student only wins if her team wins. See Johnson & Johnson (2004, pp. 63–68) for full details.
>
> *Group Test Retake*—After the individuals have taken the test, the group takes the test together. Each individual's final grade for the assessment is some combination of individual and group scores. See these variations: Retaking the Test in Groups (Johnson & Johnson, 2004, pp. 59–60); Collaborative Test-Taking (Bloom, 2009); Team-Based Learning (Fink, 2002).
>
> *Handing Back Exams*—Aldrich (2001) describes a post-exam technique where pre-existing groups work with individual exams and the answer key to improve student learning.

Group Grading means that each member of a group receives the group grade. In order for this to work, what we already addressed in previous sections must be considered. Assuming you've attended to all the issues above, here are some additional grade-related considerations:

> *Individual Accountability as Well as Group Accountability*—Individuals need to be graded on at least some portion of the work.
>
> *Group Processes*—One way to aid and encourage groups to function well is to apportion part of the overall grade to processes of group interaction. For example, you could ask group members to rate other group members on cooperation behaviors, or you could ask the group to self-assess their functioning. You could observe them at work and assign a grade on effective group functioning. Johnson and Johnson (2004) have a list on pp. 107–109.

Summary

Groups can work really well, even for assessment, as long as you know why you're using them and think through all aspects of their design and use. There's so much more to know and to say about effective groups. Check out some of the resources below.

See Also

Collaborative Testing
Peer Assessment

Resources

A themed issue of the *Journal on Excellence in College Teaching*, edited by Davidson, N., Major, C. H., & Michaelsen, L. K. (2014). *25(3&4)*.

Hodges, L. C. (2004). Group exams in science courses. *New Directions for Teaching and Learning, 100*, 89–93.

Johnson, D. W., & Johnson, R. T. (2004). *Assessing students in groups: Promoting group responsibility and individual accountability*. Thousand Oaks, CA: Corwin Press.

Millis, B. J., & Cottell, P. G. (1998). *Cooperative learning for higher education faculty*. Phoenix, AZ: American Council on Education and Oryx Press.

Roberson, B., & Franchini, B. (2014). Effective task design for the TBL classroom. *Journal on Excellence in College Teaching, 25*(3&4), 275–302.

Shimazoe, J., & Aldrich, H. (2010). Group work can be gratifying: Understanding & overcoming resistance to cooperative learning. *College Teaching, 58*(2), 52–57.

Thorley, L., & Gregory, R. (Eds.). (2013). *Using group-based learning in higher education*. New York, NY: Routledge.

References

Aldrich, H. E. (2001). How to hand exams back to your class. *College Teaching, 49*(3), 82. DOI: 10.1080/87567550109595853

Bloom, D. (2009). Collaborative test-taking: Benefits for learning and retention. *College Teaching, 57*(4), 216–220. DOI: 10.1080/87567550903218646

Fink, L. D. (2002). Beyond small groups: Harnessing the extraordinary power of learning teams. In L. K. Michaelsen, A. B. Knight, & L. D. Fink (Eds.), *Team-based learning: A transformative use of small groups*. Westport, CT: Praeger Publishers.

Johnson, D. W., & Johnson, R. T. (2004). *Assessing students in groups: Promoting group responsibility and individual accountability*. Thousand Oaks, CA: Corwin Press.

Popov, V., Brinkman, D., Biemans, H. J. A., Mulder, M., Kuznetsov, A., & Noroozi, O. (2012). Multicultural student group work in higher education: An explorative case study on challenges as perceived by students. *International Journal of Intercultural Relations, 36*, 302–317.

Rosser, S. V. (1998). Group work in science, engineering, and mathematics: Consequences of ignoring gender and race. *College Teaching, 46*(3), 82–88.

Smith, G. G., Sorensen, C., Gump, A., Heindel, A. J., Caris, M., & Martinez, C. D. (2011). Overcoming student resistance to group work: Online versus face-to-face. *Internet and Higher Education, 14*, 121–128.

Voorm, R. J. J., & Kommers, P. A. M. (2013). Social media and higher education: Introversion and collaborative learning from the student's perspective. *International Journal of Social Media and Interactive Learning Environments, 1*(1), 59–73.

Walker, A., Bush, A., Sanchagrin, K., & Holland, J. (2017). "We've got to keep meeting like this": A pilot study comparing academic performance in shifting-membership cooperative groups versus stable-membership cooperative groups in an introductory-level lab. *College Teaching, 65*(1), 9–16.

31 Humor

Should I Use Humor in Assessments?

Recommendation: Do not use humor on tests. Be very careful using humor on other assessments.

Humor is not only a natural part but also an important part of college teaching (e.g. Banas, Dunbar, Rodriguez, & Liu, 2011; Berk, 2002; Korobkin, 1988). Humor in the classroom is complex for many reasons (cf. Banas, Dunbar, Rodriguez, & Liu, 2011) including because it occurs inside of a power differential; because there are many linguistic and cultural eddies and currents in your classroom that will affect what is considered humorous; and, frankly, because not all of us are actually funny. Characteristics of assessment situations magnify these effects. Test or **evaluation anxiety*** is a critical issue as is the validity of the assessment results.

Humor seems a common-sense tool to use to reduce test anxiety. Humor is a signal of safety, of relaxed vigilance, of interpersonal comfort. However, the power differential between you and students and the stakes involved for the students mean they don't perceive humor as they would even in the middle of class on a Tuesday morning. Attempts at humor during an exam can paradoxically increase test anxiety (Banas, Dunbar, Rodriguez, & Liu, 2011). Students perceive humor to help with their anxiety but, when anxiety is directly assessed, an impact is hard to demonstrate (McMorris, Boothroyd, & Pietrangelo, 1997).

In order for humor to work, the students need to recognize it as humor. When they're focused on doing well, and perhaps anxious, they're less likely to catch the humor. If they have a different linguistic or cultural background than you, they may also miss it (McMorris, Boothroyd, & Pietrangelo, 1997). The question becomes, "Does the attempt at humor then hurt the validity of the assessment?"

With that background, here are some dos and don'ts regarding using humor on assessments.

What You Should Do

> *Be Consistent With Your Use of Humor*—If you tend to use humor during class, your students will handle it better inside of an assessment context than if you don't tend to use it in all your interactions with students.

Moderate Your Use of Humor by the Stressors Involved—A timed exam is more stressful for students than writing a paper is. Humor will be more problematic during the timed exam but might actually be facilitative on your assignment sheet for the paper.

Be Mindful of the Medium—A light-hearted verbal remark as you're passing out the test is very different than those exact same words appearing in the written directions on the test itself. Generally, the effectiveness of humor relies on a great many non-verbal cues that writing doesn't provide. So what is funny when you're talking with a student during office hours is not funny when it appears in question #19 on the mid-term exam.

What You Should NOT Do

Superiority, negative, derogatory, or defamatory humor is not beneficent (see **beneficence***) and seldom, if ever, contributes to a positive educational experience (Banas, Dunbar, Rodriguez, & Liu, 2011; Wanzer, Frymier, Wojtaszczyk, & Smith, 2006).

Using humor or sarcasm in communications about grades, deadlines, grade queries or challenges, interpretation of course policies, etc., can introduce ambiguity about your message.

Don't overuse humor (Banas, Dunbar, Rodriguez, & Liu, 2011), especially in an assessment context.

Summary

The empirical findings on humor on tests (e.g. McMorris, Boothroyd, & Pietrangelo, 1997) and the literature of the use of humor more generally in the college classroom (e.g. Banas, Dunbar, Rodriguez, & Liu, 2011) indicate that humor is a very complex social phenomenon, that demonstrations of the effectiveness of humor are at best mixed, and that the perception and the reality of humor use may be different. Some advocate for the use of humor on tests within this context (e.g. Berk, 2000, 2002). For us, this is a recipe for caution, great care, and the conservative conclusion that instructors should err on the side of avoiding the negative outcomes of using humor during assessment events, particularly tests.

See Also

Evaluation Anxiety

Resources

Banas, J. A., Dunbar, N., Rodriguez, D., & Liu, S. (2011). A review of humor in educational settings: Four decades of research. *Communication Education, 60*(1), 115–144.

McMorris, R. F., Boothroyd, R. A., & Pietrangelo, D. J. (1997). Humor in educational testing: A review and discussion. *Applied Measurement in Education, 10*(3), 269–297.

References

Banas, J. A., Dunbar, N., Rodriguez, D., & Liu, S. (2011). A review of humor in educational settings: Four decades of research. *Communication Education, 60*(1), 115–144.

Berk, R. A. (2000). Does humor in course tests reduce anxiety and improve performance? *College Teaching, 48*(4), 151–158.

Berk, R. A. (2002). *Humor as an instructional defibrillator: Evidence-based techniques in teaching and assessment.* Sterling, VA: Stylus Publishing.

Korobkin, D. (1988). Humor in the classroom: Considerations and strategies. *College Teaching, 36*(4), 154–158.

McMorris, R. F., Boothroyd, R. A., & Pietrangelo, D. J. (1997). Humor in educational testing: A review and discussion. *Applied Measurement in Education, 10*(3), 269–297.

Wanzer, M. B., Frymier, A. B., Wojtaszczyk, A. M., & Smith, T. (2006). Appropriate and inappropriate uses of humor by teachers. *Communication Education, 55*, 178–196.

32 Incomplete Grades

Recommendation: Award incomplete grades very sparingly and appropriately.

What Is an Incomplete Grade (I)?

Most institutions have a provision for permitting a student to complete work for a given course in a given semester after the grades for that given semester are due. This is referred to as an incomplete grade (I), or sometimes an X grade. Such a grade is essentially a time extension to complete the course requirements. While the individual instructor usually has discretion over many aspects of when and how an I grade works, most institutions have policies setting broad parameters. For example, some institutions have an expiration date when the I turns to an F on a student's transcript if the instructor doesn't change the grade.

You should take a moment right now to find and read your institution's incomplete grade policy. Anything else we discuss needs to be understood inside of your own institution's policies about this issue. Some institutions' policies are very broad and others are more detailed.

When to Offer or Award Incomplete Grades

Incomplete grades exist because life happens. Events beyond a student's control can interfere with getting course requirements done on schedule. For example, a student suffers a critical illness or the death of a family member late in the semester and struggles to make up the missed work. Incomplete grades are a humane way of addressing the needs of students as people.

When Not to Offer or Award Incomplete Grades

Because many institutional policies provide instructors with much discretion regarding I grades, instructors may be tempted to use them as a relief valve to handle a broad range of issues. We argue against broad use of incomplete grades because they are not designed for many of the situations for which they are deployed. For example, as a student was handing a final project in to Jay, he asked Jay if he could have an incomplete in the course. After a brief discussion, Jay determined that the student was not happy with his performance in the course and wanted an incomplete so that he could redo some of the work and earn a better grade. Jay said that "incomplete" was inappropriate because the student had, in fact, completed all assignments. The student was really asking for **extra credit***.

Some institution's policies include the specification that an incomplete can be offered when circumstances *beyond the student's control* caused the work not to get done. Illnesses, accidents, family deaths, and emergencies are all appropriate reasons. Spending an extra week away during Spring Break, for example, is not. If students had control of their circumstances, then they have chosen the consequences of their choices.

In our experience as instructors, and in Jay's experience as a department chair, we've seen lots of ways that I grades go wrong. If you are a contingent instructor—an adjunct, part-time instructor, or teaching assistant—realize that you remain responsible for resolving any incomplete grades. If you are unable or unwilling to do that, please talk to the department chair for the course about what your incomplete policies should be.

We've seen instructors who have proactively suggested to students that they should take an incomplete in order to spend more time doing "a better job" on something like a final paper. The power differential between instructor and student, the fact that work isn't actually "incomplete," and what usually are very vague criteria for the "better job," make this a minefield for the instructor and particularly for the student. Worse yet, some instructors do this as a remedial strategy for students with weak skills. Extra time is seldom the best support for such students.

Recommendations for How to Offer or Award Incomplete Grades

Communication is the real key to having incomplete grades work correctly and smoothly.

First, your syllabus should state your policy and practices for offering or awarding an incomplete grade. Those need to be clear at the beginning of the semester because they may well influence student choices. A study of syllabi showed that only 5.1% of syllabi had any mention of an incomplete policy (Parkes, Fix, & Harris, 2003). Two of those instructors explicitly said no incompletes would be given; four of them had specific conditions under which an incomplete would be granted.

Second, your students should receive information from you about missing assignments in real time. Perhaps this is the course gradebook in the learning management system (LMS), or perhaps you contact each student for whom you are missing an assignment. It's entirely possible that a student did turn in, or thought they turned in, that paper due in the third week in the semester. They should learn that it was missing and you shouldn't wait to deal with it until finals week or when you're computing and filing grades. (See **missing assignments***.)

Third, if you're communicating in real time about missing work, you can put the onus on the student to request an incomplete grade. This could be as informal as talking to you after class or during office hours, or it could be as formal as a form the student must complete. Some instructors take a contractual approach and use a document that specifies what is missing; what must be submitted to fulfill the missing assignment(s); what documentation of the reason for the I grade must be submitted (e.g. doctor's note; obituary); when the missing work must be submitted; what will happen on that deadline; how will you remind the student about the incomplete.

Frequently, in our experience, I grades are frustration- and anxiety-provoking for both instructors and students. Students often have a year from the end of the semester to resolve an incomplete, so you may find yourself grading a paper from more than a year ago whose criteria you've since changed. Students are also often a long way from the original course, which also complicates completing the assignments effectively. Students and instructors forget about I grades. Instructors retire, resign, go on sabbatical, graduate, etc., making it much harder for the student and the instructor to resolve the incomplete successfully. So if you're going to award an incomplete grade, be willing to manage all of that effectively. You, as well as the student, retain responsibility for resolving the incomplete.

Alternatives to Awarding an Incomplete Grade

Instead of using I grades as a blanket approach to solve many issues, consider addressing each one more directly and, we argue, more appropriately.

If a student's skills need to improve, make sure she is using all of the support available *during the course*: office hours, tutors, teaching assistants, writing centers, online resources, etc. Make sure all students know about these resources, talk about them often in class, and encourage their use.

Have and execute an extra credit policy. Whether you offer extra credit or not (we argue that you should not—see **extra credit***), that is often part of the incomplete picture. Students requesting an incomplete often really are wanting extra credit.

Have and execute a **late work*** policy.

Assign them the grade they have earned. If a student is missing an assignment, and your grading policy specifies a late work penalty, impose the penalty and move on. If the zero for an assignment causes the student to earn a D in your course, then that is the appropriate outcome (see **zero grades***). As long as you understand to your own satisfaction that the student's grade is within her control and can explain that to the student and anyone else who may be involved, then that is the correct resolution. To award an I grade to a student who has earned a D is not doing her a favor or even helping her (see **beneficence***), and it is definitely not fair (see **fairness***) to the students who got work done despite personal circumstances about which you know nothing and who silently accepted their D's.

Be familiar with your institution's policies about student leaves, course withdrawals, or other approaches to handling life circumstances. No, you don't need to master the intricacies of each of those policies, but you should know of their existence and to whom you can refer students for more details. A student asking you about an incomplete for your course may be better served by a full leave of absence or some other institutional approach to her particular situation.

Summary

Incomplete grades are likely overused and/or used inappropriately by instructors. Know your institution's policy particulars regarding I grades. Articulate your own policies and practices and communicate those effectively to your students. Know exactly how you will handle the resolution of an incomplete, and be committed to seeing it through. You, as well as the student, retain responsibility for resolving any incomplete.

See Also

Beneficence
Extra Credit
Missing Assignments

Resource

Read your institution's incomplete grade policy.

Reference

Parkes, J., Fix, T. K., & Harris, M. B. (2003). What syllabi communicate about assessment in college classrooms. *Journal on Excellence in College Teaching, 14*(1), 61–83.

33 Late Work

Recommendation: Have an explicit late work policy. Parkes, Fix, and Harris (2003) found that only 29.4% of syllabi listing required assignments mentioned a late work policy.

Considerations in Forming a Late Work Policy

Late work policies are icebergs. The part you actually see is but the tip, buoyed by lots of beliefs on your part about whether you see grades as an economy or as a symbolic communication system; whether you see yourself as an educator or a cop. Late work policies can also be a great source of tussling and aggravation between you and your students. A carefully considered late work policy can dampen the trouble.

Some instructors see grades as an economy. Students *earn* points by turning in assignments on time, and if work is late there is a point or percentage penalty. Often the penalty is on a point per period system: 10% per class period; 10 points per day. Students pay with points for a time extension on the assignments. Grades, however, are also a symbolic communication system. Students' scores on an assignment communicate to them how well they have mastered the material, and their final course grades communicate to anyone looking at their transcripts about what they know about the topic of your course. The deeper the penalty for turning in an assignment late, the less that grade will accurately communicate mastery. (For more, see **assessment plan***.)

Some instructors approach issues like late work as an educator and consider the learning implications of their late work policy. Some instructors act more like cops trying to catch miscreants. Is your late work policy designed to promote learning or to catch students trying to weasel an advantage? For example, a learning-oriented approach would use a due date range. Let students know that they can turn work in early. Thus, if they know they will be absent on the due date, they have options. Make explicit to students if you'll accept work through multiple means: handing in a hard copy in class, e-mailing a scan to you, sending it through the learning management system (LMS), etc.

There is also a very pragmatic set of considerations: What will be easiest for you and your students to know and to execute? There are realities to teaching human beings: students will not always meet deadlines.

Options for Late Work Policies

One option is to forbid late work. If work isn't turned in by the due date, it receives zero points (see **zero grades***). Some instructors use this option because it mimics reality. If an engineering firm doesn't get a proposal in by the deadline on the RFP, it will not be awarded the contract. If that's your approach and rationale, then teach it. Explain the policy and the reason for it. And, meet every deadline yourself. We know lots of instructors who start with this approach, only to come upon a situation in which the penalty seems overly harsh for the offense, causing them to squirm between enforcing the policy and being an understanding human being. In their next syllabi, these instructors tend to go to an exception method.

A second option is an exception method. All required assignments have to be turned in on time. In the event of an emergency and/or by prior arrangement, the instructor can choose to accept the work and to assess some penalty. The trap to this method is ensuring **fairness*** in granting exceptions. Promote fairness by listing the most common exceptions (e.g. illness), the procedures by which students communicate with you about the circumstances, the procedures by which a student documents an exception (e.g. a doctor's excuse), and any penalties or time limits for exceptions. Then be very consistent in enforcing those procedures. Don't waive the doctor's note requirement for "good" students.

Another option is a point-per-period method. A certain number of points is deducted for each time period the work is late. This approach leans heavily towards the grades-as-economy view and away from the grades-as-symbolic-communication view. Behaviorism is alive and well and works to shape behavior. This also has the advantage of being clear and undiscriminating. It only works in these ways, however, if it is in the syllabus and known before-hand by students. This, too, must be evenly meted out so as to be fair.

A fourth option is to have no due dates. Now hear us out! If you value learning above all else, and want to communicate to students that they are ultimately responsible for that learning, then give them total control. Make your due dates suggestions and not requirements. There will ultimately be a final due date—you do need to file grades eventually! But why not encourage students to manage their work themselves? This is an all-or-nothing approach which has lots of other consequences (as with conjunctive grading—see **compensatory and conjunctive grading***) but it is an approach. You'll have to consider how you'll handle cheating, for example (see **cheating and plagiarism***). If one student turns an assignment in during the fourth week but another student doesn't turn that assignment in until the 12th week, do you give the first student her graded assignment back knowing that the second student might review it before turning his in? Also, you may need to consider the grading workload for yourself. If most of the students submit their assignments at or near the end of the semester you may bear the brunt of having to grade many assignments in a short period of time. You can work all of that out, but it's a large interlocking system of policies.

A fifth option is the amalgamation approach. This is when you take some elements of each of the approaches above and cobble together some penalties and some exceptions. As long as your approach, in the end, is well thought out and consistently communicated and enforced (Pulich, 1983), it should work.

Summary

Deadlines and students who miss them are ubiquitous in college teaching. Have an explicit approach to how you will address this and communicate that thoroughly to students.

References

Parkes, J., Fix, T. K., & Harris, M. B. (2003). What syllabi communicate about assessment in college classrooms. *Journal on Excellence in College Teaching, 14*(1), 61–83.

Pulich, M. A. (1983). Student grade appeals can be reduced. *Improving College and University Teaching, 31*(1), 9–12.

34 Learning-Oriented Assessment

What Is Learning-Oriented Assessment?

Assessment is often fraught with simultaneous yet contrasting purposes: grading vs. learning, evaluating student performance vs. improving it, meeting standards vs. supporting progress (Carless, 2007). However, there are ways to mitigate these differences to create assessments to more effectively focus on student learning.

The term Learning-Oriented Assessment (LOA) refers to assessment processes that emphasize learning elements more than measurement ones. Carless (2007) identified three principles that guide LOA:

- Principle 1: Assessment tasks should be designed to stimulate sound learning practices amongst students.
- Principle 2: Assessment should involve students actively engaging with criteria, quality, their own and/or peers' performance.
- Principle 3: Feedback should be timely and forward-looking so as to support current and future student learning.

(pp. 59–60)

The first and most critical principle is that assessment tasks should be learning tasks. They should be aligned with learning objectives (see **align assessments to learning objectives***) and should help students progress toward meeting those learning objectives. Assessments should also provide real-world applications and provide spaced practice throughout the course. The second principle focuses on involving students in assessment so that they better understand the criteria and learning objectives. Involvement can take the form of helping to develop the rubric criteria by which they will be evaluated (see **rubrics***), **peer assessment***, and **self-assessment***. Lastly, **feedback*** should be timely (see **feedback timing***) and provide guidance on which students can act to support their learning (Carless, 2007).

How Do You Ensure Your Assessments Are Learning-Oriented?

Both **formative and summative assessments***** can be learning-oriented. The same is true of **selected- and constructed-response questions*****. Regardless of the format, LOA tasks should embed real-world contexts. If possible, these tasks should provide the students the opportunity to engage in solving authentic tasks such as in portfolios, projects, and performance assessments. The tasks should be cooperative rather than competitive such as with **groupwork*****. Additionally, create and provide feedback as students are engaging in the task so that students have sufficient opportunity to make use of it. Technology and online assessments may be a mechanism to help support more timely feedback (Carless, 2009).

In addition to the tasks themselves, you can engage in discussion with your students about the assessment process (Carless, 2009). This discussion could center on how to develop criteria for performance assessments, how to apply criteria to evaluate their own work, how to give feedback to peers, and how to use the assessment to inform and improve their learning. You can use these discussions to help make your **assessment philosophy***** more transparent to your students. These discussions can help you and your students co-create a classroom focused on mastering the learning objectives in the course (see **mastery opportunities*****) and avoid such things as a **grade feeding frenzy*****.

Summary

Learning-oriented assessments are aligned with learning objectives, focus on real-world applications, engage students in the assessment process, and provide timely feedback on which students can act to support their learning. You can apply these LOA principles to a variety of question formats and types.

See Also

Aligning Assessments to Learning Objectives
Mastery Opportunities

Resources

Boud, D., & Falchikov, N. (2006). Aligning assessment with long-term learning. *Assessment and Evaluation in Higher Education, 31*(4), 399–413.

Carless, D., Joughin, G., & Mok, M. (2006). Learning-oriented assessment: Principles and practice. *Assessment and Evaluation in Higher Education, 31*(4), 395–398.

References

Carless, D. (2007). Learning-oriented assessment: Conceptual bases and practical implications. *Innovations in Education and Teaching International, 44*(1), 57–66.

Carless, D. (2009). Learning-oriented assessment: Principles, practice and a project. In L. H. Meyer, S. Davidson, H. Anderson, R. Fletcher, P. M. Johnson, & M. Rees (Eds.), *Tertiary assessment & higher education student outcomes: Policy, practice & research* (pp. 79–90). Wellington, New Zealand: Ako Aotearoa.

35 Low Test Scores

Oh No! My Students Just Bombed My Test!

You click on the summary results for your students' first exam and discover that the class average is 64%. Ouch! Now what?

Do You Have a Problem?

Yes, you have a problem. The trick is diagnosing which one(s) you have. At minimum, you need to communicate the result to students and help them understand how to do better next time. See **grade feeding frenzy*** for more on this kind of communication. But don't communicate with students yet! Let's look at who owns this 64%.

Is there any aspect of this result that is your responsibility? Did you cover the material well and appropriately in class and through assignments? That is, have you done all you could to prepare students for the test? One of the problems may be the alignment between what has happened in class and what happened on the test (see **design assessments first***), or that you didn't release a study guide this time.

Have you looked at the quality of the test? Can you eliminate any bad items (e.g. see **drop a question***)? If there are parts of this score which are your responsibility, do your best to clean them up and own them.

There are likely aspects of this result which are the students' responsibility. If you've written your multiple-choice question distractors from common student misconceptions and mistakes, then item analysis would reveal how many students made that mistake. If you're using scoring guides or **rubrics***, can you discern patterns from them which would illuminate where students aren't demonstrating mastery?

Mopping Up

Now that you've diagnosed the problems, you can move on with your students. Regardless of how you move forward, we recommend you communicate openly and honestly with your students about the result and about the plan to move forward.

It is entirely possible that, after exploring these perspectives, you conclude that the grades will stand. We suspect it is rare to discover there is nothing you are willing or able to do with such a result.

We suggest you begin by addressing those aspects of the result which are within your purview. If there were faulty questions, make some adjustments. If there was a question you've used before but you didn't actually cover the material (or as thoroughly) this term, own that and provide credit. (See **drop a question*** for how to do this appropriately.) Students usually respect an instructor who honestly claims some responsibility, and doing so can deepen the trust you and your students have for one another.

Will you provide any opportunity, like a mastery opportunity, for students to have an additional chance to show you what they know and to gain some additional points for that (see **mastery opportunities***)?

Whether or not you make or provide opportunities for changes in that initial score, it is likely worth engaging students in some after-action debriefing for their benefit and yours. Whether you hold an in-class discussion, have a couple of clicker questions, or field a brief survey, getting more information for yourself and cuing students to reflect upon issues like how did they study, how much did they study, where did they see mismatches between their studying and your exam is very important. There are lots of techniques.

Williams et al. (2011) designed the Graded Exam Activity, which asks students to look at multiple-choice items which at least 40% of the class got wrong and then respond to questions like "What lectures did the information come from?" and "Why did I answer the question incorrectly, or if I answered correctly, why might my classmates answer incorrectly?" Aldrich (2001) designed the Handing Back Exams activity, a group-based approach. Lovett (2013) writes about the Exam Wrapper Activity, which centers on study skills and exam preparation.

Do Not Curve

We do *not* recommend that you curve the grades so that they are simply higher. There are several concerns with doing so. First, it sends a message to students that their grades, and not their learning, is what is most important. Second, the uncurved grades are a better representation of their actual mastery of the material than the curved grades are. Third, more nuanced approaches like dropping a question, or providing a mastery opportunity, or an after-exam activity, balance all of the concerns better because they raise the grades through those new scores, preserve mastery as the primary meaning of the scores, and acknowledge that students should learn more.

Summary

Sometimes, an entire class's performance on an assessment is below your, and their, expectations. Explore the reasons for those scores, and make adjustments that provide opportunity for students to show mastery and for you to communicate the importance of learning over grades.

See Also

Grade Feeding Frenzy

Resources

Aldrich, H. E. (2001). How to hand exams back to your class. *College Teaching, 49*(3), 82. DOI: 10.1080/87567550109595853

Lovett, M. C. (2013). Make exams worth more than the grade: Using exam wrappers to promote metacognition. In M. Kaplan, N. Silver, D. LaVaque-Manty, & D. Meizlish (Eds.), *Using reflection and metacognition to improve student learning across the disciplines, across the academy.* Sterling, VA: Stylus Publishing.

Williams, A. E., Aguilar-Roca, N. M., Tsai, M., Wong, M., Beaupré, M. M., & O'Dowd, D. K. (2011). Assessment of learning gains associated with independent exam analysis in introductory biology. *CBE-Life Sciences Education, 10*(4), 346–356.

36 Make-Up Exams

How Do I Manage Make-Up Exams?

Recommendation: Have an explicit make-up exam policy and adhere to it consistently.

Apparently, one's grandparents die with alarming frequency when one is a college student (cf. "Exams may be dangerous to grandpa's health: How inclusive fitness influences students' fraudulent excuses" (Fitzgerald & Loeffler, 2012), and "Grandma never dies during finals: A study of makeup exams" (Abernethy & Padgett, 2010)). And other life events happen, too: sporting events, job interviews, extended Spring Break trips, sisters' weddings, mono, the flu. In short, students are going to miss your class, and they're going to miss your exams sometimes, too. There are a number of issues for you to consider in how you handle such absences, three main stances for you to take, and several decision points for you to navigate in forming your make-up exam policy.

Issues to Consider

The Good Faith Contract

Most of the concerns, real and imagined, that you have about make-up exams distill to whether or not you believe the student's excuse for missing the exam. Let's disentangle that from procedures for managing make-up exams, which are where the rest of your concerns are—what a hassle! The former hinges on a Good Faith Contract between you and your students: they will be responsible in handling their obligation to take your test and you will be reasonable in accommodating student life events.

Do You Believe Your Students?

Data suggest you should be careful. First of all, there's no distinction between the excuses students use fraudulently versus legitimately (e.g. Roig & Caso, 2005), so you won't be able to discern the difference. Grandpa could well have died, even during finals week. Second, some students will take advantage of your understanding and compassion (Caron, Whitbourne, & Halgin, 1992). Once you have determined that a student's excuse is credible, however, they have fulfilled their part of the Good Faith Contract, and you need to fulfill yours.

Deterring Fraud

You definitely want to deter students from offering fraudulent excuses for missing an exam. Do this, however, through your "verification of excuse" portion, and not through the procedures for the make-up itself. Do not employ point deductions or harder exams or harder formats or unreasonable hours for the make-up. That is not fair or equitable; recall that this is a student whose excuse you have believed.

Fairness and Equity

Your make-up exam policy needs to be both fair and equitable. **Fairness*** and **equity*** need to be considered in terms of the student missing the exam as well as all the students who take the exam. Houston and Bettencourt (1999) report that reasonable make-up exam policies contribute to students' judgment of an instructor's fairness.

We argue that fairness and equity demand that, at some point under circumstances you determine, your make-up procedures acknowledge the good-faith effort of the student to perform in your class. This means that it is fundamentally unfair to design make-ups that are in a different format, knowingly more difficult, or administered at unusual times.

Test Security

By allowing some students to take the exam at a different time than other students, you do open up a security threat. Students taking the test earlier can tip off students taking it later. There are ways to address this. (See **test security***.)

Hassle

The logistical management of make-ups is a hassle. It is possible to utilize procedures which streamline the process.

The Bigger Picture

Your institution and perhaps your department likely have policies regarding excused absences and perhaps make-up exams specifically. Your policies and practices need to be consistent with the broader policies at your institution.

Communicate!

It is critical that you tell your students early and often about your policies. They need to be on your syllabus and communicated as exams approach.

Approaches to Make-Up Policies

We discern three main approaches in the literature and in our experiences to make-up exams. First is to forbid make-ups. Second is to have make-ups and to verify excuses. The third is to handle absences in some ad hoc fashion.

No Make-Ups. Period.

This takes some real intestinal fortitude because students will miss exams. It thus means saying to a student who *really did* go home for her grandmother's funeral, "Sorry, no make-ups." This can also work if you have other mechanisms in place to absorb the issue (e.g. Buchanan & Rogers, 1990). Remember, though, our advice against dropping a test score (see **drop the lowest grade***) or **extra credit***. We similarly advise against score replacement methods (e.g. Loui & Lin, 2017), although the notion of more heavily weighting the relevant portion of the comprehensive final exam in lieu of a missing mid-term (Abernethy & Padgett, 2010) nearly addresses our concerns.

Trust but Verify

Life happens. Students will miss exams. So making some provision is part of the realpolitik of college teaching. You should have some requirements for granting a make-up exam and stick to them consistently. Take "basic preventative measures" (Abernethy & Padgett, 2010, p. 105; Caron, Whitbourne, & Halgin, 1992; Roig & Caso, 2005) to prevent fraud: announce a policy and procedures early and often; define an acceptable excuse; require documentation.

This, Too, Shall Pass!

Accept every student proposal for how to handle a missed exam. This is a highly problematic approach. It causes students to think you are unfair (Houston & Bettencourt, 1999).

Decision Points

As you work on your make-up policy, here are some decision points for you to navigate.

Acceptable Excuses

You need to define what will be an acceptable excuse. That could actually be different depending on the level and content of your course. There should be a much higher standard for an acceptable excuse from an internship or student teaching experience than there is for a general education requirement, for example. You can also align acceptable excuses to ones used in the profession your students are preparing to enter.

However you do it, keep it simple and realistic. One intriguing option for avoiding splitting these hairs is offering a make-up to everyone. Roig and Caso (2005) note the possibility of permitting students a certain number of make-up exams per semester without offering any excuse. The challenge in that is creating comparable make-up versions for each of your exams.

Documentation

Some excuses come with ready documentation: student athlete events, doctor's appointments, documented disabilities, jury duty. Many others—"I awoke with a migraine," "My car wouldn't start," "My dog ate my cheat sheet" (see **cheat sheets or crib sheets***)—aren't so readily documented. Nevertheless, the consensus seems to be that asking for documentation, even when that feels intrusive or distrustful of the student, is a good prevention strategy. Even requiring a student-generated explanation with sufficient details for you to judge its credulity can help quell fraudulent excuses (Caron, Whitbourne, & Halgin, 1992; Roig & Caso, 2005).

Timing of Request

How soon before and/or how long after the regular exam time may a student request a make-up? It might be less hassle to make few if any limits here, although it would be a reasonable deterrent to have some stated deadlines.

Timing of Make-Up

When may a student do a make-up relative to the regular exam time? Taking the exam early means the make-up student has less time to study (but you shouldn't be thinking about that as a punitive deterrent) and it also means their classmates won't be handing them answers as they would if the make-up is after the test. They could be handing classmates information about the in-class exam, however.

As we've said, we believe it is inappropriate to assign unusual hours for make-ups as a deterrent.

Format for the Make-Up

The make-up exam, equitably, needs to be of the same format as the regular exam. It definitely needs to address the same learning objectives in the same way as the regular exam. This is a matter of equity and fairness.

Logistics

Know what your logistics options are before your semester begins. Do you have access to a testing center on campus that can proctor your make-ups? Are there departmental staff who can? Will you proctor them yourself? Do you have item-banking software that would speed the creation of alternate forms?

Summary

The reality is that students are going to miss your exams. Have a policy which clearly addresses what constitutes an acceptable excuse and what documentation you require. Have a set of procedures governing the notice for and administration of a make-up. Communicate these early and often to students and deploy them consistently. Be fair and equitable. Use reasonable means to deter fraudulent excuses but do not be punitive. If a student has an acceptable excuse by your standards, then they deserve the same exam experience as everyone else.

See Also

Attendance
Drop the Lowest Grade
Late Work

Resources

www.facultyfocus.com/tag/makeup-exams/
Abernethy, A. M., & Padgett, D. (2010). Grandma never dies during finals: A study of makeup exams. *Marketing Education Review, 20*(2), 103–114.
McCann, L. I. (2005). Dealing with students missing exams and in-class graded assignments. *APS Observer, 19*(6). Retrieved from www.psychologicalscience.org/observer/dealing-with-students-missing-exams-and-in-class-graded-assignments

References

Abernethy, A. M., & Padgett, D. (2010). Grandma never dies during finals: A study of makeup exams. *Marketing Education Review, 20*(2), 103–114.
Buchanan, R. W., & Rogers, M. (1990). Innovative assessment in large classes. *College Teaching, 38*(2), 69–73.

Caron, M. D., Whitbourne, S. K., & Halgin, R. P. (1992). Fraudulent excuse making among college students. *Teaching of Psychology, 19*(2), 90–93.

Fitzgerald, C. J., & Loeffler, C. (2012). Exams may be dangerous to grandpa's health: How inclusive fitness influences students' fraudulent excuses. *Evolutionary Behavioral Sciences, 6*(4), 539.

Houston, M. B., & Bettencourt, L. A. (1999). But that's not fair! An exploratory study of student perceptions of instructor fairness. *Journal of Marketing Education, 21*(2), 84–96.

Loui, M. C., & Lin, A. (2017). Estimating a missing examination score. *Journal of College Science Teaching, 46*(4), 18.

Roig, M., & Caso, M. (2005). Lying and cheating: Fraudulent excuse making, cheating, and plagiarism. *The Journal of Psychology, 139*(6), 485–494.

37 Mastery Opportunities

Exam Day does not mean that learning is now over. In fact, it is possible to provide students with opportunities to continue to learn even after an exam and perhaps to earn additional course credit for doing so. Providing students with the ability to respond to **feedback*** on written assignments or to try again on exams communicates to them that their learning, and not their grade, is what's most important. And even if you're not using an entire system and philosophy like improvement grading, there are techniques and approaches you can employ around assessments to promote learning and mastery. It also draws some of the pressure off of the grading, and lessens students' **evaluation anxiety*** and reduces the chances of a **grade feeding frenzy*** when grades are released.

Mastery opportunities are not **extra credit*** because they are additional chances for students to earn credit already present in the course and such opportunities are still related to the course learning objectives (see **align assessments to learning objectives***).

The essential elements of mastery opportunities include permitting students to revisit an assessment after it has been scored, to try again to respond to the assessment, and to gain additional credit for that assessment because they have demonstrated mastery on a subsequent occasion (Hampton, 2002). Here are several permutations on those elements:

> *Multiple-Choice Mastery Opportunity*—We've described a process we call the mastery opportunity (Parkes & Zimmaro, 2016, pp. 127–130). After a multiple-choice test is scored and scores recorded, students are provided with the exam and the scoring guide, and all students (regardless of initial score) are offered the opportunity to write about each of the questions they missed. They must write an explanation either of why the answer they chose is actually better than the correct answer, or of why the correct answer is correct. Their explanations must demonstrate that they understand the content at issue in the question. For each correct explanation, they earn half of the points that the original question was worth.

Collaborative Test Taking—Bloom (2009) collects individual test responses approximately half-way through the testing time and distributes a second scoring sheet. Students may access textbooks, notes, or classmates during the second half of the time period. We also described a similar approach which Dawn has used (Parkes & Zimmaro, 2016, pp. 127–130). Also see the entries on **groupwork*** and **collaborative testing***.

Take Two Testing—Toma and Heady (1996) describe a very similar process to Bloom's. The scores from the two halves of the testing time are averaged to achieve the final score.

Graded Exam Activity—This is an additional post-exam assignment with its own grade which requires students to reflect on items which at least 40% of the class missed on the exam (Williams et al., 2011). All students are asked to write about where the test question content came from (lectures, textbook, etc.), why the right answer is right and the wrong answers are wrong, and why they got the question wrong.

Handing Back Exams Activity—Aldrich (2001) describes this technique in which groups work with the exam and the scoring guide to understand why certain options are right or wrong. Their incentives are that a subset of the items will reappear on a quiz and a cumulative final.

With non-exam-style assessments (e.g. papers, projects, assignments), a drafting or pre-review process as well as some post-score opportunity to rewrite or rework based on feedback can also be designed and would work in similar ways.

Summary

Providing your students with a second chance to show their mastery of the course content and to improve their grade communicates that learning is more important than grades. There are several extant techniques you could adopt or adapt in your courses.

See Also

Learning-Oriented Assessment

References

Aldrich, H. E. (2001). How to hand exams back to your class. *College Teaching, 49*(3), 82. DOI: 10.1080/87567550109595853

Bloom, D. (2009). Collaborative test-taking: Benefits for learning and retention. *College Teaching, 57*(4), 216–220. DOI: 10.1080/87567550903218646

Hampton, D. R. (2002). Making complaining appealing. *College Teaching, 50*(2), 62. DOI: 10.1080/87567550209595876

Parkes, J., & Zimmaro, D. (2016). *Learning and assessing with multiple-choice questions in college classrooms.* New York, NY: Routledge.

Toma, A. G., & Heady, R. B. (1996). Take-two testing. *College Teaching, 44*(2), 61.

Williams, A. E., Aguilar-Roca, N. M., Tsai, M., Wong, M., Moravec Beaupré, M., & O'Dowd, D. K. (2011). Assessment of learning gains associated with independent exam analysis in introductory biology. *CBE-Life Sciences Education, 10,* 346–356. DOI: 10.1187/cbe.11-03-0025

38 Missing Assignments

How Do I Manage Missing Assignments?

Recommendation: Have an explicit missing assignment policy, which may be part of a make-up policy (see **make-up exams***), and adhere to it consistently.

Making the Best of a Bad Situation
(OK, There's No "Best")

You get to the end of the semester, and you realize that some students have not turned everything in. Now what? Well, at this point, your options aren't pretty. You can assign zeros to missing work, which is accurate, but that tends to have what your student and perhaps you would deem to be outsized consequences for the infraction (see **zero grades***). You can assign a failing grade for the missing assignment, but that's really giving away points. It feels humane and compassionate but isn't actually in the interests of the student's academic welfare (see **beneficence***). You can assign an incomplete for the course, but that's likely ill-fitting if not downright inappropriate (see **incomplete grades***). You can give the student notice and a couple of days in which to turn something in, which feels fair (see **fairness***), but you'll grumble about the extra grading during finals week. Someone is going to be unhappy no matter what you do.

A Few Ounces of Prevention . . .

You have several ways to avoid getting into this situation, and you'll like the prevention measures a lot better than any of those cures above.

A **late work*** policy is likely to completely eliminate the possibility of a student reaching finals week with missing work, depending on exactly how you have that policy structured. If there are penalties for late work, then those dictate what goes into the column for that assignment on your gradebook. A make-up exam policy could be expanded to include assignments. Your **attendance*** policy might also address how assignments are to be handled.

In this learning management system (LMS) age, it's a trivial task for you to keep your gradebook in the LMS where students can check it literally at any time. Communicate with them that they must take responsibility for confirming that the gradebook is accurate. They should be letting you know if a score is missing.

Summary

You and your students really will be happier having policies and procedures in place that prevent either of you reaching the end of the semester with assignments missing. Addressing missing assignments draws on many of the same considerations as **late work***, **make-up exams***, and **attendance***, so we strongly encourage you to read those entries, too.

See Also

Attendance
Late Work
Make-Up Exams

Resource

McCann, L. I. (2005). Dealing with students missing exams and in-class graded assignments. *APS Observer, 19*(6). Retrieved from www.psychologicalscience.org/observer/dealing-with-students-missing-exams-and-in-class-graded-assignments

39 Non-Cognitive Factors

What Are Non-Cognitive Factors?

Non-cognitive factors refer to behaviors, skills, attitudes, and strategies such as motivation, time management, and self-regulation (Nagaoka et al., 2013). Cognitive factors generally refer to the student's understanding of content knowledge and academic skills. Learning is an interconnection between both cognitive and non-cognitive factors (Farrington et al., 2012).

Farrington et al. (2012) identified five general categories of non-cognitive factors related to academic performance:

1) *Academic behaviors* such as going to class, doing homework, organizing materials, participating, and studying.
2) *Academic perseverance* such as grit, tenacity, delayed gratification, self-discipline, and self-control.
3) *Academic mindsets* such as sense of belongingness, belief in one's ability and competence grow with effort, belief one can succeed, and seeing value in the work.
4) *Learning strategies* such as study skills, metacognitive strategies, self-regulated learning, and goal-setting.
5) *Social skills* such as interpersonal skills, empathy, cooperation, assertion, and responsibility.

Why Are Non-Cognitive Factors Important?

Research suggests that multiple factors, including non-cognitive factors, significantly influence students' success in college. This research shows that interventions targeted at non-cognitive factors are helping to improve college retention and grades (Farrington et al., 2012). Robbins et al. (2004) conducted a meta-analysis on the relationship between college retention and non-cognitive factors defined in nine broad categories. They found a moderate relationship between college retention and academic goals, academic self-efficacy, and academic-related skills. However, prior research outcomes also show that students who have similar academic achievement have widely different outcomes in college dependent on where they attend college. While research strongly suggests that non-cognitive factors are important in college, there is not enough research on how these factors differ across different college contexts (Farrington et al., 2012).

The challenge for educators is not only to help students on what they need to know but also on how to be effective learners. The best way to improve students' academic behaviors and perseverance is through academic mindsets and learning strategies. Helping to build students' mindsets and teach them appropriate learning strategies seem to be critical areas that teachers can influence for getting students to engage in positive academic behaviors and to persevere. In turn, these academic behaviors and perseverance lead to better student learning outcomes (Farrington et al., 2012).

Assessing Non-Cognitive Factors

There are a variety of assessment instruments available to measure many of the non-cognitive factors described above. Kafka (2016) provides a resource list of many of the more prevalent instruments that aim to measure non-cognitive factors that support college success. Most of these non-cognitive assessment instruments are administered by institutions as part of students' admission process or by researchers as part of a research study. College instructors rarely try to measure these non-cognitive measures themselves (Volkwein, 2003). If such non-cognitive factors are critical in your course, then you likely have learning objectives for them. From those you could construct your own assessments which make the most sense in your discipline and with your students. However, sorting through which factors and which instruments to measure can be a daunting task. Given the vast literature and approaches to measuring non-cognitive factors, we recommend you work with teaching and learning offices on your campus to identify approaches for how to best evaluate and possibly integrate interventions related to these factors.

Non-Cognitive Factors in the Professions

The term "non-cognitive factors" is used a little differently within different professions. In medical education, for example, the term usually means communication skills, interpersonal skills, and attitudes which ultimately influence a (future) doctor's work with patients but which are not the cognitive factors such as knowledge of anatomy and diagnostic reasoning (e.g. Cushing, 2002). And in teacher preparation, instructors assess and develop "dispositions," such as the ability to be on time or the ability to handle difficult students (e.g. Choi, Benson, & Shudak, 2016; Shoffner, Sedberry, Alsup, & Johnson, 2014). Your particular profession may have its own definition of non-cognitive factors and ways to assess them.

Summary

Non-cognitive factors focus on those aspects that help students in how to be effective learners. Cognitive and non-cognitive processes are closely intertwined in supporting student learning and outcomes. Research on the role of and how to best measure non-cognitive factors continues to evolve. Campus teaching and learning offices will provide you the best support on how to assess non-cognitive factors and implement instructional approaches to support your students.

Resource

Rosen, J. A., Glennie, E. J., Dalton, B. W., Lennon, J. M., & Bozick, R. N. (2010). Non-cognitive skills in the classroom: New perspectives on education research. *RTI Press Publication No. BK-0004–1009.* Research Triangle Park, NC: RTI International. Retrieved July 22, 2017 from www.rti.org/rtipress

References

Choi, H. S., Benson, N. F., & Shudak, N. J. (2016). Assessment of teacher candidate dispositions: Evidence of reliability and validity. *Teacher Education Quarterly, 43*(3), 71.

Cushing, A. (2002). Assessment of non-cognitive factors. In G. R. Norman, C.P.M. van der Vleuten, & D. J. Newble (Eds.), *International handbook of research in medical education* (pp. 711–755). Dordrecht, Netherlands: Springer.

Farrington, C. A., Roderick, M., Allensworth, E. Nagaoka, J., Keyes, T. S., Johnson, D. W., & Beechum, N. O. (2012). Teaching adolescents to become learners: The role of non-cognitive factors in shaping school performance: A critical literature review. *University of Chicago Consortium on Chicago School Research.* Retrieved from https://raikesfoundation.org/sites/default/files/SA-Rec-Reading-CCSR-Noncog-RF-Full-Report-Revision-%281.14%29.pdf

Kafka, T. (2016). A list of non-cognitive assessment instruments. Retrieved July 22, 2017 from https://ccrc.tc.columbia.edu/images/a-list-of-non-cognitive-assessment-instruments.pdf

Nagaoka, J., Farrington, C. A., Roderick, M., Allensworth, E., Seneca Keyes, T., Johnson, D. W., & Beechum, N. O. (2013). Readiness for college: The role of noncognitive factors and context. *Voices in Urban Education, 38,* 45–52.

Robbins, S. B., Lauver, K., Le, H., Davis, D., Langley, R., & Caristrom, A. (2004). Do psychosocial and study skill factors predict college outcomes? *Psychological Bulletin, 130*(2), 261–288.

Shoffner, M., Sedberry, T., Alsup, J., & Johnson, T. S. (2014). The difficulty of teacher dispositions: Considering professional dispositions for preservice English teachers. *The Teacher Educator, 49*(3), 175–192.

Volkwein, J. F. (2003). Implementing outcomes assessment on your campus. *Center for the Study of Higher Education.* Retrieved July 22, 2017 from www.bmcc.cuny.edu/iresearch/upload/Volkwein_article1.pdf

40 Norm-Referenced Grading Approaches

Recommendation: We recommend not using norm-referenced grading approaches in college courses but prefer **criterion-referenced grading approaches*** because they award grades based on how well a student's performance is compared to an established standard. If you do need to employ a norm-referenced grading approach, use the standard deviation method.

What Is Norm-Referenced Grading?

In norm-referenced grading, a student's performance is determined by her relative standing compared to other students in the class. This grading system assumes that student performance naturally varies across a diverse set of learners because students differ in the knowledge, skills, and motivation they bring to class. Norm-referenced grading works when this variation produces a bell-shaped, or normal, distribution of scores. These scores range from low to high (F to A), with only a few scores at the ends of the grade distribution. This is why norm-referenced grading approaches are also referred to as "grading on the curve" (Snowman & Biehler, 1997). The normal curve as a grading model is based on the discovery, in the 19th century, that IQ test scores over large populations approximate a normal distribution. Norm-referenced grading is based on two assumptions:

1) One of the main objective of grading is to identify students who achieve more than their peers and to weed out those who do not do as well (see **gatekeeping***).
2) Student performance generally follows a normal distribution.
(Center for Teaching and Learning—University of North Carolina, 1991)

Advantages

Norm-referenced grading approaches tend to be easy for instructors to use. They work well in situations where instructors must differentiate students based on their performance. For example, this may happen when an academic program has limited spots for students to advance to higher level courses (Center for Teaching and Learning Services—University of Minnesota, 2003). Additionally, norm-referenced grading approaches can adjust for situations that are beyond students' control (e.g. tests that are too hard or too easy, or poor quality teaching) because the scale automatically moves up or down (Center for Teaching and Learning—University of North Carolina, 1991). If a given exam average for your class is low, the relative standing of students can account for that difficulty. Presumably, these factors would affect all the students equally, so all performance would be affected but the relative standing would stay the same (Svinicki, 1999).

Disadvantages

While it is often the case that the bigger the class, the greater chance student grades will resemble a normal curve, assuming that performance is normally distributed is unjustified, even for classes with a large number of students. College students are typically a select group and are not representative of the general population in terms of background knowledge, academic skills, or intelligence. Additionally, classroom exams are not exhaustive measures of student achievement—even standardized exams face this challenge (Center for Teaching and Learning—University of North Carolina, 1991). Student performance is not normally distributed in such situations where the class size is small or in upper-level classes. Lastly, norm-referenced grading approaches may not be appropriate for skill-based courses, such as writing-intensive or laboratory courses, in which it is hoped that all students will achieve at least minimal levels of competency (Enerson & Plank, 1997).

Research indicates grading on the curve can reduce students' motivation to learn, and increase the probability of academic dishonesty and test anxiety (see **evaluation anxiety***). Norm-referenced grading approaches also discourage effective group studying or other work, because collaboration is not rewarded. When students have to compete with each other for the few spots who will receive A's, they are less likely to be helpful to each other (Center for Teaching and Learning Services—University of Minnesota, 2003).

Additionally, normative grading does not indicate how much or how little students have learned, only where they stand in relation to the class (Committee on Undergraduate Science Education, 1997). Who the others are and how they performed influences an individual's grade in addition to her own achievement (Center for Teaching and Learning Services—University of Minnesota, 2003). Students in "high achievement" classes with a lot of high-performing students may be unfairly penalized and less skilled students in "low achievement" classes may unfairly benefit if the class as a whole is low-performing (Center for Teaching and Learning—University of North Carolina, 1991). One student may get an A in a low-achieving section while another student with the same mastery of course content and thus the same score in a higher-achieving section gets a B. Also, in a large introductory-level class, you may be justified in assuming the class is generally representative of the student population, but in small classes (under 40) the students may not be a representative sample (Center for Teaching and Learning Services—University of Minnesota, 2003).

The bottom line is that we believe that a grading system which begins with a presumption that not every member of the class can master the learning objectives, and thus earn an A, is antithetical to the learning mission of a college class. Of course not all students will master those learning objectives and earn the A, but it should still be possible.

Types of Norm-Referenced Grading Strategies

Cluster Method

One form of norm-referenced grading is to assign grades according to breaks in the distribution, called cluster grading. Using this approach, students' scores are arranged from highest to lowest, and the instructor identifies any notable gaps or breaks in the distribution. The primary advantage of cluster grading is that there are fewer complaints about borderline grades (see **borderline grade cases***), since students will likely accept the gaps as evidence of differences in performance. One disadvantage of cluster grading is that the gaps may not reflect true differences in student performance or they may not appear at realistic points in the distribution (Center for Teaching and Learning—University of North Carolina, 1991), if at all. Another disadvantage is that the instructor decides on the grade distribution after students have taken an exam or completed the course rather than on standards that are established at the beginning of the semester (Committee on Undergraduate Science Education, 1997).

Distributional Method

In this scenario, letter grades are awarded based on a predetermined percentage of students receiving each grade category. For example, the top 40% of students receive an A, the next 50% receive a B, and the bottom 10% receives a C. One advantage of the distributional method is that all sections will have the same average GPA. For example, if you teach two sections, one with 40 students and one with 50 students, using the 40% A, 50% B, and 10% C distribution, the average GPA for both sections will be 3.3.

Section 1

$(40 * .40) * 4.0 = 64$
$(40 * .50) * 3.0 = 60$
$(40 * .10) * 2.0 = 8$
$(64 + 60 + 8) / 40 = 3.3$

Section 2

(50 * .40) * 4.0 = 80
(50 * .50) * 3.0 = 75
(50 * .10) * 2.0 = 10
(80 + 75 + 10) / 50 = 3.3

A primary disadvantage is that the score needed to earn an A will vary from section to section. In the example above, the final course percentage for the top 40% in your first section may range from 88–98% and 92–100% in your second section. Students in your first section only needed to earn an 88% to be in the top 40% of the class and receive an A whereas students in your second section needed to earn a 92% in order to receive an A.

Standard Deviation Method

Statistically speaking, the soundest norm-referenced grading system is the standard deviation method. Using this approach, instructors determine students' grades based on their *distance* from the mean score for the class rather than on a subjective scale. For example, C grades span from one-half the standard deviation below the mean to one-half a standard deviation above the mean. Adding one standard deviation to the upper C grade range will yield the A–B grade levels, and subtracting one standard deviation from the lower C grade range will result in the D–F cutoff point (Center for Teaching and Learning—University of North Carolina, 1991). See Table 40.1 for how the standard deviation method works with a fractionated (+/−) grading scale.

Comparison of Norm-Referenced Grading Strategies

See Table 40.2 for a comparison of the advantages and disadvantages of the three norm-referenced grading strategies.

Table 40.1 Grade Cutoffs in the Standard Deviation Method

Grade	Minimum
A	Mean + 1.83 sd
A−	Mean + 1.50 sd
B+	Mean + 1.17 sd
B	Mean + 0.83 sd
B−	Mean + 0.50 sd
C+	Mean + 0.17 sd
C	Mean − 0.17 sd
C−	Mean − 0.50 sd
D+	Mean − 0.83 sd
D	Mean − 1.17 sd
D−	Mean − 1.50 sd
F	0

Table 40.2 Comparison of Norm-Referenced Grading Strategies

Norm-Referenced Grading Strategy	Advantages	Disadvantages
Cluster	• Identifies clear breaks in student performance. • Rewards students who are at or very near traditional cutoffs.	• With little variation in scores, clear "clusters" may be difficult to define. • Hard to justify to students how cutoff was selected. • Score needed to earn an A will vary from section to section.
Distribution Percentages	• Will set the number of A's awarded to a predetermined percentage of students. • All sections will have same GPA.	• Score needed to earn an A will vary from section to section.
Standard Deviation	• Will set the distribution of grades to match a normal distribution. • All sections will have nearly the same GPA.	• Distribution of grades in small, skills-based courses is typically not normal. • Will force some students to receive D's or F's.

Summary

Generally, if the goal of a course is to "weed out" students so that the "best" rise to the top, norm-referenced procedures may be appropriate. Additionally, norm-referenced grading is generally appropriate in large courses that require rigid differentiation among students or in multi-section courses to ensure the same course GPA across all sections and to adjust for variations in difficulty, assignments, and other factors across sections. In the end, we believe criterion-referenced grading approaches will still provide differentiation while being more consistent with a learning focus.

See Also

Criterion-Referenced Grading Approaches
Gatekeeping

References

Center for Teaching and Learning—University of North Carolina. (1991). Grading systems. Retrieved from http://ctl.unc.edu/fyc10.html

Center for Teaching and Learning Services—University of Minnesota. (2003). Grading systems. Retrieved from www1.umn.edu/ohr/teachlearn/MinnCon/grading1.html

Committee on Undergraduate Science Education. (1997). *Science teaching reconsidered: A handbook, chapter 6: Testing and grading.* Retrieved from http://books.nap.edu/readingroom/books/str/6.html

Enerson, D. M., & Plank, K. M. (1997). *The Penn State teacher II, chapter IV: Measuring and evaluating student learning.* Retrieved from www.psu.edu/idp_celt/PST/PSTchapter4.html

Snowman, J., & Biehler, R. (1997). *Psychology applied to teaching, chapter 12: Ways to evaluate student learning* (8th ed.). Retrieved from http://college.hmco.com/education/resources/res_project/students/tc/assess.html#5

Svinicki, M. S. (1999). Some pertinent questions about grading. Retrieved from www.utexas.edu/academic/cte/sourcebook/grading.html

41 Not Everything That Matters Must Be Graded

Oftentimes, grades are viewed as behavioral economics. If we want students to attend class, study thoroughly, read the readings, we must incent them to do so. Instructors who think of grades primarily in economic terms tend to want to assign points or portions of grades to every desirable student behavior. Grading systems are an economy but not only an economy. Therefore, there are limits to thinking of grades only as incentives.

Grades as an Economy

Class grades and points are an economy. Instructors can pay students with points to incent student behaviors. Students can earn points and grades by doing certain things. It is also true that "What gets measured is what matters." Operant conditioning is alive and well, and it works. Students will study a syllabus or a scoring guide for a paper to see where the points are to be earned, and they will adjust their activities accordingly. We've all known the student who, in the last week of classes, calculates that they'll earn an A in the course even with a 50% on the final exam, so they don't choose to study very much.

Weaknesses to Grades as an Economy

If your primary concept of grades in your classes is behavioral economics, there are some risks. Such a grade-oriented view tends to focus you and the students on "earning the points" rather than "mastering the learning objectives." It is possible to have designed your course and the assessments carefully enough that they are perfectly aligned with your learning objectives (see **align assessments to learning objectives***) so that those two goals are synonymous, but that's extraordinarily difficult and thus rare.

A side effect of the grade-orientation is all the haggling that will go on. Suppose you want students to be in class and ready to begin at the appointed start time. You could have a deduction for late students. "Arrive after 9:30 a.m., and I will deduct 5 points from your grade." The student who arrives at 9:31 and the student who arrives at 9:50 lose the same 5 points. Is that equitable (see **equity***)? What if the student has a good excuse? What's a good excuse? How do you keep records? How do you ensure that you know who is there precisely at 9:30? How much time and class attention will this take? Can you and your students afford the time and energy to properly account for those 5 points?

You also need to think very carefully about what you will incent. Will you incent inputs or outcomes? Class **attendance*** or **participation*** are inputs for which some instructors provide grade incentives. But they're inputs and don't guarantee mastery of learning objectives. Will you incent products or processes (or both)? For example, do students need to hand in just a final version of a term-paper (product), or must they turn in drafts of the final paper (process)? If you wish students to learn the importance of draft writing, you'll need to assign points to that.

Points and grade-based systems tend to focus you and students downward to minimums rather than upward to possibilities. Our guess is that, if you have attendance points in your class, they're expressed as a deduction for absence not as a deposit for attendance, or that you have a minimum number of acceptable absences, rather than a maximum number of presences.

Finally, you've also narrowed your options for communicating with your students about what is important and why. Due dates for homework assignments become discussions about how many points a student will lose if the homework isn't uploaded to the learning management system (LMS) by 11:59 p.m. rather than opportunities to talk about professionalism and the culture of your profession.

Not Everything That Matters Must Be Graded

We ascribe to a philosophy which says that course grades must primarily communicate the degree to which students have mastered the content of the course. As you start to "buy" behaviors from students—attendance, participation, turning work in on time, **groupwork***—the proportion of your course grade that actually communicates students' ability to comply with directions increases and erodes that primary communication. We argue, then, that there are other ways to encourage student behaviors besides points and grades which don't jeopardize that primary communication while still promoting the student behaviors you wish to promote. Here are some possibilities.

Non-Negotiable Expectations

Reflect with us for a moment on all of the things you expect from your students *that are not currently part of your grading*: you expect them to arrive in the classroom on time; you expect them to be dressed appropriately (we know that's a hedge!); you expect them to mark their answers on the bubble sheet during a test; you expect them to turn papers in written in a particular language; you expect them to use MLA or APA formatting and certain spelling conventions. You expect them to put their names on everything they hand in to you. In other words, there are a great many expectations you have for students that you probably are not spending points to get from them. Some of them may not even be explicit—like dress or that class will be conducted in English. If a student contributed to your class discussion in Mandarin (assuming that's not what you're teaching), you probably wouldn't even blink at asking them to repeat their contribution in English. In other words, you're used to having and enforcing non-negotiable expectations of students. Non-negotiable expectations, then, become an option for addressing student behaviors which you currently think you must pay for with points.

While it depends on your learning objectives, as always, what are some student behaviors you currently pay points for that perhaps you don't need to? Do you require that papers in your class conform to the seventh edition of the *APA Publication Manual*? How many points is that worth? What if that weren't a matter of points but of non-negotiable expectation? If the paper didn't comply, it isn't accepted.

Professionalism and Professional Cultural Norms

Part of what you're teaching, whether explicitly in your learning objectives or not, are the professional cultural norms in the discipline you're teaching. Tie your non-negotiable expectations to those broader professional cultural norms. Why do you assign points on a paper to margins and font sizes when, if you sent a paper to an academic journal for review and you ignored their margin and font sizes, they would simply not review it? Your approach to margins and font sizes could mimic how those expectations are addressed in the profession.

Making It Worth Their While

You have so many other ways besides points and course grades to make certain behaviors worth your students' while. Let's take being in class on time. What if, at the stroke of 9:30, something really consequential happens? Perhaps that's when you start new material, or when you answer questions about the next test, or provide information about summer internships?

Suppose you want students to participate in small group discussions. Then those discussions need to be ones worth having. The task you pitch the groups needs to be really juicy and meaty. Students will participate if they think participation is worth their efforts toward their own learning (Dallimore, Hertenstein, & Platt, 2004).

In our discussion on formative assessment we recommend that they be ungraded activities (see **formative and summative assessments***). The incentive for students is getting practice opportunities and **feedback*** on how well they understand the material to better prepare them for their summative assessments. If students see the connection between engaging with the material, even if no points are assigned, and their performance on assessments that do have grades associated with them, they are more likely to see the value in the activity as a means to support their learning.

Summary

Thinking of grades as behavioral economics is appropriate because they do function that way. But grades are not only an economic system. You have other means to incent student behavior, and we encourage you to try other means before paying for student behaviors with points.

See Also

Assessment Plan
Formative and Summative Assessments

Reference

Dallimore, E. J., Hertenstein, J. H., & Platt, M. B. (2004). Classroom participation and discussion effectiveness: Student-generated strategies. *Communication Education, 53*(1), 103–115.

42 Online Assessment and Authentication

Why Is Authentication an Issue?

There is a vast array of technologies available to deliver assessments online, often allowing students to access and complete assessments at the time and location of their choosing. However, with that capability comes the question of authentication: How do you know who is actually completing the online assessment?

In Public Law 110–315, as part of the 2008 United States Higher Education Opportunity Act, institutions are required to establish processes to ensure that the student who registers for an online or distance education course is the one who completes the program. As a result, colleges and universities have had to develop strategies around assessing and authenticating remote learners (Bailie & Jortberg, 2009).

Authentication in educational settings is fundamentally different from, say, online banking. In many electronic authentication uses, the customer is part of the security system. It is to your advantage to keep someone else from having your user ID and password. In an educational setting, we cannot assume that the learner is part of the security system. Often they consent to be, but there are lots of reasons for them to choose not to be. So you and your institution need to think a little differently about electronic authentication than many other users of authentication do.

Authentication Solutions

Solutions to address learner authentication range from fairly simple measures such as requiring an ID and password to advanced biometric techniques. Requiring a user ID and password to access an online assessment does build in some protections, but students can easily share this information with other students. Other authentication strategies include using webcam proctoring that requires the student to sit in front of a video camera while completing an assessment. Software is available that allows you to monitor a student's IP address or identify discrepancies in response patterns, for example, using keystroke recognition to identify how the student types. Advanced technologies can be used which measure biometrics such as fingerprints, signature, facial or voice recognition, and palm vein recognition (Bailie & Jortberg, 2009; Sandeen, 2013). If implementing these solutions is not technically or financially feasible, another option is requiring students to go to a physical testing center that provides in-person testing and proctoring services.

Authentication and the Purpose of Assessment

While there are technology solutions to help with authentication the type of solution you choose should be based on your purpose for giving the assessment and on the stakes attached. ("Stakes" in testing refers to the size of the consequences for the examinee.) Formative or low-stakes assessments might not need any authentication methods other than logging in to the online assessment using an ID and password (see **formative and summative assessments***). With these assessments, the focus is on scaffolding the student's learning, providing opportunities for them to struggle and make mistakes. For higher-stakes assessments, such as quizzes and exams, more stringent authentication methods may need to be used. In some cases, such as credit-by-examination programs where a student may earn college credit based on a single test score, employing physical testing centers may be warranted. Testing centers not only help address authentication issues but also aid in security of the test questions (see **online test security***).

In addition to the purpose for the assessment, you should also have a clear plan for the types of assessments you use throughout the course. Including constructed-response questions (see **selected- and constructed-response questions***) in your assessments can help reduce cheating (see **cheating and plagiarism***) and provide you with information about how the student writes and thinks. Also, if possible, having students complete projects, portfolios, concept maps, and other similar assessments, particularly as their high-stakes assessments, reduces the ability for students to cheat, making authentication issues less of a concern.

Summary

Certifying the authenticity of the student completing an online assessment is a significant concern as the number of online courses and online components in blended courses continues to grow. While many solutions exist to help authenticate learners completing an online assessment, the specific solution you use should be based on the purpose of the assessment and resources available.

See Also

Cheating and Plagiarism
Formative and Summative Assessments
Online Test Security

References

Bailie, J. L., & Jortberg, M. A. (2009). Online learner authentication: Verifying the identity of online users. *Journal of Online Learning and Teaching*, 5(2), 197–207.

Sandeen, C. (2013). Assessment's place in the new MOOC world. *Research & Practice in Assessment*, 8(2), 5–12.

43 Online Discussions

Recommendation: If your course is completely online and one or more of your learning objectives focuses on engaging in online discussions, grade online discussion contributions using a rubric focused on students' qualitative contributions to the discussion.

Should You Grade Online Discussion Contributions?

As the number of blended, hybrid, or completely online courses increases, so does the need to develop strategies that address student engagement in these online environments. Unlike the traditional classrooms where much of the instructor–student and student–student interactions happen face to face, online courses or courses with strong online components often have to rely on tools such as online discussion boards to promote instructor and peer engagement. Students with a strong sense of community are more like to persist in online courses than students who feel isolated (Rovai, 2003).

Many online discussions are done asynchronously where students reflect on the course content, questions posed by the instructor, or previous postings by other students in the class. Mason and Lockwood (1994) identified several drawbacks to online discussions, among them reduced student motivation to interact. As we acknowledge in the **not everything that matters must be graded*** entry, "What gets measured is what matters." So do you need to include student participation in online discussions as a part of the course grade in order to motivate students to interact? It depends on how important student interaction is as a part of your course, particularly if you are teaching a completely online course. Do any of your learning objectives specifically focus on students' ability to engage in online discussions (see **align assessments to learning objectives***)? If so, then grading this activity as part of your course makes sense. If you are using online discussion as a means of **participation*** then we advise against including it as a part of your course grade. Rovai (2003) suggests that including participation in online discussion as a part of the student's grade increases the number of student messages per week while simultaneously increasing a sense of community among students in the course compared to courses in which discussions were not graded. This can help to motivate students to interact in an online course.

What Grading Strategies Should You Use for Grading Online Discussions?

Rovai (2003) found that weighting participation in online discussions at 10–20% of the course grade increases student participation, but increasing the weight to 25–35% of the course grade did not result in any additional benefit to student participation. One way to grade this participation is by using a rubric to evaluate the content, quality, and frequency of participation in online discussions (for examples see Lunney & Sammarco, 2009; Rovai, 2004; Wyss, Freedman, & Siebert, 2014). **Rubrics*** primarily should focus on the students' qualitative contributions to the discussion, not the number of posts they make. Share the rubric with students to articulate your expectations for participating in the online discussions. Additionally, students should be given **feedback*** about their discussion posts and how to improve them if they do not meet the criteria outlined in the rubric. You could also consider **self-assessment*** or **peer assessment*** strategies for evaluating online discussion contributions.

Summary

While there are several strategies for how to construct online discussions to support student learning and engagement (see Rovai, 2007), we believe that, unlike classroom participation, participation in online discussions should be included in a student's grade, especially for completely online courses especially if engaging in online discussions with peers is a critical element of the course.

See Also

Feedback
Participation

References

Lunney, M., & Sammarco, A. (2009). Scoring rubric for grading students' participation in online discussions. *Computers, Informatics, Nursing, 27*(1), 26–31.

Mason. R., & Lockwood, F. (1994). *Using communications media in open and flexible learning.* London: Kogan Page.

Rovai, A. P. (2003). Strategies for grading online discussions: Effects on discussions and classroom community in Internet-based university courses. *Journal of Computing in Higher Education, 15*(1), 89–107.

Rovai, A. P. (2004). A constructivist approach to online college learning. *The Internet and Higher Education, 7*(2), 79–93.

Rovai, A. P. (2007). Facilitating online discussions effectively. *The Internet and Higher Education, 10*(1), 77–88.

Wyss, V. L., Freedman, D., & Siebert, C. J. (2014). The development of a discussion rubric for online courses: Standardizing expectations of graduate students in online scholarly discussions. *Tech Trends, 58*(2), 99–107.

44 Online Test Security

Early in Dawn's career she worked for a university testing center in which she helped instructors design quizzes and tests for classroom and online delivery. One school at the university had four large-enrollment courses and their own secure computer-based testing lab in which they would deliver their exams. Since each course had about 1,000 students and the computer lab held about 100 examinees, students could schedule their exam at any time over a two-day period. All four courses consisted of three multiple-choice exams and a cumulative multiple-choice final, each worth 25% of the course grade.

Three of the four courses used item banks where students received a randomly selected question from a pool of questions, but an instructor who taught one of the courses felt it was unfair that students did not receive the exact same questions. In this course students received the same 40 questions on their exam for that course. A savvy group of students in this class created a scheme whereby the more prepared students in the course would take the exam in the earliest time slots. Different students were assigned to memorize a certain number of questions, for example, Jane would memorize questions 1–5, John would memorize questions 6–10, etc. Immediately after leaving the exam students would call a prearranged phone number and "mind dump" their assigned questions. By the end of the first day of the exam, this group of students had the entire exam at their disposal, giving students taking the exam on the second day a significant advantage.

How did the students get caught? As part of Dawn's position, she analyzed the exams to look for any problematic items since new items were added or tested every semester. On the second exam in the semester, she noticed that the average exam scores on day two were 15% higher than the scores from day one. She also noticed that students who had barely passed the first exam were scoring above 90% on the second exam. Dawn notified the instructor and the department chair about the discrepancy and it was they who uncovered the elaborate scheme the students had constructed. Over 200 students were involved, the exam scores were all thrown out, and the course underwent a significant overhaul to its exam process.

Online Assessment—Are All My Test Questions Available Online?

When you deliver your assessments online, you not only need to be concerned about issues with student authentication (see **online assessment and authentication***), but also about security of the assessments themselves. As we mentioned in our **cheating and plagiarism*** entry, we know students cheat. The opportunities for cheating and unauthorized sharing of information become even more prevalent in an online environment. However, your level of concern should primarily be influenced by whether you are using the assessment for formative or summative purposes (see **formative and summative assessments***). You may be less concerned about formative assessments given they are typically ungraded with a focus on practice and **feedback*** for students. You may be interested in protecting graded summative assessments, particularly those that include selected-response question types as these can be time-consuming and challenging to create (see **selected- and constructed-response questions***).

There are some technological solutions that can help address security issues for online assessments. Some examples include:

- Item randomization: each student receives questions and answer choices presented in a different order.
- Time limits: instructors can set time limits that start once a student has opened an assessment, such as one minute per question or 20 minutes to complete an entire assessment.
- Item pooling: students receive questions randomly selected from a "pool" of questions so that each student has a different set of questions.
- Secure browsers: students are required to use a secure browser plug-in that prevents them from accessing other sites or programs.
- Remote proctoring: students are required to log in to a secure website and take their assessment in front of a webcam; external companies monitor students as they complete the assessment looking for signs of suspicious behavior.
- Remote test centers: students must go to a physical testing center location to take their assessment via computer.

One particular strategy that has been found to be effective for online assessments is using parameterized questions whereby each student receives a randomly generated parameter from a particular set (Sosnovsky, Shcherbinina, & Brusilovsky, 2003). For example, to measure a learning objective about students' ability to add single-digit whole numbers you could set up the following question in your online course: In the equation $X + Y = ?$, set X and Y to be any value between 0 and 9. Parameterized questions are typically limited to fields such as math, statistics, or computer programming where the underlying formula or principle can be explicitly defined. However, when used, these types of questions evaluate the same underlying process (e.g. do students know how to add two single-digit numbers between 0 and 9?) while simultaneously providing a different set of values for each student.

Some instructors and institutions combine several approaches for completely online courses. For example, Troy University in Alabama has their online students purchase and install a 360-degree webcam permitting visual and auditory proctoring and software that prevents students from accessing anything but tests during exams (Clark, 2008). While these measures may seem extreme, for high-stakes online assessments that contribute to course grades and awarding course credit, they may be necessary. However, for a majority of online assessments, particularly those used as part of a flipped or hybrid course, the focus should be on providing low-stakes assessments with frequent feedback. That removes the need for extreme security measures and makes the focus on providing students guidance about their learning as part of the online assessment.

Summary

The level of concern and security measures you implement to safeguard online assessments should be influenced by your assessment purpose. A range of technological solutions, from fairly simple and inexpensive to complex and costly, exist to help you manage maintaining the integrity of your online assessments.

See Also

Cheating and Plagiarism
Formative and Summative Assessments
Online Assessment and Authentication

Resources

Eisenberg, A. (2013, March 2). Keeping an eye on online test-takers. *New York Times*. Retrieved from www.nytimes.com/2013/03/03/technology/new-technologies-aim-to-foil-online-course-cheating.html?_r=1&

Online Schools Center. (2014, July). How students cheat online. Retrieved from www.onlineschoolscenter.com/cheating-online/

Wollack, J. A., & Fremer, J. (Eds.). (2013). *Handbook of test security*. New York, NY: Routledge.

Young, J. R. (2013, June 3). Online classes see cheating go high-tech. *Chronicle of Higher Education*. Retrieved from www.chronicle.com/article/Cheating-Goes-High-Tech/132093/

References

Clark, K. (2008, October 3). Professors use technology to fight cheating. *U.S. News and World Report.* Retrieved from www.usnews.com/education/articles/2008/10/03/professors-use-technology-to-fight-student-cheating

Sosnovsky, S., Shcherbinina, O., & Brusilovsky, P. (2003). Web-based parameterized questions as a tool for learning. Retrieved July 14, 2017 from www.pitt.edu/~peterb/papers/ELearn03.pdf

45 Open-Book Exams

By "open-book exam" we mean students are allowed to bring pre-existing resources with them, or access them via the internet, during an in-class examination. That's enough different from **cheat sheets or crib sheets*** that we've got a separate entry for those. They do share several similarities, along with **take-home exams***, so those three entries will sound a bit alike.

Let's tackle this right up front: you're concerned that open-book exams are easier and that you're "selling the store" in giving them to students. You think students like them better because they're easier, so your evaluations may be impacted by whether you let students do open-book exams or not. You may also be wondering whether these choices influence student studying, that, for example, if they have an open-book then they won't study or study as well. In short, while there are many empirical studies which address these issues, for every study which leans in one direction, there is seemingly another leaning in the other direction. Nonetheless, the research literature on open-book tests has some lessons we'd like to share.

Larwin, Gorman, and Larwin (2013) conducted a meta-analysis of 14 effect sizes from 15 studies conducted between 1958 and 2009 comparing open-book exam conditions to closed-book exam conditions. They found that, indeed, students do better in an open-book condition than a closed-book condition across the studies they examined (mean effect size, d, of +0.257).

Matthew (2012) found that, while undergraduate psychology and statistics students preferred open-book or cheat-sheet exam conditions to closed-book exam conditions, the condition didn't actually change their self-reported study behaviors or study time. Some studies have indicated that students engage in more adaptive studying behaviors for open-book exams than closed-book exams (e.g. Theophilides & Koutselini, 2000). Other suggest they use better strategies for closed-book tests (e.g. Heijne-Penninga, Kuks, Hofman, & Cohen-Schotanus, 2008).

There are some potential benefits to open-book exams documented in the literature reviewed by Larwin, Gorman, and Larwin (2013): test anxiety may be lessened (see **evaluation anxiety***), textbook reading comprehension may increase, and open-book exams focus more on application and authentic problems.

When deciding whether to employ open-book exams, we recommend you think through several issues. First, what meets your learning objectives (see **align assessments to learning objectives***)? Second, how are your students prepared? And third, how will this actually work?

What Meets Your Learning Objectives?

Open-book exams work really well for learning objectives that include accessing resources, and such learning objectives are valid. Hasn't your doctor turned to a reference work during a medical appointment? Using resources is a professional skill (Heijne-Penninga, Kuks, Schönrock-Adema, Snijders, & Cohen-Schotnus, 2006). It is critical to anchor your choices about open-book options in what you want students to know and to be able to do.

This has to align with the resources you permit them to bring as well as the questions you ask. Depending on the resources and the questions, the open-book can either represent a place for students to *locate* a correct answer or a resource they use to *arrive* at a correct answer. The former is a crutch that could have negative consequences for student studying and exam preparation while the latter acknowledges that some problems require the use of resources. It depends on what questions are on the test.

"Time's Winged Chariot"

Allowing students to access resources during an in-class exam means they will take longer to respond to the same number of questions than they would in a closed-book format. One study documented medical school students using four to five minutes *per question* during an open-book examination (Westerkamp, Hiejne-Penninga, Kuks, & Cohen-Schotanus, 2013).

So you and your students need to think that through. For you, it becomes a matter of testing real estate. You only have so much time, and thus so many questions, you can reasonably ask students to respond to. The fewer the questions in a sitting, the more valuable each one is in terms of the learning objectives you are assessing and how thoroughly, deeply, and broadly you're assessing each one. Thus one consideration in choosing open-book is the tradeoff of the advantages of doing so against less testing real estate to work with.

Preparing and Supporting Students

Before the exam, talk with them about how to prepare. Students think that open-book means they do not need to study or prepare in any way. That's not true. They should spend time organizing the resources they will access during the exam and being very familiar with them. Students who used a deeper learning approach to studying took less time to do the open-book exam (Heijne-Penninga, Kuks, Hofman, & Cohen-Schotanus, 2011).

Especially with less experienced students, talk explicitly with them before the test about how to handle resources during the test. Help them develop strategies to combat the gross inefficiencies of using resources. For example, teach them to go through the test first without referring to any resource, answering every question and providing a confidence rating: completely sure, not sure, no idea. Then, once they've responded to every question, they should use resources to check their "not sure" questions first, which shouldn't take them as long to confirm as the "no idea" items.

During the exam, help them to manage their time and navigate the test. You can do things like write the time remaining on the board, or make announcements about time remaining. Number the exam pages "Page 2 of 12" so that they have a "progress bar" to refer to.

Variations

Partial Open-Book—Students spend the first part of the in-class examination time working without the book or other supports, then during a second time period they may consult resources to check answers. A subvariant is that they turn in one answer sheet midway and then a second one after they've consulted resources.

Questions Ahead Then Write in Class—You can choose to give students the entire test ahead of time but ask them to take it in class without resources. Another variation is to give them, say, 12 short-essay questions, of which eight will actually be on the test when they come to class.

Online Administration

If you are administering your exam online, you'll need to consider authentication (see **online assessment and authentication***) and **online test security*** issues in addition to the resources you want your students to access. While there are some technological solutions you can employ to combat unauthorized use of resources, no system is completely fool-proof, particularly in online administration. Matching your assessment to your learning objectives, considering time constraints, and preparing your students are also critical elements to address with online assessments. Given that your students potentially will have greater access to resources in an online environment, you might want to design your online assessments with the "open-book exam" approach in mind.

Summary

When deciding whether to employ open-book exams, we recommend you think through several issues. First, what meets your learning objectives? Second, how are your students prepared? And third, how will this actually work?

See Also

Cheat Sheets or Crib Sheets
Take-Home Exams

Resource

Heijne-Penninga, M., Kuks, J.B.M., Hofman, W.H.A., & Cohen-Schotanus, J. (2011). Directing students to profound open-book test preparation: The relationship between deep learning and open-book test time. *Medical Teacher, 33*(1), e16–e21.

References

Heijne-Penninga, M., Kuks, J., Hofman, W. H., & Cohen-Schotanus, J. (2008). Influence of open- and closed-book tests on medical students' learning approaches. *Medical Education, 42*(10), 967–974.

Heijne-Penninga, M., Kuks, J.B.M., Hofman, W.H.A., & Cohen-Schotanus, J. (2011). Directing students to profound open-book test preparation: The relationship between deep learning and open-book test time. *Medical Teacher, 33*(1), e16–e21.

Heijne-Penninga, M., Kuks, J. B., Schönrock-Adema, J., Snijders, T. A., & Cohen-Schotanus, J. (2008). Open-book tests to complement assessment-programmes: Analysis of open and closed-book tests. *Advances in Health Sciences Education, 13*(3), 263–273.

Larwin, K. H., Gorman, J., & Larwin, D. A. (2013). Assessing the impact of testing aids on post-secondary student performance: A meta-analytic investigation. *Educational Psychology Review, 25*(3), 429–443.

Matthew, N. (2012, March). Student preferences and performance: A comparison of open-book, closed book, and cheat sheet exam types. *Proceedings of the National Conference on Undergraduate Research*, Ogden, UT.

Theophilides, C., & Koutselini, M. (2000). Study behavior in the closed-book and the open-book examination: A comparative analysis. *Educational Research & Evaluation, 6*(4), 379–393.

Westerkamp, A. C., Hiejne-Penninga, M., Kuks, J.B.M., & Cohen-Schotanus, J. (2013). Open-book tests: Search behaviour, time used and test scores. *Medical Teacher, 35*, 330–332.

46 Our Policy on Policies

We advocate often in this book for having policies—**late work*** policy, **attendance*** policy, etc. There are some principles and pitfalls here, however, that you should be aware of. First, though, we should share our definition of a policy. In your courses, a "policy" sets forth the way you will view and act on certain instructor and/or student behaviors.

Advantages of Policies

By setting a "policy," you decide for yourself before you're faced with the particulars of a situation how you will address certain eventualities. This gives you the opportunity to think thoroughly and dispassionately about the issues at hand. For example, how do you weigh the various influences on a late work policy? Being handed an assignment late when you haven't thought through how that should be addressed will likely get you into trouble. We've seen colleagues overly swayed by the circumstances, like when it's their star pupil who turns a paper in late.

You will then communicate that policy to students before they face the particulars of a situation. This is an ounce of prevention that will reduce the number of discussions, debates, arguments you have with students.

When a student presents you with a set of circumstances, you've got somewhere to turn to address them. Jay had a senior colleague who always marveled at how, if he said something in class, students would argue with him about it, but if the same policy appeared in writing on the syllabus, there was much less fuss. Same policy, same instructor; but having it in writing made a difference.

Perhaps most importantly, having policies and enforcing them tremendously aids the consistency and **fairness*** of decision-making. When students know and you know what the "rules" are, it will shape their behavior and yours.

The Goldilocks Rule of Policy-Making

The Goldilocks Rule of Policy-Making has two elements to it. First, each policy itself has to be of appropriate specificity—not too general and not too specific. If a policy is too general, it won't be actionable. If a policy is too specific, it won't be flexible and allow you to handle truly unique circumstances. If your syllabus says, "Attendance is expected in this course," that is likely too general. There are no consequences; there's no real definition of attendance. If that's all you want to say about attendance, perhaps you should say nothing at all and let the importance of attendance be unspoken as one of the unwritten rules of college success (see **not everything that matters must be graded***). On the other hand, if your syllabus says, "Attendance is mandatory. Each missed class will result in 5 points being deducted from the final course grade," that is likely too specific. There's no wiggle room for an excused absence, that is, a legitimate reason for missing class.

The second element of the Goldilocks Rule of Policy-Making is that your course needs to have the right number of policies—not too many and not too few. A 30-page syllabus is likely one students won't read. Have policies for the most frequent and/or the most consequential issues that arise in your courses. Over time, you'll hone that balance.

Your course's policy environment needs to aid learning, help to keep your decisions fair and consistent, and not be cumbersome to navigate for you or your students.

Every Rule Has Exceptions

The purpose of a rule or policy is to address 85–90% of circumstances while still providing you with the ability to use your professional judgment and discretion in the other 10–15% of circumstances. You want to use policies to cut the line outside your office hours or the e-mails in your inbox from 20 to 4. Part of the paradox of rules is, if you try to write them to address 100% of situations, that will actually increase the number of exceptions you need to make.

Be careful that you don't foreclose your ability to deploy your professional judgment as circumstances warrant. Every rule has exceptions, and you want to be able to handle that. You can use what linguists call "hedges" to provide some wiggle room, words like "usually" or "typically." You can write exceptions in directly; for example, "unexcused absences" instead of "absences" provides for some discretion on your part.

Don't overcorrect after an unsatisfying occurrence. Due dates are a great example, especially with electronic submissions being so common. In "the old days," if a paper was due on Wednesday, February 23, that meant during the class session on that date. But with electronic submission, that could mean any time prior to 11:59 p.m. on February 23. We've seen instructors who felt students exploited the ambiguity of a due date of "February 23" when their classmates turned the paper in in class or submitted it before class while the "offending" student waited until after any comments you make in class about the assignment to make changes and submit the paper by midnight. The aggrieved instructor, in the next semester, puts the due dates as "11:59 p.m." Now, however, someone's internet connection blinked and it was submitted at

12:03 a.m. Our advice is to think very carefully about changing your policy based on a specific event.

Summary

There are very good reasons to have written policies, but you don't want to overdo it. Your course's policy environment needs to be facilitative of learning and as un-cumbersome as possible for you and your students.

47 Participation

Recommendation: Strongly encourage, but do not grade, participation.

Participation is a very important learning behavior which you should encourage or even require as a non-negotiable. *But don't pay for it with points or grades* even though most instructors do (Rogers, 2013). Not everything that is important is graded, and what is graded are not the only important things (see **not everything that matters must be graded*** and **assessment plan***).

Class participation is an extraordinarily complex and multifaceted topic (e.g. Rocca, 2010). Here, we will confine ourselves to the issue of how class participation should affect grades in the class.

Participation Is Important; Why Not Grade It?

Of course participation is important to you and to your students! But why (Jones, 2008)? And what is participation anyway?

Students' active engagement with the course content enhances their mastery of it. Further, student participation during class enriches the learning environment for everyone. Those are likely the two major reasons you're interested in promoting student participation.

If those two main outcomes are to be achieved, students have to be engaged in lots of ways, at lots of levels, and in rich ways that prove difficult to condense into a grade. It's a classic case of the quantification of something as complex as student participation producing at best a signaling or flagging system that communicates bare minimums to you and your students.

When you think "participation," what do you imagine? Responding to your questions. Asking their own questions. Talking with a peer about a course-related topic. Taking good notes. Being prepared for class. Contributing effectively to group activities. Yes, and probably lots of other things (e.g. Petress, 2006). How would you measure all of that?

Participation is usually a learning input, not a learning output. Participation is not an end in itself. It's the route to what you want from students;

it's not the outcome itself. We advise you to measure, assess, and grade what you really want.

Students are clear that they love to have participation graded (e.g. Dallimore, Hertenstein, & Platt, 2004). We wager, though, that's because it's usually ill-defined, poorly measured, and contributes a significant amount to their grade (Bean & Peterson, 1998). In other words, they know a good deal when they see one.

If participation is important, but you're not going to grade it, then you should promote it.

Promoting Participation

We advocate that you promote active participation by students rather than incenting it (see the next section). Promoting participation is an excellent thing to do! Here's an all-too-brief list of ways to promote participation:

Is Your Course Full of Good Stuff?—No really! Useful and interesting content, tied to students' personal or professional lives, on issues whose implications they're eager to explore will help students participate (Dallimore, Hertenstein, & Platt, 2004).

Do You Ask Good Questions?—Are you asking questions or designing activities that provoke students to think (Dallimore, Hertenstein, & Platt, 2004)? Teacher questioning is a huge topic, beyond the scope of this book, but it may well be worth your time to investigate (see Gayle, Preiss, & Allen, 2006).

What Happens When You Ask a Questions of the Class?—You ask a question and three high-performing students' hands shoot up. The same three hands most of the time. So you call on one of them. Let's look behind the scenes on this one. All the students in your class are so used to this dynamic. They know one of those three will answer. So they don't need to. They don't even need to consider your question. They can just sit there, and they know it. Imagine a slightly different dynamic. Suppose you ask your question, and ask every student to jot down an answer, and then you call on one of them (randomly or not, see below). All of a sudden, they know they must engage. Or suppose you pose your question via a student response system (i.e. "clickers") or a backchannel system? Now whether and how everyone responds is noticeable. Something that simple can really alter the dynamic of student engagement, even if only one student speaks, in your class.

How Do You Pick a Student to Respond?—Cold-calling participation systems or systems that ask students to engage at random have some pros and cons. The pros are that every student must be prepared in the event they are randomly called upon. It eliminates all the reasons why a student might not be participating. It disengages all the instructor biases which drive who you call on to participate. On the downside, it forces students to engage publicly when there may be good reasons for them not to. It also doesn't permit you to select students who can make the best contribution at a given point in the class. There are lots of permutations on cold-calling which attempt to balance these considerations and mitigate the concerns. If you're inclined toward such a system, check out:

Mehvar, R. (2010). A participation requirement to engage students in a pharmacokinetics course synchronously taught at a local and distant campus. *American Journal of Pharmaceutical Education*, *74*(7), 118.

Dallimore, E. J., Hertenstein, J. H., & Platt, M. B. (2004). Classroom participation and discussion effectiveness: Student-generated strategies. *Communication Education*, *53*(1), 103–115.

Dallimore, E. J., Hertenstein, J. H., & Platt, M. B. (2006). Nonvoluntary class participation in graduate discussion courses: Effects of grading and cold calling. *Journal of Management Education*, *30*(2), 354–377.

Dallimore, E. J., Hertenstein, J. H., & Platt, M. B. (2013). Impact of cold-calling on student voluntary participation. *Journal of Management Education*, *37*(3), 305–341.

Are Students Participating or Contributing?—Once a student answers your question, respond. Say something else. Tie their contribution to the course objectives, or better yet, support them to do so. Let the students truly contribute to, not just "participate" in, the course.

(Dallimore, Hertenstein, & Platt, 2004)

Pitfalls to (Grading) Participation

Many approaches to participation attempt to incent student involvement during class, essentially (or literally! (Chylinski, 2010)) paying students to contribute to the class. Such systems, in our view, draw students' attention to the minimums necessary—"what do I have to do to get a B?"—rather than drawing their attention to maximizing their involvement in the course. If you require two substantive contributions to each class session, if a student makes her two contributions in the first ten minutes, she's off the hook for the other 40 minutes.

Does the portion of the course grade allocated to participation indicate mastery of the course learning objectives? Indirectly at best. And yet, it is not uncommon to see a large percentage (Parkes, Fix and Harris (2003) report a median of 10%), even up to half, of a course grade defined as participation.

Similarly, a great many factors contribute to when, how, and how much a student speaks up or pitches in in class (Rocca, 2010; Weaver & Qi, 2005). Your personality, your aggressiveness and argumentativeness (Goodboy & Bolkan, 2009; Myers, Edwards, Wahl, & Martin, 2007; Rocca, 2008), your perceived openness to questions, and how you handle them when they're asked—just to name a short list that *you* have more influence over than the student does—influence how much students speak up in class. So counts of vocalizations, for example, may not actually measure a student's engagement with the course material or even with peers (Frymier & Houser, 2016). Meyer (2009) actually argues that silence can be participation.

Considerations in Grading Participation (If You Must Grade Participation)

If we haven't convinced you and you feel you must provide some portion of the course grade to participation, do it in a way that honors these considerations. Have a systematic approach which is clear and clearly communicated to students. The system needs to focus on the quality, not just the quantity, of participation. It should focus on the behaviors that promote learning (e.g. O'Connor, 2013). It should actually capture participating, not simply attending (see **attendance***). You will need to wrestle with who is the best judge of student participation. There are systems that use the instructor, the student herself, and peers, and systems which use combinations of those (Gopinath, 1999; Ryan, Marshall, Porter, & Jia, 2007). Finally, it should represent a pretty small fraction of the course grade (less than 5%).

If a portion or all of your course is taught online and you embed discussion boards in your online system, you might have different considerations for whether or not to include participation in these forums as a part of the course grade. For a further discussion of this issue see **online discussions***.

Summary

Student participation is so critical to student success that you definitely should expect it. Do not grade it, however. Promote it!

See Also

Attendance
Not Everything That Matters Must Be Graded
Online Discussions

Resources

Bean, J. C., & Peterson, D. (1998). Grading classroom participation. *New Directions for Teaching and Learning, 1998*(74), 33–40.

Jones, R. C. (2008). The "why" of class participation: A question worth asking. *College Teaching, 56*(1), 59–63.

O'Connor, K. (2013). Class participation: Promoting in-class student engagement. *Education, 133*(3), 340–344.

Rocca, K. A. (2010). Student participation in the college classroom: An extended multidisciplinary literature review. *Communication Education, 59*(2), 185–213.

References

Bean, J. C., & Peterson, D. (1998). Grading classroom participation. *New Directions for Teaching and Learning, 1998*(74), 33–40.

Chylinski, M. (2010). Cash for comment: Participation money as a mechanism for measurement, reward, and formative feedback in active class participation. *Journal of Marketing Education, 32*(1), 25–38.

Dallimore, E. J., Hertenstein, J. H., & Platt, M. B. (2004). Classroom participation and discussion effectiveness: Student-generated strategies. *Communication Education, 53*(1), 103–115.

Frymier, A. B., & Houser, M. L. (2016). The role of oral participation in student engagement. *Communication Education, 65*(1), 83–104.

Gayle, B. M., Preiss, R. W., & Allen, M. (2006). How effective are teacher-initiated classroom questions in enhancing student learning? *Classroom Communication and Instructional Processes: Advances through Meta-Analysis*, 279–293.

Goodboy, A. K., & Bolkan, S. (2009). College teacher misbehaviors: Direct and indirect effects on student communication behavior and traditional learning outcomes. *Western Journal of Communication, 73*(2), 204–219.

Gopinath, C. (1999). Alternatives to instructor assessment of class participation. *Journal of Education for Business, 75*(1), 10–14.

Jones, R. C. (2008). The "why" of class participation: A question worth asking. *College Teaching, 56*(1), 59–63.

Meyer, K. R. (2009). *Student classroom engagement: Rethinking participation grades and student silence* (Doctoral dissertation, Ohio University).

Myers, S. A., Edwards, C., Wahl, S. T., & Martin, M. M. (2007). The relationship between perceived instructor aggressive communication and college student involvement. *Communication Education, 56*(4), 495–508.

Parkes, J., Fix, T. K., & Harris, M. B. (2003). What syllabi communicate about assessment in college classrooms. *Journal on Excellence in College Teaching, 14*(1), 61–83.

Petress, K. (2006). An operational definition of class participation. *College Student Journal, 40*(4), 821–824.

Rocca, K. A. (2008). Participation in the college classroom: The impact of instructor immediacy and verbal aggression. *The Journal of Classroom Interaction*, 22–33.

Rocca, K. A. (2010). Student participation in the college classroom: An extended multidisciplinary literature review. *Communication Education, 59*(2), 185–213.

Rogers, S. L. (2013). Calling the question: Do college instructors actually grade participation? *College Teaching, 61*(1), 11–22.

Ryan, G. J., Marshall, L. L., Porter, K., & Jia, H. (2007). Peer, professor and self-evaluation of class participation. *Active Learning in Higher Education, 8*(1), 49–61.

Weaver, R. R., & Qi, J. (2005). Classroom organization and participation: College students' perceptions. *The Journal of Higher Education, 76*(5), 570–601.

48 Peer Assessment

What Is Peer Assessment?

Similar to **self-assessment***, peer assessment involves having classmates evaluate each other's work, typically using a rubric (see **rubrics***). Peer assessment can be used as a formative assessment as a means to provide feedback to classmates or can be used as a summative assessment where a score contributes to their classmate's course grade (see **formative and summative assessments***).

Falchikov and Goldfinch (2000) conducted a meta-analysis review of research comparing peer and instructor evaluations of student work in college courses. Peer assessments more closely aligned with instructor assessments when holistic ratings were used compared to asking peers to evaluate several dimensions of performance. Additionally, peer and instructor assessments were more strongly aligned when the task focused on academic products and processes rather than professional practice. The researchers did not find any differences across disciplines or when a single or multiple peer raters were used.

Advantages

There are several advantages to using peer assessment. The process of evaluating a classmate's work can help students reflect on the strengths and weaknesses of their own performance. Additionally, peer assessment helps students develop skills in making judgments, which is a skill often needed in their professional career (Bostock, n.d.; Boud, 1989). Peers can often allocate more time and provide more detailed **feedback*** than the instructor can provide (Weaver & Cotrell, 1986). While peer assessment might not provide the same level of expertise as from an instructor, the potential for peers to provide feedback quickly and in greater depth could compensate for this (Topping, 1998). If peer assessment is used as formative feedback on a paper or other performance assessment, the student receiving the feedback can edit and make corrections before completing the final version (Froyd, 2002).

Disadvantages

The primary disadvantage of peer assessment is whether peers can provide reliable, insightful evaluations and feedback, particularly when that evaluation is included as part of a grade. Students who receive low scores or critical comments from their peers might not accept the feedback as accurate (Topping, 1998). Training students to use a rubric or provide constructive feedback can be time-consuming, especially if you have to develop sample exemplars to use for the training. Some instructors are concerned that peers might not be able to objectively evaluate their classmates, particularly if ensuring anonymity is not possible. Lastly, students may put varying levels of effort into the peer assessment which may necessitate some oversight from the instructor.

How Can Peers Be Trained to Give Their Classmates Good Feedback?

Based on their meta-analysis findings, Falchikov and Goldfinch (2000) developed several recommendations for implementing peer assessment in higher education:

- Focus peer assessment tasks on academic products and processes.
- Have students provide overall global ratings (i.e. use a holistic rubric) instead of rating several dimensions.
- Involve your students in discussions about evaluation criteria.

Along with involving your students in the discussion about the rubric criteria, there are also several software programs you can use to train students in the peer assessment process. The general premise for most of these programs is that the instructor rates several exemplars either developed by the instructor or taken from a previous semester. Students then evaluate these exemplars with the same rubric the instructor used. Students must match or be close to the instructor's rating on a certain number of exemplars before being able to proceed to evaluate artifacts from peers in their course. In this way, the system is calibrating the students' ratings of their peers to that of the instructor.

In addition to the above recommendations, we also suggest the following when doing peer assessment:

- Tell students why you are doing peer review and explain the expectations you have for giving scores and/or feedback.
- If you are asking students to provide feedback/comments as part of the peer review process, model how to give useful feedback.

- If the peer assessment primarily includes a score from a rubric and not qualitative feedback, peers should be asked to provide written justification for their score.
- If possible, remove any identifying information from assignments before having peers review them.
- Give students the opportunity to practice doing peer assessment either through an online software product for training or through in-class activities with exemplars.

Should I Include Peer Assessment Scores as Part of a Grade?

The primary focus of peer assessment should be on giving and receiving feedback about a task, not on awarding a grade. However, if students have been adequately trained in how to apply the rubric, scores from peers can be used as a small part of the grading for the task. We discuss these processes in more detail in **groupwork***, and you could also consult Johnson and Johnson (2004).

Summary

Peer assessment can be an effective and efficient method to provide students formative or summative evaluation of papers, projects, and other performance assessments. Students should be given well-defined criteria on a holistic rubric, training and practice on how to give scores and constructive feedback, and a mechanism to give ratings and feedback anonymously.

See Also

Feedback
Rubrics
Self-Assessment

References

Bostock, S. (n.d.). Student peer assessment. *The Higher Education Academy.* Retrieved July 16, 2017 from www.reading.ac.uk/web/files/engageinassessment/student_peer_assessment_-_stephen_bostock.pdf

Boud, D. (1989). The role of self-assessment in student grading. *Assessment and Evaluation in Higher Education, 14,* 20–30.

Falchikov, N., & Goldfinch, J. (2000). Student peer assessment in higher education: A meta-analysis comparing peer and teacher marks. *Review of Educational Research, 70*(3), 287–322.

Froyd, J. (2002). Peer assessment and peer evaluation. Retrieved July 16, 2017 from www.foundationcoalition.org/publications/brochures/2002peer_assessment.pdf

Johnson, D. W., & Johnson, R. T. (2004). *Assessing students in groups: Promoting group responsibility and individual accountability.* Thousand Oaks, CA: Corwin Press.

Topping, K. (1998). Peer assessment between students in colleges and universities. *Review of Educational Research, 68*(3), 249–276.

Weaver, R. L., & Cotrell, H. W. (1986). Peer evaluation: A case study. *Innovative Higher Education, 11*, 25–39.

49 Personal Disclosures

How Do I Handle Personal Disclosures?

Recommendation: Know your institutional landscape for student issues and be prepared to address personal disclosures in your classes.

In Dawn's very first teaching assignment as a graduate student she assigned her small undergraduate summer class of about 15 students to give a five-minute oral presentation on someone who significantly influenced their lives. She sat poised in the back of the room with her grading rubric (see **rubrics***) ready to evaluate their performances. Student after student got up in front of the class and revealed very personal information about their lives and the individuals who influenced them. She vividly remembers most of the class in tears by the end of the presentations.

It's going to happen to you, too. At some point, a student is going to disclose personal information to you. You may even be planning and intending for students to make personal disclosures. We are not only referring here to disclosures of sexual assault or harassment or illegal activity like underage drinking, but also to disclosures which may, at first, seem more innocuous, like a spat with a dorm roommate.

Your first response is likely to be your very natural, humane, and empathic response (Rosenthal, 2017), which is wholly appropriate. You are not only another human being, however, in this situation. You are also a representative of your institution, so you also need to take those considerations into account when responding.

We advise that you know your institution's policies regarding personal disclosures and that you think through your responses before the disclosure happens.

Know Your Institutional Landscape for Such Issues

Even an off-handed comment from a student could trigger a vast array of important and complex issues from student well-being, to harassment, to criminal or other legal considerations. Because how you respond not only has ramifications for you and the student but may also affect your institution, we can't urge you strongly enough to *know now what your campus advises you to do for various kinds of disclosures and have that information readily available if needed.* Every campus has different approaches to such issues, different regulatory requirements, different resources available. It is critical that you know where on campus you could or should refer students and whether and to whom you're obligated to report such disclosures.

The type of institution you work at, the web of federal and state laws and regulations, and the structures and resources available on your campus all play into how you are expected to respond. Even the extent to which you are to discuss the disclosure with the student depends on those issues. So please know as soon as you can how such matters are to be addressed on your campus.

Know What You're Going to Do

If you are teaching courses where you have students writing from their personal experiences, or in professional fields where students must engage personal issues in class or classwork, you definitely want to have formal policies and procedures worked out and clearly communicated to students. Your profession likely has ethical guidelines for addressing such disclosures in addition to the considerations we just mentioned.

Even if you're not planning or intending disclosures, know what your options are and plan ahead. For example, at the end of Dawn's class she was able to mention several campus resources to the students and communicate with the summer program coordinator who was supporting this cohort of students about the need for follow-up as a result of the assignment. What she didn't have prepared was contact information for the appropriate campus offices that she could immediately provide the students. Ever since, and congruent with her institution's policies and approaches, whenever Dawn teaches she now prepares a handout for students as a resource should the need arise. It was a valuable lesson that what may seem an innocuous assignment might evoke personal disclosures and to be prepared for that eventuality.

Summary

You have an obligation to act in professionally responsible ways when students disclose personal information. You also have the right to respond in a humane and empathetic way. How you respond may make a huge difference to the student's well-being. In addition, how you respond may end up having legal implications for you, the student, and your institution, depending on what it is they disclose.

See Also

Beneficence
FERPA

Resource

Rosenthal, M. N. (2017, April 7). Responding to students' trauma disclosures with empathy [Blog post]. Retrieved from www.insidehighered.com/advice/2017/04/07/how-professors-can-best-respond-when-students-experience-trauma-essay

50 Pop Quizzes

Should I Give Pop Quizzes?

Recommendation: Do not give pop quizzes.

Why We Give Pop Quizzes

Instructors get frustrated with poor student engagement such as poor attendance and being unprepared for class. Somewhere in their frustration, they recall their own intro psych class and those experiments on how to get the pigeon to tap a button to get food. The way to get the pigeon to tap like crazy is to have the food come after a random number of taps rather than a predictable number of taps. It's called intermittent reinforcement, and it is why lotteries are so lucrative for the lottery sponsor (and a big part of why gambling is addictive). It's an extremely powerful way to shape human behavior. Why not use it in the classroom?

Sometimes instructors get so frustrated that they snap and declare a pop quiz that even they didn't see coming, the punitive pop quiz. These are particularly damaging. Aside from the chances that a quiz you write on the spot when you're angry will be of good quality, such an action really tears at the fabric of the relationship you have with your students.

Intermittent reinforcement works, as does a coercive power play, but at a tremendous cost. Your students aren't pigeons. They're learners and people, just like you are. Part of why they come to class eager and prepared is the relationship they have with you. The Latin root of the word "assessment" is *assidere*, which means to sit beside. When you pop a quiz, or worse, punitively pop a quiz, you oppose the learners rather than come alongside them.

Pop quizzes are not learning-oriented strategies but rather are performance-oriented. When reading examples in the higher education teaching literature, we noted how often the writer who advocated for pop quizzes to drive **attendance***, engagement, or for **extra credit*** mentioned that students liked the impact on their grades. That is, however, maladaptive for lasting learning. We thus encourage you to read testimonials for pop quizzes in the higher education teaching literature very carefully.

A great deal of empirical literature is clear that (frequent) quizzing works to promote learning but it does so without needing to be unannounced. There's little evidence that the "pop" adds anything to the "quiz" (Kamuche, 2011), and nearly all evidence that supports pop quizzes relies on the "quiz," not the "pop" (e.g. Graham, 1999). When frequent (announced) quizzes are used, students tend to have better attitudes about their learning, about the instructor, about the course, better class attendance, less test anxiety, a sense of being better prepared (Kuo & Simon, 2009), and they did their readings (Schrank, 2016)!

What You Should Do

Give announced and relatively frequent quizzes. See **quizzing frequency***.

If you're concerned about whether students attend class, there are many better strategies for encouraging attendance. If you need methods to take attendance, there are many better strategies for that, too. See **attendance***.

If you're concerned about students being prepared for class, there are many better strategies for encouraging them to be prepared. The Readiness Assessment Tests (e.g. Weinstein & Wu, 2009) are an example.

If you're tempted to conduct a punitive pop quiz when students aren't engaged during class, don't do it. See Carbone (1999) for an excellent discussion of *Students Behaving Badly in Large Classes*.

If you would like instructional feedback about your teaching, consider using the anonymous pop quiz (Bell, 1997).

If you're going to use pop quizzes despite all we've just discussed, consider using the Monte Carlo Quiz (Fernald, 2004). It meets several of these needs while mitigating some of the dangers above because each class period the class rolls a die to determine whether there's a quiz that class or not, and the potential quiz questions—one of which is chosen for that class period by the die—are always the same.

Summary

Quizzes are good—fabulous, actually—at promoting learning. Not announcing the quizzes adds nothing to the value of quizzing while introducing lots of potential negatives.

See Also

Attendance
Extra Credit
Participation
Quizzing Frequency

Resources

Carbone, E. (1999). Students behaving badly in large classes. *New Directions for Teaching and Learning, 1999*(77), 35–43.

Fernald, P. S. (2004). The Monte Carlo quiz: Encouraging punctual completion and deep processing of assigned readings. *College Teaching*, 95–99.

References

Bell, J. T. (1997). Anonymous quizzes: An effective feedback mechanism. *Chemical Engineering Education (CEE), 31*(1), 56–57.

Graham, R. B. (1999). Unannounced quizzes raise test scores selectively for mid-range students. *Teaching of Psychology, 26*(4), 271–273.

Kamuche, F. U. (2011). The effects of unannounced quizzes on student performance: Further evidence. *College Teaching Methods & Styles Journal (CTMS), 3*(2), 21–26.

Kuo, T., & Simon, A. (2009). How many tests do we really need? *College Teaching, 57*(3), 156–160.

Schrank, Z. (2016). An assessment of student perceptions and responses to frequent low-stakes testing in introductory sociology classes. *Teaching Sociology, 44*(2), 118–127.

Weinstein, S. E., & Wu, S. W. (2009). Readiness assessment tests versus frequent quizzes: Student preferences. *International Journal of Teaching and Learning in Higher Education, 21*(2), 181–186.

51 Prior Knowledge

Recommendation: Whenever possible, administer a prior knowledge assessment to evaluate students' knowledge about the prerequisite learning objectives that are critical to support learning in your course.

What Is Prior Knowledge and Why Is It Important?

Prior knowledge is the knowledge your students have about your subject matter before they start your course. Dochy (1994) provided a comprehensive definition of prior knowledge that we summarize below.

Prior knowledge is:

- the knowledge your students have available to them before completing a task or assessment,
- organized into units that have connections among them,
- both knowledge about facts (what) and processes (how),
- partly knowledge that can be accessed and verbalized and partly intuitive and unarticulated knowledge that cannot be communicated,
- capable of action or change, and
- stored in the learner's knowledge base.

(Dochy, 1994)

Research has shown that there is a strong relationship between prior knowledge and student performance. Dochy, Segers, and Beuhl (1999) conducted a meta-analysis of research on prior knowledge and the majority of studies (91.5%) demonstrated positive effects of prior knowledge on student performance. Prior knowledge influences how students perceive and organize new information and how they make connections between ideas.

Determining what your students' prior knowledge is can help you identify specific gaps in their knowledge (Angelo & Cross, 1993), evaluate any misconceptions they might have that could interfere with how well they learn new material (Ambrose, Bridges, DiPietro, Lovett, & Norman, 2010), and create connections between what students already know and new concepts introduced in your class. Understanding what your students know and can do as they start your course can help inform your instructional activities.

How Do You Determine What Your Students Know as They Begin Your Course?

You might have certain assumptions about your students' prior knowledge that could hinder or halt their learning, so developing an assessment to evaluate their prior knowledge is an effective strategy particularly given the influence of prior knowledge on new learning. However, it can be challenging to evaluate all the prior knowledge that your students possess that could influence learning in your course. While you can't check *everything* they should know, there are, no doubt, core concepts that would be well worth checking. You might want to look at the learning objectives from the prerequisite course(s) to help you identify some of those core concepts. However, you should also consider other core concepts that you might assume they learned (for example, in high school) that wouldn't show up in the learning objectives for a prerequisite course but are foundational concepts critical to learning and success in your course.

While knowing what students know and can do when they start your course is important, you may also want to assess their prior knowledge before you begin a new topic. As we mentioned above, you can't check everything, so multiple, shorter prior knowledge assessments before major units may be better than a single, larger assessment. As with a prior knowledge assessment at the beginning of the course, the focus should be on evaluating the key concepts students should have *before* they started your class. This tactic may also be useful for you as some just-in-time feedback about any deficient core concepts students have that you may need to address before progressing to the next unit.

In a meta-analysis on prior knowledge assessments, Dochy, Segers, and Beuhl (1999) found that prior knowledge was often measured through multiple-choice tests, open questions/completion tests, association tests, recognition tests, free recall, and self-evaluation by the students. Angelo and Cross (1993) describe some less formal techniques such as the quick inventory, background knowledge probe, and focused listing that attempt to evaluate students' prior knowledge. While **self-assessment*** can be a useful instructional tool, we recommend not using this method to evaluate prior knowledge as students are often not the best judges of their own learning. In general, most instructors use an assessment with some type of selected- or constructed-response questions (see **selected- and constructed-response questions***) to evaluate students' prior knowledge. These assessments should be ungraded and used to inform their learning as well as your teaching. Whichever format you choose, if you choose to administer a prior knowledge assessment the primary focus should be on creating questions that align with what you believe are the prerequisite learning objectives for your course.

What Should You Do If Your Students Don't Have the Prerequisite Prior Knowledge?

You have several strategies at your disposal if you identify that a majority of your students have weak or little understanding of a concept that is critical to learning in your course. You could teach the concept as a part of your class, provide a review session outside of class, or create an online module that students have to complete on their own. If you discover one or more students have significant deficiencies in their prior knowledge you may refer them to a prerequisite course to address those deficiencies. Regardless of which strategy you use, identifying and remediating weaknesses in students' prior knowledge is a critical process to support their learning new content in your course.

Summary

Prior knowledge is the knowledge students bring with them into your course and has been found to play a significant role in learning and performance. You should administer a prior knowledge assessment to evaluate if there are any deficiencies in your students' prior knowledge that you need to address either as part of your instructional activities or by asking students to address them outside of class.

See Also

Align Assessments to Learning Objectives

References

Ambrose, S. A., Bridges, M. W., DiPietro, M., Lovett, M. C., & Norman, M. K. (2010). *How learning works: Seven research-based principles for smart teaching*. San Francisco, CA: Jossey-Bass.

Angelo, T., & Cross, P. (1993). *Classroom assessment techniques: A handbook for college teachers*. San Francisco: Jossey-Bass.

Dochy, F. J.R.C. (1994). Prior knowledge and learning. In T. Husen & T. N. Postlethwaite (Eds.), *International encyclopedia of education* (2nd ed., pp. 4698–4702). Oxford/New York: Pergamon Press.

Dochy, F. J.R.C., Segers, M., & Beuhl, M. M. (1999). The relation between assessment practices and outcomes of studies: The case of research on prior knowledge. *Review of Educational Research, 69*(2), 145–186.

52 Quizzing Frequency

How Often Should I Give Quizzes?

Recommendation: Quiz students frequently (at least once per week). Give more than two exams (about one per month) per semester. Give them a practice test prior to the exams.

The Testing Effect and Test-Enhanced Learning

Giving students frequent quizzes enhances both short- and long-term learning, does so better than other kinds of study strategies, and is known as the *testing effect* (e.g. Adesope, Trevisan, & Sundararajan, 2017; Rowland, 2014). The testing effect is a long-standing, well-known, robust effect. Its use in the classroom has been referred to as "test-enhanced learning."

Giving students frequent tests or quizzes has a direct effect on their learning and there is also the indirect effect that, in preparing for more frequent quizzes, students tend to study more than they otherwise would. There are also ancillary benefits: students tend to have better attitudes about their learning, about the instructor, about the course, better class attendance, less test anxiety (see **evaluation anxiety***), a sense of being better prepared (Kuo & Simpson, 2009), and they did their readings (Schrank, 2016)!

Considerations in Harnessing the Testing Effect for Your Students

Providing frequent quizzes for your students is a great thing to do! Here are some considerations:

> *Graded or Ungraded?*—They can be graded or ungraded, that is, worth points or not worth points. If they're worth points, lots of additional issues arise, like whether quizzes should be announced or unannounced (see **pop quizzes***), and how to handle absences (see **attendance***) and make-ups (see **make-up exams***). Some

evidence suggests that graded opportunities have a greater impact on subsequent test performance than ungraded opportunities do (Hautau et al., 2006).

Feedback—They can include **feedback*** or no feedback. We would argue feedback is a good thing for reasons other than its contribution to the testing effect, which appears to be negligible (Adesope, Trevisan, & Sundararajan, 2017).

Formats—The testing effect works regardless of the test format (e.g. multiple-choice, short answer, etc.; see **selected- and constructed-response questions***) and whether the practices and the final test are similar or dissimilar in format (Adesope, Trevisan, & Sundararajan, 2017). Though it works with lots of formats, the testing effect works best on multiple-choice tests (Adesope, Trevisan, & Sundararajan, 2017). Having the practice test be of open-ended formats (e.g. short answer, short essay) seems to produce better learning than closed-format practice tests (McDaniel, Roediger, & McDermott, 2007).

Types of Learning/Information—The testing effect works for recall learning (e.g. facts) but also for transfer learning, that is, for novel situations on the exam (Adesope, Trevisan, & Sundararajan, 2017). It may not work as well for complex learning (van Gog & Sweller, 2015), though there is debate (cf. Rawson, 2015).

When Should Students Take Practice Tests?—As a test preparation activity, testing effects will definitely work for at least a week. So encouraging your students to do practice testing in the week prior to the exam should yield benefits. There is evidence that spacing material out over a series of quizzes may promote long-lasting learning (Hopkins, Lyle, Hieb, & Ralston, 2016), though the time between quizzes, and whether that timing is constant, doesn't seem to matter (Karpicke & Bauernschmidt, 2011).

How Many Practice Tests Do They Need?—One practice test before an exam works better than multiple practice tests (Adesope, Trevisan, & Sundararajan, 2017).

So . . . How Often Should I Quiz?

There are actually several different questions inherent in what we've already looked at. Let's take them one by one.

How Often Should I Quiz Students?—There's actually a literature on daily quizzes (e.g. Batsell, Perry, Hanley, & Hostetter, 2017; Leeming, 2002; Pennebaker, Gosling, & Ferrell, 2013) or other daily activities (e.g. Hautau et al., 2006). From a learning perspective that is defensible while the downsides would be the logistics for you as well as the class time. Without taking other contexts into account (see below), we recommend quizzing about once per week.

How Often Should I Test?—One (e.g. a final exam) or two (mid-term and final) are generally seen as not enough to promote learning. Kuo and Simon (2009) synthesized the issues involved and concluded that one test per month is optimal, that is, about three or four exams in addition to the final exam (see **assessment plan***).

Should I Give Students Practice Tests Prior to Exams?—One practice test within a week of an exam is our recommendation for maximizing learning.

Caveats

In addressing the question of how often you should give quizzes, we've focused entirely on the outcome of maximizing student learning and examined that through the testing effect. There are some caveats to that and some additional context you should consider.

> *Caveat #1*—The studies on the testing effect are largely laboratory based, largely on list-learning, and largely on short recall periods. There is a growing literature on the testing effect in living classrooms, with lots of different learning content and contexts. Our recommendations are based on both, but we wanted to alert you to that.
>
> *Caveat #2*—The literatures on the testing effect and on test-enhanced learning are muddled on the distinction between several weekly quizzes building to a mid-term exam versus four mid-term exams that don't build to a cumulative final. Both should be advantageous, but the research isn't clear on such a point.
>
> *Caveat #3*—The distinction between a quiz, a test, and an exam is arbitrary.

There are other contextual factors which weigh on the question of how many quizzes you should give in a term. First, what other kinds of assessments and activities do you want or need to do? Are the quizzes your only assessment, or will there be other elements in your assessment plan? Second, how much of the course grade will be allocated to these quizzes? Third, what are the grading policy implications for your choices? What are your policies regarding attendance and make-up quizzes? Fourth, what about time? How much class time can you devote to quizzing? Fifth, what about logistics? How much time and energy do you have for writing and grading the quizzes? How will you use technology?

In the end, more frequent assessment is a good thing for your students on lots of levels, so we recommend you err on the side of too many, rather than too few, assessment and learning opportunities for your students.

Summary

The testing effect is a long-standing, well-known, robust effect. Quiz students frequently (at least once per week). Give more than two exams (about one per month) per semester. Give them a practice test prior to the exams.

See Also

Assessment Plan
Formative and Summative Assessments
Pop Quizzes

Resources

Adesope, O. O., Trevisan, D. A., & Sundararajan, N. (2017). Rethinking the use of tests: A meta-analysis of practice testing. *Review of Educational Research, 80,* 207–245.
Brame, C. J., & Biel, R. (2015). Test-enhanced learning: The potential for testing to promote greater learning in undergraduate science courses. *CBE-Life Sciences Education, 14*(2), es4.
Kuo, T., & Simon, A. (2009). How many tests do we really need? *College Teaching, 57*(3), 156–160.

References

Adesope, O. O., Trevisan, D. A., & Sundararajan, N. (2017). Rethinking the use of tests: A meta-analysis of practice testing. *Review of Educational Research, 80,* 207–245.
Batsell, W. R., Perry, J. L., Hanley, E., & Hostetter, A. B. (2017). Ecological validity of the testing effect the use of daily quizzes in introductory psychology. *Teaching of Psychology, 44*(1), 18–23.
Hautau, B., Turner, H. C., Carroll, E., Jaspers, K., Parker, M., Krohn, K., & Williams, R. L. (2006). Differential daily writing contingencies and performance on major multiple-choice exams. *Journal of Behavioral Education, 15*(4), 256–273.
Hopkins, R. F., Lyle, K. B., Hieb, J. L., & Ralston, P. A. (2016). Spaced retrieval practice increases college students' short- and long-term retention of mathematics knowledge. *Educational Psychology Review, 28*(4), 853–873.
Karpicke, J. D., & Bauernschmidt, A. (2011). Spaced retrieval: Absolute spacing enhances learning regardless of relative spacing. *Journal of Experimental Psychology: Learning, Memory, and Cognition, 37*(5), 1250.
Kuo, T., & Simon, A. (2009). How many tests do we really need? *College Teaching, 57*(3), 156–160.
Leeming, F. C. (2002). The exam-a-day procedure improves performance in psychology classes. *Teaching of Psychology, 29*(3), 210–212.
McDaniel, M. A., Roediger, H. L., & McDermott, K. B. (2007). Generalizing test-enhanced learning from the laboratory to the classroom. *Psychonomic Bulletin & Review, 14*(2), 200–206.
Pennebaker, J. W., Gosling, S. D., & Ferrell, J. D. (2013). Daily online testing in large classes: Boosting college performance while reducing achievement gaps. *PloS One, 8*(11), e79774.

Rawson, K. A. (2015). The status of the testing effect for complex materials: Still a winner. *Educational Psychology Review, 27*(2), 327–331.

Rowland, C. A. (2014). The effect of testing versus restudy on retention: A meta-analytic review of the testing effect. *Psychological Bulletin, 140*(6), 1432–1463.

Schrank, Z. (2016). An assessment of student perceptions and responses to frequent low-stakes testing in introductory sociology classes. *Teaching Sociology, 44*(2), 118–127.

van Gog, T., & Sweller, J. (2015). Not new, but nearly forgotten: The testing effect decreases or even disappears as the complexity of learning materials increases. *Educational Psychology Review, 27*(2), 247–264.

53 Rubrics

How Can You Develop a Reliable Rubric to Score Open-Ended Assessments?

Recommendation: Whenever possible, use a task-specific analytic rubric to evaluate students' performance on open-ended assessments. Give students a copy of the rubric along with the assignment so they know the criteria by which they will be evaluated.

What Is a Rubric?

A rubric is a systematic scoring guideline that contains a detailed description of standards that you can use to evaluate students' performance (papers, speeches, problem solutions, portfolios, cases).

What Questions Do Rubrics Answer?

Spending the time to develop a systematic scoring guide by which to evaluate student performance not only helps you create objectivity and consistency in your grading, but also is a way to communicate to students the benchmarks against which their performance will be scored. It is a way for you to show students how their work will be evaluated and the expectations for different levels of performance. Rubrics can help you address these questions:

- What are the criteria I should use to evaluate students' performance?
- How should I describe the different levels of quality and how do I distinguish them from one another?
- What does the range in quality performance look like?
- How do I determine validly, reliably, and fairly what score should be given to a student and what that score means?

Types of Rubrics

Rubrics can be holistic or analytic and within those two categories rubrics can be general or specific to the task. A holistic rubric provides a single score based on an overall impression of a student's performance on an assignment, for example on a score of 1 = Poor to 5 = Excellent. An analytic rubric provides multiple scores along several criteria. For example, you may evaluate the persuasiveness, supportive evidence, conclusion, and mechanics in a writing assignment, each one rated on a scale of 1 to 3.

Holistic rubrics provide quick scoring and an overall impression of student performance on an assignment. However, they do not provide detailed information for the student to know where her strengths and deficiencies lie, so they may require you to provide written comments or other **feedback***. Additionally, it can be a challenge to decide on an overall score when a student does really well on several parts of the assignment but is weak in a few others. Analytic rubrics provide more detailed feedback and scoring tends to be more consistent across students and graders (for example, if you have multiple teaching assistants doing the scoring). The biggest disadvantage is that they can be time-consuming to use, depending on how many criteria you use in your rubric.

General rubrics contain criteria that are common across different assignments. Using the writing example described above, you could have students complete four different writing assignments all of which are evaluated based on the same criteria: persuasiveness, supportive evidence, conclusion, and mechanics. The ability to use the same rubric across different tasks is an advantage of the general rubric, but this type of rubric may also suffer from lack of specificity in the feedback. In contrast, task-specific rubrics are unique to a specific assignment and include elements in the criteria specific to that assignment. Task-specific rubrics provide more reliable measures of performance, but can be difficult to construct for all tasks, particularly if you are evaluating content accuracy as a part of the rubrics. They also don't focus students on the generalizable skills you wish them to learn across a series of assignments in the way that general rubrics can.

Whether you use a holistic general, holistic task-specific, analytic general, or analytic task-specific rubric is dependent upon several factors.

How Can I Involve Students With Rubrics?

At a minimum, you should share the rubric with your students as part of the assignment. This clearly communicates to them your expectations for performance and it helps motivate students to reach the standards you have set for the assignment. Depending on the level and size of your class, you may even ask students to give feedback on or to add more detail to a rubric you created. This helps students take more personal ownership of the evaluation criteria. Lastly, you can have peers (see **peer assessment***) or students themselves apply the rubric to a work product (see **self-assessment***) as formative assessments focused on feedback and improvement (see **formative and summative assessments***).

Summary

When done well, rubrics are an effective way to create and apply detailed criteria to help you score and evaluate students' open-ended assessments (see **scoring essay tests, papers, or assignments***). They also communicate to your students your expectations and standards for the assignment and remove some of the subjectivity often found when grading students' performance.

See Also

Peer Assessment
Scoring Essay Tests, Papers, or Assignments
Self-Assessment

Resources

Andrade, H. G. (1997). Understanding rubrics. *Educational Leadership, 54*(4), 14–17.
Brookhart, S. M., & Nitko, A. J. (2014). *Educational assessment of students* (7th ed.). NJ: Pearson.
Taggart, G. L., Phifer, S. J., Nixon, J. A., & Wood, M. (Eds.). (n.d.). *Rubrics: Handbook for construction and use.* Lancaster, PA: Technomic Publishing Co.
Wiggins, G. (1998). *Educative assessment: Designing assessments to inform and improve student performance.* San Francisco, CA: Jossey-Bass Publishers.

54 Scoring Essay Tests, Papers, or Assignments

There are lots of opportunities when you are scoring student work for positive and negative biases to impact your scoring. Some simple logistics and mechanics can mitigate those biases.

Objective Scoring Is a Myth

Human beings are subject to numerous conscious and unconscious biases when they are scoring essays and papers. By "bias" here we mean some consideration other than student mastery of the learning objective (see **align assessments to learning objectives***) as evidenced in the assignment you're scoring which influences the student's score. It's actually a long list, but here are some of the more prominent:

> *Caprice*—If you don't have a scoring guide or rubric (see **rubrics***) that articulates how many points will be earned or deducted for various aspects of the work, you may be capricious in your scoring. You might deduct 5 points from one student but 7 from another student for making the same error. Using a well-articulated scoring guideline or rubric will help you stay consistent.
>
> *Recency*—You read a magnificent answer to a short-essay exam question, and you think, "This is why I teach!" Then you flip to the next exam. Ugh! "This is why I will retire the moment I'm eligible!" Is the second response really that bad, or does it seem bad because you just read that awesome one?
>
> *Drift*—As you work your way through a stack of 35 homework assignments, you change how you think about the criteria. In the first five or so, you're getting the criteria set in your head. By the last ten or so, you're understanding the question, the acceptable answer, and your criteria differently.
>
> *Fatigue*—As you're reading the 32nd homework assignment from a class of 35, you're tired. You're not reading as carefully. Your attention is drifting.

Switching Criteria—If you have multiple scoring guides, **rubrics***, or criteria in one assessment, e.g. one set of criteria for question #1 and different criteria for question #2, you are constantly switching from criteria to criteria throughout your scoring. This can lead to inconsistent application.

Halo—As you're reading short-essay exam responses, a student really aces question #1. When you're reading that student's response to question #2, it doesn't seem as good, but since they really knew what they were writing for question #1, you assign them a somewhat higher grade on question #2. In other words, the shine or halo from their first response colors your perception of their second response.

Personality—You see one of your problematic student's name on the top of the exam paper. She always sits in the back. She texts during class . . . when she's there. Ugh! Then you start reading her responses. It takes a strong, conscious resolve, if it's possible at all, not to let those impressions you have of her not to color your scoring of her responses.

There are numerous other biases which also can operate such as biases related to gender, ethnicity, language, culture, religious beliefs, age, appearance, etc. Any and all of these biases can happen unconsciously. They can even happen when we think we are consciously working against them. It is possible, however, to deploy some relatively straightforward procedures which will mitigate, diffuse, or at times eliminate the impact of bias on student scores.

Some Simple Procedures

Here are some relatively straightforward procedures you can enact which will reduce the impact of your biases on student scores:

Use a Scoring Guide or Rubric—There are many, many good reasons for using scoring guides or rubrics. **Rubrics***, used well, are one of the "superfoods" of educational assessment. We recommend them here because they give you a firm grounding in what truly matters in each assessment and greatly helps you score consistently.

Score Anonymously—One of the most powerful techniques you can employ is to score anonymously. If you're collecting papers, simply have students write their names on the backs, not on the fronts, of their papers. Or otherwise devise a way so their identity is not right there where you must see it while scoring. Some learning management systems have a blind feature for grading work. It's important to explain the procedures to students and the reasons for them so they will not put their name somewhere where you can see it.

Dry Score—Go through the first several papers or exams with your scoring guide and "practice score" or "dry score" them. Then return to them, or put them on the bottom of the pile, and actually score them. This lets you settle in to the criteria and adjust your thinking a little bit. Those first several papers thus don't suffer from being the first ones you've read.

Score by Question, not by Student—Imagine again that stack of 35 exam papers with seven short-essay questions. Typically, you score student #1's responses to all seven questions, then student #2's, etc. But scoring by student permits halo, personality, and switching criteria errors to occur. We recommend that you score every student's response to question #1 first, then every student's response to question #2, etc. Doing so makes it much harder for halo and switching criteria errors to occur.

Shuffle the Stack—If you're scoring by question instead of by student, when you are done scoring all responses to question #1, shuffle the stack of papers before you read the responses to question #2. This changes the impact that order, recency, fatigue, and halo effects will have on the same student. If you don't shuffle the stack each time, the same student is always last and gains the same benefits or suffers the same impacts on every question.

Start and Stop in Logical Places—If at all possible, read all of question #1 in one sitting. Try to avoid getting interrupted in the middle of a question. This will help you stay consistent in your understanding and application of the criteria.

These are relatively simple procedures to adopt, but they make such a difference in how bias affects student scores.

Summary

Bias is inevitable when human beings score other humans' work. With some relatively simple procedures, you can mitigate, diffuse, or eliminate the impact of those biases on students' scores.

See Also

Rubrics

55 Selected- and Constructed-Response Questions

Recommendation: Your selection of whether to use selected- or constructed-response questions on your assessments should first be guided by your learning objectives and secondarily by the resources available for developing and scoring.

What Is a Selected-Response Question?

A selected-response question requires students to select an answer from a set of choices developed by the instructor. Examples of selected-response questions include multiple-choice, true-or-false, check all that apply, and matching.

What Is a Constructed-Response Question?

A constructed-response question requires students to provide a written response to an open-ended prompt. Examples of constructed-response questions include essays, short-answer, numeric input, and fill-in-the-blank questions.

How Do Selected- and Constructed-Response Questions Compare?

See Table 55.1 for an overview of how selected- and constructed-response questions compare.

When Should I Use Selected- or Constructed-Response Questions?

Factors such as alignment with the learning objectives (see **align assessments to learning objectives***) and the resources available to develop and/or score the assessment can influence whether or not you use a selected-response or constructed-response question type on your assessment. A learning objective that states "Students will be able to identify the definition of

Table 55.1 Comparison of Selected- and Constructed-Response Questions

	Selected-Response	*Constructed-Response*
Instructor Effort	Takes more time to write	Takes more time to grade
Influence of Guessing	Somewhat susceptible to guessing since choices are provided	Less susceptible to guessing since students construct their answers
Scoring	Fairly objective scoring (correct/incorrect)	Scoring can be somewhat subjective and influenced by the grader (see **rubrics*** to address this issue)
Student Performance	More heavily influenced by students' reading comprehension skills	More heavily influenced by students' writing skills
Content Coverage	Generally can be used to cover a large amount of content	Generally used to cover a smaller amount of content in greater detail

a psychological disorder" is best assessed with a selected-response question asking students to identify the definition from a list of choices. For a learning objective that states "Students will be able to draw the structure of saturated fatty acids," the best format would be a constructed-response question asking students to compose a drawing of a fatty acid structure. A learning objective that states "Students will be able to calculate the mean of a set of numbers" could be either format. For this learning objective for both a selected- or constructed-response format, students would be given a set of numbers and asked to calculate the mean. The selected-response version would provide students a set of answer choices from which to select and in the constructed-response version students would be asked to write or type in a numerical value. In the latter case, you should provide students with guidelines about rounding (e.g. round to the nearest tenth). The learning objective you are trying to evaluate should be the primary factor you consider when deciding on the question format. If the learning objective you've created asks students to "explain" a concept and you assess that using a selected-response question, you should evaluate whether you truly want students to be able to "explain" the concept and modify the learning objective if not, or if the behavior you want to evaluate is the ability to explain a concept then you need to modify your assessment format to match the learning objective.

With respect to the resources available, you need to weigh such factors as class size and grading support. For example, in a course with several hundred students it may not be feasible to grade constructed-response assessments that contain lengthy essay questions. In that case, you may be limited to using more selected-response question formats. Alternatively, if you have human or technology resources to support grading short-answer and/or numerical input questions you may be able to use constructed-response questions even in large classes.

Summary

Selected-response questions require students to select an answer from a set of choices developed by the instructor, and constructed-response questions require students to provide a written response to an open-ended prompt. The question type you use should align to your learning objectives and be informed by what resources you have to support creating and scoring your assessments.

See Also

Align Assessments to Learning Objectives
Rubrics

Resource

Waugh, C. K., & Gronlund, N. E. (2013). *Assessment of student achievement* (10th ed.). Upper Saddle River, NJ: Pearson.

56 Self-Assessment

Recommendation: Have students engage in self-assessment as a formative assessment to help them evaluate and revise their work. How much students are involved in setting the criteria and providing feedback as part of the self-assessment process should be guided by the level of the course and ability of the students to evaluate their own learning.

What Is Self-Assessment?

Self-assessment is the process by which students evaluate their own performance on a specific learning task typically against a set of criteria, called a rubric (see **rubrics***). Self-assessment should be done as a formative assessment to help students evaluate and revise their work (see **formative and summative assessments***). The focus should not be on self-grading (Andrade & Valtcheva, 2009). In addition to having students evaluate their own work, you also can have them help define the criteria included in the self-assessment.

McMillan and Hearn (2008) provide an expanded definition of self-assessment to include the process that students engage in to evaluate their own thinking during learning and to create strategies for improving their understanding. According to these authors, self-assessment includes having students identify the discrepancies between current and desired performance and using that information to develop strategies for improvement.

Arguments in Favor of Self-Assessment

Student self-assessment helps support motivation, engagement in the learning process, and learning outcomes. Students learn to reflect on and monitor their learning progress. The reflection process inherent in self-assessment helps students to develop their skills evaluating and improving their work (Kear, 2011), which includes deepening their understanding of learning objectives.

Research also shows that students can use the self-assessment process as a source of **feedback*** (Andrade & Boulay, 2003; Andrade, Du, & Wang, 2008; Ross, Rolheiser, & Hogaboam-Gray, 1999). In this sense, students can help identify where they might have misconceptions or inadequate understanding about a concept. You could also ask students to identify where they have demonstrated evidence of having met the criteria outlined in a rubric. They can then use this feedback about whether they have met the criteria and where they are deficient to guide revisions on their work (Andrade & Valtcheva, 2009).

Successful self-assessment often requires that you provide students with some type of training in how to engage in the self-assessment process. McMillan and Hearn (2008, p. 47) describe four stages of teaching student self-assessment (see Table 56.1).

Table 56.1 Adaptation of McMillan and Hearn's Four Stages of Teaching Student Self-Assessment

	Stage 1	*Stage 2*	*Stage 3*	*Stage 4*
Level of Implementation	*Establishing Criteria*	*Teaching Students How to Apply Criteria*	*Providing Feedback to Students on Application of Criteria*	*Setting Learning Goals and Strategies*
Beginning	Students are given the criteria and asked to provide feedback to the instructor	Students are show examples of how to apply the criteria (e.g. exemplars with rubric scores)	The instructor gives students feedback on how well they did applying the criteria	The instructor determines the goals and strategies
Intermediate	Students are given a set of criteria to select from and include on their rubric	The instructor describes for students how to apply the criteria	The instructor and student both reflect on how well the student did in applying the criteria	Students are given a set of goals and strategies from which to select
Full	Students create the criteria by which they will be evaluated	The instructor models how to apply the criteria by scoring exemplars	The students have to provide a justification for their self-assessment scores	Students create the goals and strategies

Source: McMillan, J. H., & Hearn, J. (2008). Student self-assessment: The key to stronger student motivation and higher achievement. *Educational Horizons, 87,* 40–49.

As shown above, there are three levels of implementation from which you can choose. Beginning level of self-assessment might be best suited for introductory-level courses and/or students early in their college courses who may not have the sophistication to direct their own learning and establish their own criteria by which they should be evaluated. At the other end of the spectrum, full implementation might be best suited for upper-level courses and/or upper-division students who are well versed in the discipline they are studying and have the learning strategies to be able to determine their own learning goals and evaluation criteria.

Once students are adequately trained in how to do self-assessment, you need to determine whether to count the self-assessment as part of a grade and if so, how it will be graded. Will the self-assessment be averaged with a **peer assessment*** grade? Will it count a certain number of points as part of an instructor grade? While the focus of a self-assessment should be on improvement, providing some incentive to engage in the self-assessment might help students take the process more seriously.

Arguments Against Self-Assessment

Students can become frustrated if the criteria by which they need to evaluate their work are not clear. Additionally, if the focus is on self-grading and not improvement, students may not seriously engage in the self-reflection process. For example, they may give themselves the highest marks on each category of the rubric so as to maximize their grade, regardless of whether the product warrants those scores. You will need to be clear that the purpose of the self-assessment is on reflection and improvement and not on self-grading.

Summary

Self-assessment can be an effective formative assessment tool to help students evaluate and revise their work. Using self-assessment, students learn to reflect on and monitor their learning progress. You will need to train students in how to engage in self-assessment in both applying criteria using a rubric and being able to provide feedback on their own learning.

See Also

Feedback
Formative and Summative Assessments
Peer Assessment
Rubrics

Resource

Rolheiser, C. (Ed.). (1996). *Self-evaluation . . . Helping students get better at it! A teacher's resource book.* Toronto: Cooperative Learning Evaluation & Assessment Research Group.

References

Andrade, H., & Boulay, B. (2003). Gender and the role of rubric-referenced self-assessment in learning to write. *Journal of Educational Research, 97,* 21–34.

Andrade, H., Du, Y., & Wang, X. (2008). Putting rubrics to the test: The effect of a model, criteria generation, and rubric-referenced self-assessment on elementary school students' writing. *Educational Measurement: Issues and Practices, 27*(2), 3–13.

Andrade, H., & Valtcheva, A. (2009). Promoting learning and achievement through self-assessment. *Theory into Practice, 48*(1), 12–19.

Kear, K. (2011). *Online and social networking communities: A best practice guide for educators.* Abingdon: Routledge.

McMillan, J. H., & Hearn, J. (2008). Student self-assessment: The key to stronger student motivation and higher achievement. *Educational Horizons, 87,* 40–49.

Ross, J. A., Rolheiser, C., & Hogaboam-Gray, A. (1999). Effects of self-evaluation training on narrative writing. *Assessing Writing, 6,* 107–132.

57 Student Choice

Can I Let My Students Make Choices in Assessment?

Recommendation: Use student choice judiciously.

Permitting student choice of assessments and/or during assessments can be a great way of engaging student interests, nurturing student autonomy and engagement, and helping them grow as professionals and people. Making choices is an important part of critical thinking, after all.

While that all sounds good in theory, the way students actually make assessment choices when they have them often works in an entirely different way. Students tend to be more pragmatic than principled when making assessment choices (Stefanou & Parkes, 2003). They will make assessment choices based on their familiarity with the formats and the topics and out of a sense of grade security—which choice will get them the better grade. So it is really important if you're going to provide students with choices that you try to keep the choices comparable in difficulty and that you provide guidance and support so that they fully embrace their ability to choose.

Another genuine concern with choosing is that it can present real problems of grading and grade comparability. We address this more fully in the entry **drop the lowest grade***.

Let's consider two different examples of instructors who gave students a choice:

- Lecturer I.L.L. Conceived assigns a project about what life was like in pre-Revolutionary War Boston (1763–1775). Students may choose to write a 20-page paper, construct a diorama, present a poster, do a 15-minute speech with PowerPoint slides, or prepare a creative work like a song or poem.
- Instructor Jen Eralizable places an essay question on her mid-term exam asking students to provide an example from their own experience to which the Thomas–Kilmann Model of Conflict Resolution would have been applicable and to detail how use of the model would have played out in that situation from their experience.

We've all experienced, or at least heard of, these kinds of student choice in assessment. Some of these choices are more defensible than others. Let's have a look at several of the ways these are different and the implications of these differences.

Lecturer Conceived is offering a choice of modality through which students will respond. Instructor Eralizable provides students the opportunity to select the setting about which an assessment question is asked.

What relationship does each of those choices have to the learning objective(s) being assessed? Letting students choose a modality of response could work but the variation of possibilities that Lecturer Conceived offers likely means that different learning objectives will be assessed. How could a 20-page paper and a song possibly represent the same learning objectives here? In Instructor Eralizable's case the question is essentially the same—give an example of the Thomas–Kilmann Model of Conflict Resolution—while the particulars of each student's response may be different. There's a much higher chance here that the same learning objectives will be assessed (see **align assessments to learning objectives***).

It is important then to have student choice operate *within* the learning objective, not between learning objectives. This is particularly true when choosing is part of the learning objective or when the student's choice itself is part of your measurement of the learning objective.

What exactly are students choosing? In order to gain the benefits of choice for student learning while avoiding the pitfalls, it's important for you to articulate what students are actually choosing. Choices that permit student interests to work are good choices. Choices also have to be meaningful to students in order to work (Flowerday, Schraw, & Stevens, 2004). Dictating the 12-slide outline for class presentations but letting students pick the fonts and background colors does not involve meaningful choices.

Summary

Giving students choices within assessments can work really well to drive student learning. Giving students choices among assessments, or the wrong kinds of choices within assessments, can be counterproductive. Know why and exactly how you are offering students choices.

See Also

Align Assessments to Learning Objectives

References

Flowerday, T., Schraw, G., & Stevens, J. (2004). The role of choice and interest in reader engagement. *The Journal of Experimental Education*, 72(2), 93–114.

Stefanou, C., & Parkes, J. (2003). Effects of classroom assessment on student motivation in fifth-grade science. *The Journal of Educational Research*, 96(3), 152–162.

58 Take-Home Exams

A "take-home exam" to us is one which you transmit to students, provide them with some time limit, and then ask them to submit it online or return to you without using in-class time to complete the exam itself. For purposes of this discussion, "take-home exams" can be either in paper format or delivered online; the issues are the same. It shares some similarities and overlapping issues with **open-book exams*** and with **cheat sheets or crib sheets***. You may notice that these three entries follow a similar structure.

"Should I give a take-home exam or give the exam in class?" is not the best place to start in making that decision because that decision relies on many other factors and is never a decision you would make in and of itself. Whether you should offer a take-home exam depends on your learning objectives, what kind of assessment you think best matches those objectives (see **align assessments to learning objectives***), your students, and how you're feeling and what you're already doing about cheating (see **cheating and plagiarism***), mastery learning (see **mastery opportunities***), authenticity in assessment, and a host of other issues.

Aren't Take-Home Exams Easier?

Let's cut to the chase. You're afraid of "selling the store" when giving a take-home exam. You're worried that all your students will get an A on the exam because they'll consult numerous resources, they'll google every question, they'll talk to classmates, they'll work on it together, and, thus, they'll get a perfect score. There's at least one study that does indicate that scores are higher on take-home exams versus in-class exams. Andrada and Linden (1993) established that, while take-home scores were higher on average than in-class scores on the same test, all other aspects were indistinguishable: the reliability of the scores was about the same; the distribution of scores was about the same. In other words, both formats differentiated different levels of student mastery of the material.

Andrada and Linden used two equivalent forms of the same test which were randomly counterbalanced. For the purposes of determining whether taking a test at home versus in-class influenced performance and test discrimination, this was a very important thing to do. For the purposes of assessing student mastery of the learning objectives in your course, why would you do that?

So there's at least one study that validates your fears: students will score higher on a take-home exam than on an in-class exam. That's a red herring, however. The real issue is *why* did they score better? Is it because they "cheated" or is it because they did a better job of demonstrating their mastery of the learning objectives? The first is definitely a problem; the second is highly desirable. Let's break this down.

Considerations in Take-Home Exams

Let's make four groups of considerations: one about instructional economics, one about what you're trying to achieve with your test, one about the test itself, and one about your own students.

First are your instructional economics. "Had we but world enough, and time" we could always assess perfectly. We are, regrettably, always constrained by limited resources, limited time, and limited attention (ours and theirs). Whether to permit take-home or not is in some respects a decision of instructional economics. Of all the things you want students spending out-of-class time on, how "worth it" is this assessment? Is the assessment of these learning objectives worth the take-home exam time, or could students be assigned more articles to read, or another journal entry, or a site visit somewhere? Another instructional economy angle is how you're spending in-class time. By having the students complete the test outside of class, you're freeing up in-class time that you can use for something else. Crannell (1999) also writes that the instructional economics issues of take-homes mean you don't need to answer the "what will be on the test" questions nor do you need to hold review sessions. You can thus construct a cost/benefit ledger for where this time is better spent.

Second, what are you trying to achieve? What are the learning objectives in your course? Consider these two learning objectives: A) "students will synthesize an historical argument from primary historical texts," and B) "students will justify the choice of historical texts supporting an historical argument." While at first they look similar, they are actually quite different, and so are the range of possibilities for the kinds of demonstrations you would need from students in order to know whether they've mastered them or not. Objective A requires that students actually construct an argument in some medium while Objective B does not. Thus some of your learning objectives may lend themselves to a take-home format while others would not or could be done in class.

One aspect here is the role that authenticity will play in your learning objectives and in your assessment. By authenticity, we mean how much like the "real world" your assessments are. If, on the job, it would be appropriate for students to google some things and ask a couple of co-workers and then take three days to write up 1,000 words, then doing so on your assessments has some extra validation. If, however, the learning objective of interest is one aligned with being called on during a staff meeting to give a knowledge-level answer to a technical question on the spot, then take-home isn't as authentic to how that learning objective appears in the real world.

Third, there are some considerations about the test itself. As we mentioned above, we hope you're taking advantage of a take-home test to do things which you could not do during an in-class exam. While students could be given a ten-item multiple-choice quiz to complete online outside of class, this does not take full advantage of the take-home format. A take-home exam provides more time, access to resources, and the ability to collaborate. Hopefully, then, you're capitalizing on this by the formats of the exam questions.

A key consideration then also becomes testing real estate. If you're asking more extensive questions, then you're not asking as many questions. This requires a much more careful consideration of mapping test questions to learning objectives to ensure you're covering the ground the way you need to.

Fourth, there are considerations about your students. What are they prepared and able to handle? What instructions and preparation have you given them?

If you're going to employ take-home exams, take some in-class time, particularly early in the semester before the first exam, to talk with them about why you're doing it, what your expectations are, and how they should be thinking about and approaching them. Students perceive take-home exams as being better for them and perhaps even easier. Those perceptions may not be adaptive for them. So work with them so they are approaching the take-home appropriately.

If you're worried about cheating or the security of your questions (see **test security***** and **online test security***), then don't give a take-home test. They will consult resources. They will talk to each other. For some instructors, for some learning objectives, those activities are not cheating, they're effective strategies. So if you find yourself thinking a lot about "cheating" in making the decision about whether to do take-home or in-class, then do in-class where you have greater control.

Options for Take-Home Exams

Partial Take-Home—Take-home doesn't have to be an all-or-nothing proposition. You can do hybrids where some aspects are done inside the classroom and some outside the classroom. This helps balance the concerns and considerations we've discussed. Crannell (1999) has an individual oral component to see what they know on their own.

Online Testing—Using a learning management system (LMS) to deliver assessments does not fundamentally alter the dynamics we've discussed.

At-Home Test Preparation–In-Class Test Administration—Another approach to balance the concerns is to give a test in class but ask students to do certain kinds of preparations before the test on their own time. We talk about **cheat sheets or crib sheets*** and **open-book exams*** elsewhere. An example here is to provide students with, say, 12 short-essay questions ahead of time of which six will be on the exam when students come to class to write the test. This way, they can benefit from all that take-home provides but you also benefit from the in-class aspects.

Summary

Deciding between take-home versus in-class exams should be based on instructional economics and learning objectives and ultimately understood as an assessment design question.

See Also

Open-Book Exams

Resources

Andrada, G. N., & Linden, K. W. (1993, April). Effects of two testing conditions on classroom achievement: Traditional in-class versus experimental take-home conditions. *Paper presented at the Annual Meeting of the American Educational Research Association*, Atlanta, GA.

Crannell, A. (1999). Collaborative oral take home examinations. In B. Gold, S. Z. Keith, & W. A. Marion (Eds.), *Assessment practices in undergraduate mathematics*. Washington, DC: The Mathematical Association of America.

References

Andrada, G. N., & Linden, K. W. (1993, April). Effects of two testing conditions on classroom achievement: Traditional in-class versus experimental take-home conditions. *Paper presented at the Annual Meeting of the American Educational Research Association*, Atlanta, GA.

Crannell, A. (1999). Collaborative oral take home examinations. In B. Gold, S. Z. Keith, & W. A. Marion (Eds.), *Assessment practices in undergraduate mathematics*. Washington, DC: The Mathematical Association of America.

59 Test Security

How Do I Safeguard My Test Questions?

You might spend hours crafting the perfect multiple-choice exam, ensuring that your questions align with your learning objectives (see **align assessments to learning objectives***), creating questions and answer choices that address common student misconceptions at various levels of difficulty. You administer the exam in class and collect it and the students' bubble sheets at the end of the period. The item analysis results from your institution's testing center shows that the exam worked well to identify students who mastered the concepts and those who didn't and identified areas on which you need to provide more instruction to the whole class before moving on. You go on to reuse this masterpiece the next time you teach the course only to discover your exams are posted on a website (one such website, postyourtest.com, operated in 2008–2010 to systematically allow students to do this (Guess, 2008)).

Not only does this reduce your return on investment for all that effort, cause you to have to invest more effort to create another exam, and vex you extremely, but it also means some students have an unfair advantage over other students. As we mention in our **cheating and plagiarism*** entry, we know students will cheat. However, there are some strategies you can use to help safeguard your test questions.

In the **assessment plan*** and **quizzing frequency*** entries we advocate that frequent, low-stakes assessments are helpful in not only supporting short- and long-term learning but also in reducing the **evaluation anxiety*** students feel when the course contains only a few assessments that influence their grades. So your first strategy should be creating an assessment plan that has multiple opportunities for students to demonstrate how well they have mastered the learning objectives in the course.

Second, providing students with good study guides and test preparation should not only reduce their anxiety but also assuage their need to know what to expect on the test. Providing **mastery opportunities*** and letting students know they'll be available also draws off some of the pressure to cheat.

In addition to having a sufficient number of assessments, the types of questions you include on your assessments should be diversified. For example, complex constructed-response questions are harder to memorize and require an examinee to demonstrate their skill rather than recall information in the case of selected-response questions (see **selected- and constructed-response questions***). However, it is often easier for students to recall the general idea of a constructed-response question, particularly if there are fewer included on the assessment (Wollack & Fremer, 2013). Creating a balance in selected- and constructed-response question types might help address some security issues, but certainly not all.

If you are restricted to using selected-response questions for your classroom exams, perhaps due to class size or limited resources to score constructed-response questions, another strategy to help maintain test security is to use item pools. Item pools work particularly well with multiple-choice exams in that you can create "pools" of questions that measure the same learning objective at the same level of difficulty. Students in the same class receive a different set of questions from the pool, reducing the opportunities for cheating. Additionally, if you reuse the exams from semester to semester, drawing questions from item pools reduces the probability that your exact exam questions are available to future students. You can use software or manually create paper-based tests from a set of item pools. See Parkes and Zimmaro (2016) for a review of strategies to create item pools for multiple-choice questions.

If you have strong suspicions that your test questions from previous semesters have been released, you might want to take on the task of writing new questions each term. You might want to even consider using **open-book exams*** which focus more on application and authentic problems and therefore reduce the need for test security.

Summary

If you reuse test questions from semester to semester, there is a good chance that some or all of those questions have been exposed. While varying your question types, using item pools, and writing new questions are some strategies to maintain test security, the best strategy is to create a comprehensive assessment plan that includes formative assessments (see **formative and summative assessments***), low-stakes quizzes, papers, projects, etc., so that students have multiple opportunities to demonstrate outside of traditional exams how well they have mastered the learning objectives in the course.

See Also

Cheating and Plagiarism
Online Test Security

Resources

Wollack, J. A., & Fremer, J. J. (Eds.). (2013). *Handbook of test security*. New York, NY: Routledge.
Wright, B. D., & Bell, S. R. (1984). Item banks: What, why, how. *Journal of Educational Measurement, 21*(4), 331–345.

References

Guess, A. (2008, June 10). Finished with your exam? Good: Now share it. *Inside Higher Education*. Retrieved from www.insidehighered.com/news/2008/06/10/postyourtest
Parkes, J., & Zimmaro, D. (2016). *Learning and assessing with multiple-choice questions in college classrooms*. New York, NY: Routledge.
Wollack, J. A., & Fremer, J. J. (2013). Introduction: The test security threat. In J. A. Wollack & J. J. Fremer (Eds.), *Handbook of test security* (pp. 1–13). New York, NY: Routledge.

60 Zero Grades

Should I Assign Zeros for Grades?

Recommendation: Arrange your course policies so that assigning a zero is a highly unlikely possibility and so that doing so doesn't become an outsized consequence for students.

If a student does not turn in an assignment, the logical consequence is that a zero gets entered into the gradebook for that exam or assignment. Simple, right? Not really. Let's have a look.

Arguments in Favor of Zeros

If an assignment isn't turned in, there is nothing to grade, so the grade should be a zero. That's hard to argue with.

If a student cheats or plagiarizes (see **cheating and plagiarism***), a zero on that assignment or exam is often the penalty. As a punishment, a zero may be justifiable, though some of the other issues below remain unaddressed.

Arguments Against Zeros

A zero may not actually be valid if the grade is supposed to represent primarily what students know of the course content. A missing assignment means you don't know what the student knows, not that the student knows nothing. In that sense, a zero isn't valid.

A zero can be an outsized consequence for a student who doesn't turn in an assignment. If a paper or assignment represents 15% of that grade, and a student doesn't turn it in, does her maximum possible grade of 85% (in most grading schemes a B) truly represent her mastery of the course content?

If a student turns in work—and we don't mean a piece of paper with her name on it; we mean a genuine attempt—it's highly unlikely that she knows absolutely nothing about the topic. Your scoring guide or rubric (see **rubrics***) should provide for some points on the assignment.

Guskey (2004) makes the argument that instructors often use zeros as punishment for behavior such as not turning assignments in on time even though there is no evidence to support that they work as a deterrent to such behavior. Further, when a zero results in a large consequence to a student's semester grade, she is more likely to disengage further or withdraw from the course.

Avoid the Zero

You (really) don't want to assign a zero and the student really doesn't want to receive a zero. So craft and deploy policies on lots of issues which provide you and your students not only with clear notice about when a zero could be assigned but that also provide for contingencies for how to avoid a zero. Doing so is a deterrent for students and provides you with options for dealing with situations where the issue of a zero are likely to arise. Have a look at the entries on **cheating and plagiarism***, **incomplete grades***, **late work***, **attendance***, and **participation***.

If a zero for a single missing assignment seems to be an oversized consequence, it likely means you don't have enough assessments in your course. If you're using the "one mid-term/one final" approach to your course grade, that's likely not enough (see **assessment plan***). Exactly how a zero impacts the final course grade depends on the grading system you are using (e.g. **compensatory and conjunctive grading***).

Communicate to students that it is ALWAYS better to turn something in than not to turn something in. Then use your scoring guide or rubric to score what they did turn in. Chances are they will earn some credit so that the grade you enter, even if it's 45%, better represents the student's level of mastery than a zero does.

One alternative is a minimum grade policy (Carifio & Carey, 2015) in which you assign a failing grade, such as 50% or 60% or 69%, instead of a zero. Doing this still acknowledges failure but doesn't provide an outsized response. We think this is a compromise measure that leaves all considerations we've already mentioned unsatisfactorily addressed.

Summary

Arrange your course policies so that assigning a zero is a highly unlikely possibility and so that doing so doesn't become an outsized consequence for students.

See Also

Compensatory and Conjunctive Grading
Late Work

Resource

Guskey, T. R. (2004). Are zeros your ultimate weapon? *The Education Digest*, 70(3), 31–35.

References

Carifio, J., & Carey, T. (2015). Further findings on the positive effects of minimum grading. *Journal of Education and Social Policy*, 2(4), 130–136.

Guskey, T. R. (2004). Are zeros your ultimate weapon? *The Education Digest*, 70(3), 31–35.

Resources

Many of our entries included resources you could consult and which would provide you more information about that entry. We've pulled them all together here and labeled each with the entries in which they are mentioned.

Resource	Entry Mentioned
A themed issue of the *Journal on Excellence in College Teaching*, edited by Davidson, N., Major, C. H., & Michaelsen, L. K. (2014). *25*(3&4).	Groupwork
Abernethy, A. M., & Padgett, D. (2010). Grandma never dies during finals: A study of makeup exams. *Marketing Education Review, 20*(2), 103–114.	Make-Up Exams
Adesope, O. O., Trevisan, D. A., & Sundararajan, N. (2017). Rethinking the use of tests: A meta-analysis of practice testing. *Review of Educational Research, 80*, 207–245.	Quizzing Frequency
Aldrich, H. E. (2001). How to hand exams back to your class. *College Teaching, 49*(3), 82. DOI: 10.1080/87567550109595853.	Low Test Scores
Alley, D. (2011). The role of extra-credit assignments in the teaching of world languages. *Hispania, 94*(3), 529–536.	Extra Credit
Andrada, G. N., & Linden, K. W. (1993, April). Effects of two testing conditions on classroom achievement: Traditional in-class versus experimental take-home conditions. Paper presented at the Annual Meeting of the American Educational Research Association. Atlanta, GA.	Take-Home Exams
Andrade, H. G. (1997). Understanding rubrics. *Educational Leadership, 54*(4), 14–17.	Rubrics
Angelo, T., & Cross, P. (1993). *Classroom assessment techniques: A handbook for college teachers.* San Francisco: Jossey-Bass.	Formative and Summative Assessments
Astin, A. W. (1990). Educational assessment and educational equity. *American Journal of Education, 98*(4), 458–478.	Equity

(*Continued*)

(Continued)

Resource	Entry Mentioned
Banas, J. A., Dunbar, N., Rodriguez, D., & Liu, S. (2011). A review of humor in educational settings: Four decades of research. *Communication Education, 60*(1), 115–144.	Humor
Bean, J. C., & Peterson, D. (1998). Grading classroom participation. *New Directions for Teaching and Learning, 1998*(74), 33–40	Participation
Bloom, L. Z. (2004). The seven deadly virtues. *The Journal of the Assembly for Expanded Perspectives on Learning, 10*(1), 3.	Gatekeeping
Boud, D., & Falchikov, N. (2006). Aligning assessment with long-term learning. *Assessment and Evaluation in Higher Education, 31*(4), 399–413.	Learning-Oriented Assessment
Brame, C. J., & Biel, R. (2015). Test-enhanced learning: The potential for testing to promote greater learning in undergraduate science courses. *CBE-Life Sciences Education, 14*(2), es4.	Quizzing Frequency
Brookhart, S. M., & Nitko, A. J. (2014). *Educational assessment of students* (7th ed.). New Jersey: Pearson.	Design Assessments First; Rubrics
Carbone, E. (1999). Students behaving badly in large classes. *New Directions for Teaching and Learning, 1999*(77), 35–43.	Pop Quizzes
Carless, D., Joughin, G., & Mok, M. (2006). Learning-oriented assessment: Principles and practice. *Assessment and Evaluation in Higher Education, 31*(4), 395–398.	Learning-Oriented Assessment
Carroll, J. (2013). *Handbook for deterring plagiarism in higher education* (2nd ed.). Oxford Brookes University, UK: Oxford Center for Staff and Learning Development.	Cheating and Plagiarism
Chester, M. D. (2003). Multiple measures and high-stakes decisions: A framework for combining measures. *Educational Measurement: Issues and Practice, 22*(2), 33–41.	Compensatory and Conjunctive Grading
Close, D. (2009). Fair grades. *Teaching Philosophy, 32*(4), 361–398.	Effort
Crannell, A. (1999). Collaborative oral take home examinations. In B. Gold, S. Z. Keith, & W. A. Marion (Eds.), *Assessment practices in undergraduate mathematics.* Washington, DC: The Mathematical Association of America.	Take-Home Exams
Credé, M., Roch, S. G., & Kieszczynka, U. M. (2010). Class attendance in college: A meta-analytic review of the relationship of class attendance with grades and student characteristics. *Review of Educational Research, 80*(2), 272–295.	Attendance
Eisenberg, A. (2013, March 2). Keeping an eye on online test-takers. *New York Times.* Retrieved from www.nytimes.com/2013/03/03/technology/new-technologies-aim-to-foil-online-course-cheating.html?_r=1&.	Online Test Security
Elwood, J. (2006). Gender issues in testing and assessment. In C. Skelton, B. Francis, & L. Smulyan (Eds.), *The Sage handbook of gender and education.* Thousand Oaks, CA: Sage.	Equity

Resource	Entry Mentioned
Erbe, B. (2007). Reducing test anxiety while increasing learning: The cheat sheet. *College Teaching, 55*(3), 96–98.	Cheat Sheets or Crib Sheets
www.facultyfocus.com/tag/makeup-exams/	Make-Up Exams
Fernald, P. S. (2004). The Monte Carlo quiz: Encouraging punctual completion and deep processing of assigned readings. *College Teaching*, 95–99.	Pop Quizzes
Fink, L. D. (2005). A self-directed guide to designing courses for significant learning. Retrieved April 19, 2017 from www.deefinkandassociates.com/GuidetoCourseDesignAug05.pdf.	Align Assessments to Learning Objectives
Frisbie, D. A., & Waltman, K. K. (1992). Developing a personal grading plan. *Educational Measurement: Issues and Practice, 11*(3), 35–42.	Assessment Philosophy
Georgia State University. (1999). Mager's tips on instructional objectives. Adapted from R. F. Mager. (1984). *Preparing instructional objectives* (2nd ed.), Belmont, CA: David S. Lake.	Align Assessments to Learning Objectives
Gordon, M. E., & Fay, C. H. (2010). The effects of grading and teaching practices on students' perceptions of grading fairness. *College Teaching, 58*(3), 93–98.	Fairness
Guskey, T. R. (2004). Are zeros your ultimate weapon? *The Education Digest, 70*(3), 31–35.	Zero Grades
Heijne-Penninga, M., Kuks, J.B.M., Hofman, W.H.A., & Cohen-Schotanus, J. (2011). Directing students to profound open-book test preparation: The relationship between deep learning and open-book test time. *Medical Teacher, 33*(1), e16–e21.	Open-Book Exams
Hodges, L. C. (2004). Group exams in science courses. *New Directions for Teaching and Learning, 100*, 89–93.	Groupwork
Hunt, L. H. (Ed.). (2008). *Grade inflation: Academic standards in higher education.* Albany, NY: State University of New York Press.	Grade Inflation
Johnson, D. W., & Johnson, R. T. (2004). *Assessing students in groups: Promoting group responsibility and individual accountability.* Thousand Oaks, CA: Corwin Press.	Groupwork
Jones, R. C. (2008). The "why" of class participation: A question worth asking. *College Teaching, 56*(1), 59–63.	Participation
Knapp, C. (2007). Assessing grading. *Public Affairs Quarterly, 21*(3), 275–294.	Beneficence
Kuo, T., & Simon, A. (2009). How many tests do we really need? *College Teaching, 57*(3), 156–160.	Quizzing Frequency
Lang, J. M. (2013). *Cheating lessons: Learning from academic dishonesty.* Cambridge, MA: Harvard University Press.	Cheating and Plagiarism
Leach, L., Neutze, G., & Zepke, N. (2000). Learners' perceptions of assessment: Tensions between philosophy and practice. *Studies in the Education of Adults, 32*(1), 107–119.	Assessment Philosophy

(Continued)

Resource	Entry Mentioned
Leathwood, C. (2005). Assessment policy and practice in higher education: Purpose, standards and equity. *Assessment and Evaluation in Higher Education, 30*(3), 307–324.	Equity
LeJeune, N. (2010). Contract grading with mastery learning in CS 1. *Journal of Computing Sciences in Colleges, 26*(2), 149–156.	Contract Grading and Learning Contracts
LoGiudice, A. B., Pachai, A. A., & Kim, J. A. (2015). Testing together: When do students learn more through collaborative tests? *Scholarship of Teaching and Learning in Psychology, 1*(4), 377.	Collaborative Testing
Lovett, M. C. (2013). Make exams worth more than the grade: Using exam wrappers to promote metacognition. In M. Kaplan, N. Silver, D. LaVaque-Manty, & Meizlish, D. (Eds.), *Using reflection and metacognition to improve student learning across the disciplines, across the academy.* Sterling, VA: Stylus Publishing.	Low Test Scores
McCabe, D. L., Butterfield, K. D., & Trevino, L. K. (2012). *Cheating in college: Why students do it and what educators can do about it.* Baltimore, MD: Johns Hopkins University Press.	Cheating and Plagiarism
McCann, L. I. (2005). Dealing with students missing exams and in-class graded assignments. *APS Observer, 19*(6). Available at www.psychologicalscience.org/observer/dealing-with-students-missing-exams-and-in-class-graded-assignments.	Make-Up Exams; Missing Assignments
McMorris, R. F., Boothroyd, R. A., & Pietrangelo, D. J. (1997). Humor in educational testing: A review and discussion. *Applied Measurement in Education, 10*(3), 269–297.	Humor
Millis, B. J., & Cottell, P. G. (1998). *Cooperative learning for higher education faculty.* Phoenix, AZ: American Council on Education and Oryx Press.	Groupwork
Moore, R. (2003). Helping students succeed in introductory biology classes: Does improving students' attendance also improve their grades? *Bioscene, 29*(3), 17–25.	Attendance
Moore, R. (2005). Attendance: Are penalties more effective than rewards? *Journal of Developmental Education, 29*(2), 26–32.	Attendance
Nath, L., & Lovaglia, M. (2009). Cheating on multiple choice exams: Monitoring, assessment, and an optional assignment. *College Teaching, 57*(1), 3–8.	Cheating and Plagiarism
O'Connor, K. (2013). Class participation: Promoting in-class student engagement. *Education, 133*(3), 340–344.	Participation
Online Schools Center (2014, July). How students cheat online. Retrieved from www.onlineschoolscenter.com/cheating-online/.	Online Test Security

Resource	Entry Mentioned
Pynes, C. A. (2014). Seven arguments against extra credit. *Teaching Philosophy, 37*(2), 191–214.	Extra Credit
Ramirez, C. A. (2009). *FERPA: Clear and Simple.* San Francisco, CA: Jossey-Bass.	FERPA
Roberson, B., & Franchini, B. (2014). Effective task design for the TBL classroom. *Journal on Excellence in College Teaching, 25*(3&4), 275–302.	Groupwork
Rocca, K. A. (2010). Student participation in the college classroom: An extended multidisciplinary literature review. *Communication Education, 59*(2), 185–213.	Participation
Rolheiser, C. (Ed.). (1996). *Self-evaluation . . . Helping students get better at it! A teacher's resource book.* Toronto: Cooperative Learning Evaluation & Assessment Research Group.	Self-Assessment
Rosen, J. A., Glennie, E. J., Dalton, B. W., Lennon, J. M., & Bozick, R. N. (2010). Noncognitive skills in the classroom: New perspectives on education research. *RTI Press publication no. BK-0004–1009.* Research Triangle Park, NC: RTI International. Retrieved July 22, 2017 from www.rti.org/rtipress.	Non-Cognitive Factors
Rosenthal, M. N. (2017, April 7). Responding to students' trauma disclosures with empathy. [Blog post]. Retrieved from www.insidehighered.com/advice/2017/04/07/how-professors-can-best-respond-when-students-experience-trauma-essay.	Personal Disclosures
Sandahl, S. S. (2009). Collaborative testing as a learning strategy in nursing education: A review of the literature. *Nursing Education Perspectives, 30*(3), 171–175.	Collaborative Testing
Shimazoe, J., & Aldrich, H. (2010). Group work can be gratifying: Understanding & overcoming resistance to cooperative learning. *College Teaching, 58*(2), 52–57.	Groupwork
Shon, P.C.H. (2006). *How college students cheat on in-class examinations: Creativity, strain, and techniques of innovation.* Ann Arbor, MI: Publishing, University of Michigan Library. http://hdl.handle.net/2027/spo.5240451.0001.010.	Cheating and Plagiarism
Shute, V. J. (2008). Focus on formative feedback. *Review of Educational Research, 78*(1), 153–189.	Feedback Timing
Spencer, S. J., Logel, C., & Davies, P. G. (2016). Stereotype threat. *Annual Review of Psychology, 67,* 415–437.	Equity
Svinicki, M., & McKeachie, W. J. (2011). The ABCs of assigning grades. In *McKeachie's teaching tips: Strategies, research, and theory for college and university teachers* (13th ed.) (pp. 125–128). Belmont, CA: Wadsworth, Cengage.	Borderline Grade Cases
Taggart, G. L., Phifer, S. J., Nixon, J. A., & Wood, M. (Eds.) (n.d.). *Rubrics: Handbook for construction and use.* Lancaster, PA: Technomic Publishing Co.	Rubrics

(Continued)

(Continued)

Resource	Entry Mentioned
Tanner, K. D. (2013). Structure matters: Twenty-one teaching strategies to promote student engagement and cultivate classroom equity. *CBE-Life Sciences Education, 12*, 322–331.	Equity
The American Test Anxieties Association—http://amtaa. org/.	Evaluation Anxiety
The Stress and Anxiety Research Society—www.star-society.org/.	Evaluation Anxiety
Thorley, L., & Gregory, R. (Eds.) (2013). *Using group-based learning in higher education.* New York, NY: Routledge.	Groupwork
Tierney, R. D. (2012). Fairness in classroom assessment. In J. McMillan (Ed.), *Sage handbook of research on classroom assessment* (pp. 125–144). Thousand Oaks, CA: Sage.	Fairness
von der Embse, N., Barterian, J., & Segool, N. (2012). Test anxiety interventions for children and adolescents: A systematic review of treatment studies from 2000–2010. *Psychology in the Schools, 50*(1), 57–71.	Equity
Ware, M. C. (2011). Insuring self-direction and flexibility in distance learning for adults: Using contracts. In *Encyclopedia of information communication technologies and adult education integration* (pp. 322–336). IGI Global.	Contract Grading and Learning Contracts
Waugh, C. K., & Gronlund, N. E. (2013). *Assessment of student achievement, tenth edition.* Upper Saddle River, NJ: Pearson.	Selected- and Constructed-Response Questions
Wiggins, G. (1998). *Educative assessment: Designing assessments to inform and improve student performance.* San Francisco, CA: Jossey-Bass Publishers.	Rubrics
Wiggins, G., & McTighe, J. (2005). *Understanding by design, expanded 2nd edition.* Alexandria, VA: Association for Supervision and Curriculum Development.	Design Assessments First
Williams, A. E., Aguilar-Roca, N. M., Tsai, M., Wong, M., Beaupré, M. M., & O'Dowd, D. K. (2011). Assessment of learning gains associated with independent exam analysis in introductory biology. *CBE-Life Sciences Education, 10*(4), 346–356.	Low Test Scores
Wollack, J. A., & Fremer, J. (Eds.). (2013). *Handbook of test security.* New York, NY: Routledge.	Online Test Security; Test Security
Wright, B. D., & Bell, S. R. (1984). Item banks: What, why, how. *Journal of Educational Measurement, 21*(4), 331–345.	Test Security
Young, J. R. (2013, June 3). Online classes see cheating go high-tech. *Chronicle of Higher Education.* Retrieved from www.chronicle.com/article/Cheating-Goes-High-Tech/132093/.	Online Test Security

References

Abedi, J., & Lord, C. (2001). The language factor in mathematics tests. *Applied Measurement in Education, 14*(3), 219–234.

Abernethy, A. M., & Padgett, D. (2010). Grandma never dies during finals: A study of makeup exams. *Marketing Education Review, 20*(2), 103–114.

Adams, J. B. (2005). What makes the grade? Faculty and student perceptions. *Teaching of Psychology, 32*(1), 21–24.

Adesope, O. O., Trevisan, D. A., & Sundararajan, N. (2017). Rethinking the use of tests: A meta-analysis of practice testing. *Review of Educational Research, 80*, 207–245. DOI: 0034654316689306.

Aldrich, H. E. (2001). How to hand exams back to your class. *College Teaching, 49*(3), 82. DOI: 10.1080/87567550109595853

Alley, D. (2011). The role of extra-credit assignments in the teaching of world languages. *Hispania, 94*(3), 529–536.

Ambrose, S. A., Bridges, M. W., DiPietro, M., Lovett, M. C., & Norman, M. K. (2010). *How learning works: Seven research-based principles for smart teaching.* San Francisco, CA: Jossey-Bass.

The American Association of University Professors. (2009). Statement of professional ethics. Retrieved January 4, 2017 from www.aaup.org/report/statement-professional-ethics

American Educational Research Association, American Psychological Association, & National Council on Measurement in Education. (2014). *The standards for educational and psychological testing.* Washington, DC: AERA.

Anderson, G., Boud, D., & Sampson, J. (1996). *Learning contracts.* New York, NY: Psychology Press.

Anderson, G., Boud, D., & Sampson, J. (1998). Qualities of learning contracts. In J. Stephenson & M. Yorke (Eds.), *Capability and quality in higher education* (pp. 162–173). New York, NY: Routledge.

Andrada, G. N., & Linden, K. W. (1993, April). Effects of two testing conditions on classroom achievement: Traditional in-class versus experimental take-home conditions. *Paper presented at the Annual Meeting of the American Educational Research Association,* Atlanta, GA.

Andrade, H. (2005). Teaching with rubrics: The good, the bad, and the ugly. *College Teaching, 53*(1), 27–31.

Andrade, H., & Boulay, B. (2003). Gender and the role of rubric-referenced self-assessment in learning to write. *Journal of Educational Research, 97*, 21–34.

Andrade, H., Du, Y., & Wang, X. (2008). Putting rubrics to the test: The effect of a model, criteria generation, and rubric-referenced self-assessment on elementary school students' writing. *Educational Measurement: Issues and Practices, 27*(2), 3–13.

Andrade, H., & Valtcheva, A. (2009). Promoting learning and achievement through self-assessment. *Theory into Practice, 48*(1), 12–19.

Andrews, B. W. (2004). Musical contracts: Fostering student participation in the instructional process. *International Journal of Music Education, 22*(3), 219–229.

Angelo, T., & Cross, P. (1993). *Classroom assessment techniques: A handbook for college teachers.* San Francisco: Jossey-Bass.

Angus, S. D., & Watson, J. (2009). Does regular online testing enhance student learning in the numerical sense? Robust evidence from a large data set. *British Journal of Educational Technology, 40*(2), 255–272.

Babb, K. A., & Ross, C. (2009). The timing of online lecture slide availability and its effect on attendance, participation, and exam performance. *Computers and Education, 52,* 868–881.

Babcock, P. (2010). Real costs of nominal grade inflation? New evidence from student course evaluations. *Economic Inquiry, 48*(4), 983–996.

Bailie, J. L., & Jortberg, M. A. (2009). Online learner authentication: Verifying the identity of online users. *Journal of Online Learning and Teaching, 5*(2), 197–207.

Banas, J. A., Dunbar, N., Rodriguez, D., & Liu, S. (2011). A review of humor in educational settings: Four decades of research. *Communication Education, 60*(1), 115–144.

Barnes, L. L., Bull, K. S., Campbell, N. J., & Perry, K. M. (2001). Effects of academic discipline and teaching goals in predicting grading beliefs among undergraduate teaching faculty. *Research in Higher Education, 42*(4), 455–467.

Batsell, W. R., Perry, J. L., Hanley, E., & Hostetter, A. B. (2017). Ecological validity of the testing effect the use of daily quizzes in introductory psychology. *Teaching of Psychology, 44*(1), 18–23.

Bell, J. T. (1997). Anonymous quizzes: An effective feedback mechanism. *Chemical Engineering Education (CEE), 31*(1), 56–57.

Berk, R. A. (2000). Does humor in course tests reduce anxiety and improve performance? *College Teaching, 48*(4), 151–158.

Berk, R. A. (2002). *Humor as an instructional defibrillator: Evidence-based techniques in teaching and assessment.* Sterling, VA: Stylus Publishing.

Black, P., & Wiliam, D. (1998). Assessment and classroom learning. *Assessment in Education, 5*(1), 70–73.

Bledsoe, T. S., & Baskin, J. J. (2014). Recognizing student fear: The elephant in the classroom. *College Teaching, 62*(1), 32–41.

Bloom, D. (2009). Collaborative test-taking: Benefits for learning and retention. *College Teaching, 57*(4), 216–220. DOI: 10.1080/87567550903218646

Bostock, S. (n.d.). Student peer assessment. *The Higher Education Academy.* Retrieved July 16, 2017 from www.reading.ac.uk/web/files/engageinassessment/student_peer_assessment_-_stephen_bostock.pdf

Boud, D. (1989). The role of self-assessment in student grading. *Assessment and Evaluation in Higher Education, 14,* 20–30.

Brookhart, S. M. (1991). Grading practices and validity. *Educational Measurement: Issues and Practice, 10*(1), 35–36.

Brookhart, S. M., Guskey, T. R., Bowers, A. J., McMillan, J. H., Smith, J. K., Smith, L. F., Stevens, M. T., & Welsh, M. E. (2016). A century of grading research: Meaning and value in the most common educational measure. *Review of Educational Research, 86*(4), 803–848.

Buchanan, R. W., & Rogers, M. (1990). Innovative assessment in large classes. *College Teaching, 38*(2), 69–73.

Butler, D. L., & Winne, P. H. (1995). Feedback and self-regulated learning: A theoretical synthesis. *Review of Educational Research, 65*(3), 245–281.

Byrd, G. G., Coleman, S., & Werneth, C. (2004). Exploring the universe together: Cooperative quizzes with and without a classroom performance system in astronomy 101. *Astronomy Education Review, 3*(1), 26–30.

Cairney, T., Hodgdon, C., & Sewon, O. (2008). The effects of individual, institutional, and market factors on business school faculty beliefs about grades. *Review of Business Research, 8*(3), 131–138.

Carifio, J., & Carey, T. (2015). Further findings on the positive effects of minimum grading. *Journal of Education and Social Policy, 2*(4), 130–136.

Carless, D. (2007). Learning-oriented assessment: Conceptual bases and practical implications. *Innovations in Education and Teaching International, 44*(1), 57–66.

Carless, D. (2009). Learning-oriented assessment: Principles, practice and a project. In L. H. Meyer, S. Davidson, H. Anderson, R. Fletcher, P. M. Johnson, & M. Rees (Eds.), *Tertiary assessment & higher education student outcomes: Policy, practice & research* (pp. 79–90). Wellington, New Zealand: Ako Aotearoa.

Caron, M. D., Whitbourne, S. K., & Halgin, R. P. (1992). Fraudulent excuse making among college students. *Teaching of Psychology, 19*(2), 90–93.

Center for Teaching and Learning—University of North Carolina. (1991). Grading systems. Retrieved from http://ctl.unc.edu/fyc10.html

Center for Teaching and Learning Services—University of Minnesota. (2003). Grading systems. Retrieved from www1.umn.edu/ohr/teachlearn/MinnCon/grading1.html

Choi, H. S., Benson, N. F., & Shudak, N. J. (2016). Assessment of teacher candidate dispositions: Evidence of reliability and validity. *Teacher Education Quarterly, 43*(3), 71.

Chylinski, M. (2010). Cash for comment: Participation money as a mechanism for measurement, reward, and formative feedback in active class participation. *Journal of Marketing Education, 32*(1), 25–38.

Chyung, S. Y. (2007). Invisible motivation of online adult learners during contract learning. *Journal of Educators Online, 4*(1), n1.

Cizek, G. J. (1999). *Cheating on tests: How to do it, detect it, and prevent it.* New York, NY: Routledge.

Cizek, G. J., & Burg, S. S. (2006). *Addressing test anxiety in a high-stakes environment.* Thousand Oaks, CA: Corwin Press.

Cizek, G. J., & Wollack, J. A. (Eds.). (2016). *Handbook of quantitative methods for detecting cheating on tests.* New York, NY: Taylor & Francis.

Clariana, R. B., Wagner, D., & Roher Murphy, L. C. (2000). Appling a connectionist description of feedback timing. *Educational Technology Research and Development, 48*(3), 5–22.

Clark, K. (2008, October 3). Professors use technology to fight cheating. *U.S. News and World Report.* Retrieved from www.usnews.com/education/articles/2008/10/03/professors-use-technology-to-fight-student-cheating

Committee on Undergraduate Science Education. (1997). *Science teaching reconsidered: A handbook, chapter 6: Testing and grading.* Retrieved from http://books.nap.edu/readingroom/books/str/6.html

Corbett, A. T., & Anderson, J. R. (2001). Locus of feedback control in computer-based tutoring: Impact on learning rate, achievement and attitudes. *Proceedings of ACM CHI 2001 Conference on Human Factors in Computing Systems*, 245–252.

Covey, S. R. (2004). *The 7 habits of highly effective people*. New York, NY: Free Press.

Crannell, A. (1999). Collaborative oral take home examinations. In B. Gold, S. Z. Keith, & W. A. Marion (Eds.), *Assessment practices in undergraduate mathematics*. Washington, DC: The Mathematical Association of America.

Credé, M., Roch, S. G., & Kieszczynka, U. M. (2010). Class attendance in college: A meta-analytic review of the relationship of class attendance with grades and student characteristics. *Review of Educational Research, 80*(2), 272–295.

Cross, L. H., & Frary, R. B. (1999). Hodgepodge grading: Endorsed by students and teachers alike. *Applied Measurement in Education, 12*(1), 53–72.

Cross, L. H., Frary, R. B., & Weber, L. J. (1993). College grading: Achievement, attitudes, and effort. *College Teaching, 41*(4), 143–148.

Cushing, A. (2002). Assessment of non-cognitive factors. In G. R. Norman, C.P.M. van der Vleuten, & D. J. Newble (Eds.), *International handbook of research in medical education* (pp. 711–755). Dordrecht, Netherlands: Springer.

Dallimore, E. J., Hertenstein, J. H., & Platt, M. B. (2004). Classroom participation and discussion effectiveness: Student-generated strategies. *Communication Education, 53*(1), 103–115.

Dallimore, E. J., Hertenstein, J. H., & Platt, M. B. (2006). Nonvoluntary class participation in graduate discussion courses: Effects of grading and cold calling. *Journal of Management Education, 30*(2), 354–377.

Dallimore, E. J., Hertenstein, J. H., & Platt, M. B. (2013). Impact of cold-calling on student voluntary participation. *Journal of Management Education, 37*(3), 305–341.

Deci, E. L., & Ryan, R. M. (2000). The "what" and "why" of goal pursuits: Human needs and the self-determination of behavior. *Psychological Inquiry, 11*, 227–268.

Dochy, F.J.R.C. (1994). Prior knowledge and learning. In T. Husen & T. N. Postlethwaite (Eds.), *International encyclopedia of education* (2nd ed., pp. 4698–4702). Oxford/New York: Pergamon Press.

Dochy, F.J.R.C., Segers, M., & Beuhl, M. M. (1999). The relation between assessment practices and outcomes of studies: The case of research on prior knowledge. *Review of Educational Research, 69*(2), 145–186.

Duke, R. (2008, April 18). Why students don't learn what we think we teach. Retrieved July 27, 2017 from www.cornell.edu/video/robert-duke-why-students-dont-learn-what-we-think-we-teach

Enerson, D. M., & Plank, K. M. (1997). *The Penn State teacher II, chapter IV: Measuring and evaluating student learning*. Retrieved from www.psu.edu/idp_celt/PST/PSTchapter4.html

Erbe, B. (2007). Reducing test anxiety while increasing learning: The cheat sheet. *College Teaching, 55*(3), 96–98.

Falchikov, N., & Goldfinch, J. (2000). Student peer assessment in higher education: A meta-analysis comparing peer and teacher marks. *Review of Educational Research, 70*(3), 287–322.

Family Educational Rights and Privacy Act (FERPA) (20 U.S.C. § 1232g; 34 CFR Part 99).

Farrington, C. A., Roderick, M., Allensworth, E., Nagaoka, J., Keyes, T. S., Johnson, D. W., & Beechum, N. O. (2012). Teaching adolescents to become learners: The role of noncognitive factors in shaping school performance: A critical literature review.

University of Chicago Consortium on Chicago School Research. Retrieved from https://raikesfoundation.org/sites/default/files/SA-Rec-Reading-CCSR-Noncog-RF-Full-Report-Revision-%281.14%29.pdf

Fendler, R. J., & Godbey, J. M. (2016). Cheaters should never win: Eliminating the benefits of cheating. *Journal of Academic Ethics, 14*(1), 71–85.

Fink, L. D. (2002). Beyond small groups: Harnessing the extraordinary power of learning teams. In L. K. Michaelsen, A. B. Knight, & L. D. Fink (Eds.), *Team-based learning: A transformative use of small groups*. Westport, CT: Praeger Publishers.

Fitzgerald, C. J., & Loeffler, C. (2012). Exams may be dangerous to grandpa's health: How inclusive fitness influences students' fraudulent excuses. *Evolutionary Behavioral Sciences, 6*(4), 539.

Flowerday, T., Schraw, G., & Stevens, J. (2004). The role of choice and interest in reader engagement. *The Journal of Experimental Education, 72*(2), 93–114.

Frisbie, D. A., & Waltman, K. K. (1992). Developing a personal grading plan. *Educational Measurement: Issues and Practice, 11*(3), 35–42.

Froyd, J. (2002). Peer assessment and peer evaluation. Retrieved July 16, 2017 from www.foundationcoalition.org/publications/brochures/2002peer_assessment.pdf

Frymier, A. B., & Houser, M. L. (2016). The role of oral participation in student engagement. *Communication Education, 65*(1), 83–104.

Gasiewski, J. A., Eagan, M. K., Garcia, G. A., Hurtado, S., & Chang, M. J. (2012). From gatekeeping to engagement: A multicontextual, mixed method study of student academic engagement in introductory STEM courses. *Research in Higher Education, 53*(2), 229–261.

Gayle, B. M., Preiss, R. W., & Allen, M. (2006). How effective are teacher-initiated classroom questions in enhancing student learning? *Classroom Communication and Instructional Processes: Advances Through Meta-Analysis*, 279–293.

Goodboy, A. K., & Bolkan, S. (2009). College teacher misbehaviors: Direct and indirect effects on student communication behavior and traditional learning outcomes. *Western Journal of Communication, 73*(2), 204–219.

Gopinath, C. (1999). Alternatives to instructor assessment of class participation. *Journal of Education for Business, 75*(1), 10–14.

Gordon, M. E., & Fay, C. H. (2010). The effects of grading and teaching practices on students' perceptions of grading fairness. *College Teaching, 58*(3), 93–98.

Graham, R. B. (1999). Unannounced quizzes raise test scores selectively for mid-range students. *Teaching of Psychology, 26*(4), 271–273.

Groopman, J. (2007). *How doctors think*. Boston, MA: Houghton Mifflin.

Guess, A. (2008, June 10). Finished with your exam? Good: Now share it. *Inside Higher Education*. Retrieved from www.insidehighered.com/news/2008/06/10/postyourtest

Hampton, D. R. (2002). Making complaining appealing. *College Teaching, 50*(2), 62. DOI: 10.1080/87567550209595876

Harris, D. (1940). Factors affecting college grades: A review of the literature 1930–1937. *Psychological Bulletin, 37*(3), 125–166.

Harrison, M. A., Meister, D. G., & LeFevre, A. J. (2011). Which students complete extra-credit work? *College Student Journal, 45*(3), 550–555.

Hassel, H., & Lourey, J. (2005). The dea(r)th of student responsibility. *College Teaching, 53*(1), 2–13.

Hattie, J. A. (1999, August). Influences on student learning (Inaugural Lecture, University of Auckland, New Zealand). Retrieved April 22, 2015 from http://growthmindseteaz.org/files/Influencesonstudent2C683_1_.pdf

Hattie, J. A., & Timperley, H. (2007). The power of feedback. *Review of Educational Research, 77*(1), 81–112.

Hautau, B., Turner, H. C., Carroll, E., Jaspers, K., Parker, M., Krohn, K., & Williams, R. L. (2006). Differential daily writing contingencies and performance on major multiple-choice exams. *Journal of Behavioral Education, 15*(4), 256–273.

Hayes, N., & Introna, L. D. (2005). Cultural values, plagiarism, and fairness: When plagiarism gets in the way of learning. *Ethics & Behavior, 15*(3), 213–231.

Heijne-Penninga, M., Kuks, J., Hofman, W. H., & Cohen-Schotanus, J. (2008). Influence of open- and closed-book tests on medical students' learning approaches. *Medical Education, 42*(10), 967–974.

Heijne-Penninga, M., Kuks, J. B., Schönrock-Adema, J., Snijders, T. A., & Cohen-Schotanus, J. (2008). Open-book tests to complement assessment-programmes: Analysis of open and closed-book tests. *Advances in Health Sciences Education, 13*(3), 263–273.

Hill, G. W., Paladino, J. J., & Eison, J. A. (1993). Blood, sweat, and trivia: Faculty ratings of extra-credit opportunities. *Teaching of Psychology, 20*(3), 209–213.

Hofstee, W. K. (1983). The case for compromise in educational selection and grading. In S. B. Anderson & J. S. Helmick (Eds.), *On educational testing*. San Francisco, CA: Jossey-Bass.

Hopkins, R. F., Lyle, K. B., Hieb, J. L., & Ralston, P. A. (2016). Spaced retrieval practice increases college students' short- and long-term retention of mathematics knowledge. *Educational Psychology Review, 28*(4), 853–873.

Houston, M. B., & Bettencourt, L. A. (1999). But that's not fair! An exploratory study of student perceptions of instructor fairness. *Journal of Marketing Education, 21*(2), 84–96.

Immerwahr, J. (2011). The case for motivational grading. *Teaching Philosophy, 34*(4), 335–346.

Inoue, A. B. (2012). Grading contracts: Assessing their effectiveness on different racial formations. In A. B. Inoue & M. Poe (Eds.), *Race and writing assessment* (pp. 78–94). New York, NY: Peter Lang.

Jamieson, S. (2016). Is it plagiarism or patchwriting? Toward a nuanced definition. In T. A. Bretag (Ed.), *Handbook of academic integrity* (pp. 503–518). Singapore: Springer.

Jaschik, S. (2016, March 29). Grade inflation, higher and higher. *Inside Higher Education*. Retrieved May 19, 2017 from www.insidehighered.com/news/2016/03/29/survey-finds-grade-inflation-continues-rise-four-year-colleges-not-community-college

Jensen, M., Moore, R., & Hatch, J. (2002). Cooperative learning—Part 3: Electronic cooperative quizzes. *The American Biology Teacher, 64*(3), 169–174.

Johnson, D. W., & Johnson, R. T. (2004). *Assessing students in groups: Promoting group responsibility and individual accountability*. Thousand Oaks, CA: Corwin Press.

Jones, R. C. (2008). The "why" of class participation: A question worth asking. *College Teaching, 56*(1), 59–63.

Junn, E. N. (1995). Empowering the marginal student: An innovative skills-based extra credit assignment. *Office of the Provost Scholarship*. Paper 11. Retrieved February 1, 2016 from http://scholarworks.sjsu.edu/provost_schol/11

Kafka, T. (2016). A list of non-cognitive assessment instruments. Retrieved July 22, 2017 from https://ccrc.tc.columbia.edu/images/a-list-of-non-cognitive-assessment-instruments.pdf

Kamber, R., & Biggs, M. (2003). Grade inflation: Metaphor and reality. *The Journal of Education, 184*(1), 31–37.

Kamuche, F. U. (2011). The effects of unannounced quizzes on student performance: Further evidence. *College Teaching Methods & Styles Journal (CTMS)*, 3(2), 21–26.

Karpicke, J. D., & Bauernschmidt, A. (2011). Spaced retrieval: Absolute spacing enhances learning regardless of relative spacing. *Journal of Experimental Psychology: Learning, Memory, and Cognition*, 37(5), 1250.

Kear, K. (2011). *Online and social networking communities: A best practice guide for educators.* Abingdon: Routledge.

Kearns, K. D., & Sullivan, C. S. (2011). Resources and practices to help graduate students and postdoctoral fellows write statements of teaching philosophy. *Advances in Physiology Education*, 35(2), 136–145.

Kohil, S. (2014, October 7). Princeton is giving up ground in its fight against grade inflation. *Quartz*. Retrieved from https://qz.com/277288/princeton-is-giving-up-ground-in-its-fight-against-grade-inflation/

Korobkin, D. (1988). Humor in the classroom: Considerations and strategies. *College Teaching*, 36(4), 154–158.

Kulik, J. A., & Kulik, C. C. (1988). Timing of feedback and verbal learning. *Review of Educational Research*, 58(1), 79–97.

Kuo, T., & Simon, A. (2009). How many tests do we really need? *College Teaching*, 57(3), 156–160.

Lang, J. M. (2013). *Cheating lessons: Learning from academic dishonesty.* Cambridge, MA: Harvard University Press.

Larwin, K. H., Gorman, J., & Larwin, D. A. (2013). Assessing the impact of testing aids on post-secondary student performance: A meta-analytic investigation. *Educational Psychology Review*, 25(3), 429–443.

Leeming, F. C. (2002). The exam-a-day procedure improves performance in psychology classes. *Teaching of Psychology*, 29(3), 210–212.

Lindemann, D. F., & Harbke, C. R. (2011). Use of contract grading to improve grades among college freshmen in introductory psychology. *Sage Open*, DOI: 10.1177/2158244011434103

Litterio, L. M. (2016). Contract grading in a technical writing classroom: A case study. *Journal of Writing Assessment*, 9(2).

Lluka, L., & Chunduri, P. (2015). A grading matrix assessment approach to align student performance to Threshold Learning Outcomes (TLOs) in a large first year biology class. *The International Journal of the First Year in Higher Education*, 6(1), 49–60. DOI: 10.5204/intjfyhe.v6i1.262

Loui, M. C., & Lin, A. (2017). Estimating a missing examination score. *Journal of College Science Teaching*, 46(4), 18.

Lunney, M., & Sammarco, A. (2009). Scoring rubric for grading students' participation in online discussions. *Computers, Informatics, Nursing*, 27(1), 26–31.

Manager Tools. (2012, January 8). Routine town hall meetings—Part 1. *Manager Tools*. Retrieved from www.manager-tools.com/2012/01/routine-town-hall-meetings-part-1

Mason. R., & Lockwood, F. (1994). *Using communications media in open and flexible learning.* London: Kogan Page.

Matthew, N. (2012, March). Student preferences and performance: A comparison of open-book, closed book, and cheat sheet exam types. *Proceedings of the National Conference on Undergraduate Research*, Ogden, UT.

McCabe, D. L., Butterfield, K. D., & Trevino, L. K. (2012). *Cheating in college: Why students do it and what educators can do about it.* Baltimore, MD: Johns Hopkins University Press.

McCarthy, J. M., Bauer, T. N., Truxillo, D. M., Campion, M. C., Van Iddekinge, C. H., & Campion, M. A. (2017). Using pre-test explanations to improve test-taker reactions: Testing a set of "wise" interventions. *Organizational Behavior and Human Decision Processes, 141*, 43–56.

McCrickerd, J. (2012). What can be fairly factored in to final grades? *Teaching Philosophy, 35*(3), 275–291.

McDaniel, M. A., Roediger, H. L., & McDermott, K. B. (2007). Generalizing test-enhanced learning from the laboratory to the classroom. *Psychonomic Bulletin & Review, 14*(2), 200–206.

McKeachie, W., & Svinicki, M. (2013). *McKeachie's teaching tips.* Boston, MA: Cengage Learning.

McMillan, J. H., & Hearn, J. (2008). Student self-assessment: The key to stronger student motivation and higher achievement. *Educational Horizons, 87*, 40–49.

McMorris, R. F., Boothroyd, R. A., & Pietrangelo, D. J. (1997). Humor in educational testing: A review and discussion. *Applied Measurement in Education, 10*(3), 269–297.

Mehvar, R. (2010). A participation requirement to engage students in a pharmacokinetics course synchronously taught at a local and distant campus. *American Journal of Pharmaceutical Education, 74*(7), 118.

Meyer, K. R. (2009). *Student classroom engagement: Rethinking participation grades and student silence* (Doctoral dissertation, Ohio University).

Moore, R. (2003). Helping students succeed in introductory biology classes: Does improving students' attendance also improve their grades? *Bioscene, 29*(3), 17–25.

Moore, R. (2005). Attendance: Are penalties more effective than rewards? *Journal of Developmental Education, 29*(2), 26–32.

Myers, S. A., Edwards, C., Wahl, S. T., & Martin, M. M. (2007). The relationship between perceived instructor aggressive communication and college student involvement. *Communication Education, 56*(4), 495–508.

Nagaoka, J., Farrington, C. A., Roderick, M., Allensworth, E., Seneca Keyes, T., Johnson, D. W., & Beechum, N. O. (2013). Readiness for college: The role of noncognitive factors and context. *Voices in Urban Education, 38*, 45–52.

National Research Council. (2000). *How people learn: Brain, mind, experience, and school, expanded edition.* Washington, DC: National Academies Press.

Norcross, J. C., Horrocks, L. J., & Stevenson, J. F. (1989). Of barfights and gadflies: Attitudes and practices concerning extra credit in college courses. *Teaching of Psychology, 16*, 199–203.

Oosterhof, A., Conrad, R. M., & Ely, D. P. (2008). *Assessing learners online.* NJ: Pearson.

Owasso Independent School District v. Falvo, 534 US 426 (2002).

Owens, L. W., Miller, J. J., & Grise-Owens, E. (2014). Activating a teaching philosophy in social work education: Articulation, implementation, and evaluation. *Journal of Teaching in Social Work, 34*(3), 332–345.

Padilla-Walker, L. M., Zamboanga, L., Thompson, R. A., & Schmersal, L. A. (2005). Extra credit as incentive for voluntary research participation. *Teaching of Psychology, 32*(3), 150–153.

Parkes, J., Fix, T. K., & Harris, M. B. (2003). What syllabi communicate about assessment in college classrooms. *Journal on Excellence in College Teaching, 14*(1), 61–83.

Parkes, J., & Harris, M. B. (2002). The purposes of a syllabus. *College Teaching, 50*(2), 55–61.

Parkes, J., & Zimmaro, D. (2016). *Learning and assessing with multiple-choice questions in college classrooms.* New York, NY: Routledge.

Pattison, E., Groadsky, E., & Muller, C. (2013). Is the sky falling? Grade inflation and the signaling power of grades. *Educational Research, 42*(5), 259–265.

Paul, A. M. (2015, August 1). Researchers find that frequent tests can boost learning. *Scientific American.* Retrieved July 8, 2017 from www.scientificamerican.com/article/researchers-find-that-frequent-tests-can-boost-learning/

Pennebaker, J. W., Gosling, S. D., & Ferrell, J. D. (2013). Daily online testing in large classes: Boosting college performance while reducing achievement gaps. *PloS One, 8*(11), e79774.

Petress, K. (2006). An operational definition of class participation. *College Student Journal, 40*(4), 821–824.

Polczynski, J. J., & Shirland, L. E. (1977). Expectancy theory and contract grading combined as an effective motivational force for college students. *The Journal of Educational Research, 70*(5), 238–241.

Popov, V., Brinkman, D., Biemans, H. J. A., Mulder, M., Kuznetsov, A., & Noroozi, O. (2012). Multicultural student group work in higher education: An explorative case study on challenges as perceived by students. *International Journal of Intercultural Relations, 36*, 302–317.

Pulich, M. A. (1983). Student grade appeals can be reduced. *Improving College and University Teaching, 31*(1), 9–12.

Pynes, C. A. (2014). Seven arguments against extra credit. *Teaching Philosophy, 37*(2), 191–214.

Quinn, B. L., & Peters, A. (2017). Strategies to reduce nursing student test anxiety: A literature review. *Journal of Nursing Education, 56*(3), 145–151.

Rainsberger, R. (2007). Ensure that letters of recommendation don't violate FERPA. *Successful Registrar, 7*(1), 3.

Rawson, K. A. (2015). The status of the testing effect for complex materials: Still a winner. *Educational Psychology Review, 27*(2), 327–331.

Robbins, S. B., Lauver, K., Le, H., Davis, D., Langley, R., & Caristrom, A. (2004). Do psychosocial and study skill factors predict college outcomes? *Psychological Bulletin, 130*(2), 261–288.

Rocca, K. A. (2008). Participation in the college classroom: The impact of instructor immediacy and verbal aggression. *The Journal of Classroom Interaction,* 22–33.

Rocca, K. A. (2010). Student participation in the college classroom: An extended multidisciplinary literature review. *Communication Education, 59*(2), 185–213.

Rogers, S. L. (2013). Calling the question: Do college instructors actually grade participation? *College Teaching, 61*(1), 11–22.

Roig, M., & Caso, M. (2005). Lying and cheating: Fraudulent excuse making, cheating, and plagiarism. *The Journal of Psychology, 139*(6), 485–494.

Rojstaczer, S., & Healy, C. (2012). Where A is ordinary: The evolution of American college and university grading, 1940–2009. *Teachers College Record, 114*(7), 1–23.

Ross, J. A., Rolheiser, C., & Hogaboam-Gray, A. (1999). Effects of self-evaluation training on narrative writing. *Assessing Writing, 6*, 107–132.

Rosser, S. V. (1998). Group work in science, engineering, and mathematics: Consequences of ignoring gender and race. *College Teaching, 46*(3), 82–88.

Rovai, A. P. (2003). Strategies for grading online discussions: Effects on discussions and classroom community in Internet-based university courses. *Journal of Computing in Higher Education, 15*(1), 89–107.

Rovai, A. P. (2004). A constructivist approach to online college learning. *The Internet and Higher Education, 7*(2), 79–93.

Rovai, A. P. (2007). Facilitating online discussions effectively. *The Internet and Higher Education, 10*(1), 77–88.

Rowland, C. A. (2014). The effect of testing versus restudy on retention: A meta-analytic review of the testing effect. *Psychological Bulletin, 140*(6), 1432–1463.

Ryan, G. J., Marshall, L. L., Porter, K., & Jia, H. (2007). Peer, professor and self-evaluation of class participation. *Active Learning in Higher Education, 8*(1), 49–61.

Sabini, J., & Monterosso, J. (2003). Moralization of college grading: Performance, effort, and moral worth. *Basic and Applied Social Psychology, 25*(3), 189–203.

Sandeen, C. (2013). Assessment's place in the new MOOC world. *Research & Practice in Assessment, 8*(2), 5–12.

Scanlon, P. M. (2003). Student online plagiarism: How do we respond? *College Teaching, 51*(4), 161–165.

Schönwetter, D. J., Sokal, L., Friesen, M., & Taylor, K. L. (2002). Teaching philosophies reconsidered: A conceptual model for the development and evaluation of teaching philosophy statements. *International Journal for Academic Development, 7*(1), 83–97.

Schrank, Z. (2016). An assessment of student perceptions and responses to frequent low-stakes testing in introductory sociology classes. *Teaching Sociology, 44*(2), 118–127.

Shoffner, M., Sedberry, T., Alsup, J., & Johnson, T. S. (2014). The difficulty of teacher dispositions: Considering professional dispositions for preservice English teachers. *The Teacher Educator, 49*(3), 175–192.

Shute, V. J. (2008). Focus on formative feedback. *Review of Educational Research, 78*(1), 153–189.

Simpson, D. (2016). Academic dishonesty: An international student perspective. *Academic Perspectives in Higher Education, 2*(1), 5.

Slavov, S. (2013, December 6). How to fix grade inflation. *U.S. News & World Report.* Retrieved from www.usnews.com/opinion/blogs/economic-intelligence/2013/12/26/why-college-grade-inflation-is-a-real-problem- and-how-to-fix-it

Smith, G. (2007). How does student performance on formative assessments relate to learning assessed by exams? *Journal of College Science Teaching, 36*(7), 28–34.

Smith, G. G., Sorensen, C., Gump, A., Heindel, A. J., Caris, M., & Martinez, C. D. (2011). Overcoming student resistance to group work: Online versus face-to-face. *Internet and Higher Education, 14*, 121–128.

Smith, J. (1997). Students' goals, gatekeeping, and some questions of ethics. *College English, 59*(3), 299–320.

Snowman, J., & Biehler, R. (1997). *Psychology applied to teaching, chapter 12: Ways to evaluate student learning* (8th ed.). Retrieved from http://college.hmco.com/education/resources/res_project/students/tc/assess.html#5

Sosnovsky, S., Shcherbinina, O., & Brusilovsky, P. (2003). Web-based parameterized questions as a tool for learning. Retrieved July 14, 2017 from www.pitt.edu/~peterb/papers/ELearn03.pdf

Spencer, S. J., Logel, C., & Davies, P. G. (2016). Stereotype threat. *Annual Review of Psychology, 67*, 415–437.

Spidell, C., & Thelin, W. H. (2006). Not ready to let go: A study of resistance to grading contracts. *Composition Studies, 34*(1), 35–68.

Staats, S. K. (2007). An intensive option for developmental algebra: Student achievement on extra credit test problems. *Research and Teaching in Developmental Education, 23*(2), 49–61.

Stefanou, C., & Parkes, J. (2003). Effects of classroom assessment on student motivation in fifth-grade science. *The Journal of Educational Research, 96*(3), 152–162.

Stiggins, R. J., & Conklin, N. (1992). *In teachers' hands: Investigating the practice of classroom assessment.* Albany, NY: SUNY Press.

Sung, Y. T., Chao, T. Y., & Tseng, F. L. (2016). Reexamining the relationship between test anxiety and learning achievement: An individual-differences perspective. *Contemporary Educational Psychology, 46*, 241–252.

Suresh, R. (2006–2007). The relationship between barrier courses and persistence in engineering. *Journal of College Student Retention, 8*(2), 215–239.

Svinicki, M. S. (1999). Some pertinent questions about grading. Retrieved from www.utexas.edu/academic/cte/sourcebook/grading.html

Swinton, O. H. (2010). The effect of effort grading on learning. *Economics of Education Review, 29*(6), 1176–1182.

Theophilides, C., & Koutselini, M. (2000). Study behavior in the closed-book and the open-book examination: A comparative analysis. *Educational Research & Evaluation, 6*(4), 379–393.

Tierney, R. D. (2012). Fairness in classroom assessment. In J. McMillan (Ed.), *Sage handbook of research on classroom assessment* (pp. 125–144). Thousand Oaks, CA: Sage.

Tippin, G. K., Lafreniere, K. D., & Page, S. (2012). Student perception of academic grading: Personality, academic orientation, and effort. *Active Learning in Higher Education, 13*(1), 51–61.

Toma, A. G., & Heady, R. B. (1996). Take-two testing. *College Teaching, 44*(2), 61.

Topping, K. (1998). Peer assessment between students in colleges and universities. *Review of Educational Research, 68*(3), 249–276.

van Gog, T., & Sweller, J. (2015). Not new, but nearly forgotten: The testing effect decreases or even disappears as the complexity of learning materials increases. *Educational Psychology Review, 27*(2), 247–264.

Velliaris, D. M. (Ed.). (2016). *Handbook of research on academic misconduct in higher education.* Hershey, PA: IGI Global.

Volkwein, J. F. (2003). Implementing outcomes assessment on your campus. *Center for the Study of Higher Education.* Retrieved July 22, 2017 from www.bmcc.cuny.edu/iresearch/upload/Volkwein_article1.pdf

Vonderwell, S., Liang, X., & Alderman, K. (2007). Asynchronous discussions and assessment in online learning. *Journal of Research on Technology in Education, 39*(3), 309–328.

Voorm, R. J. J., & Kommers, P. A. M. (2013). Social media and higher education: Introversion and collaborative learning from the student's perspective. *International Journal of Social Media and Interactive Learning Environments, 1*(1), 59–73.

Walker, A., Bush, A., Sanchagrin, K., & Holland, J. (2017). "We've got to keep meeting like this": A pilot study comparing academic performance in shifting-membership cooperative groups versus stable-membership cooperative groups in an introductory-level lab. *College Teaching, 65*(1), 9–16.

Wanzer, M. B., Frymier, A. B., Wojtaszczyk, A. M., & Smith, T. (2006). Appropriate and inappropriate uses of humor by teachers. *Communication Education, 55*, 178–196.

Weaver, R. L., & Cotrell, H. W. (1986). Peer evaluation: A case study. *Innovative Higher Education, 11*, 25–39.

Weaver, R. R., & Qi, J. (2005). Classroom organization and participation: College students' perceptions. *The Journal of Higher Education, 76*(5), 570–601.

Weeks, K. M. (2001). Family-friendly FERPA policies: Affirming parental partnerships. *New Directions for Student Services, 94*, 39–50.

Weinstein, S. E., & Wu, S. W. (2009). Readiness assessment tests versus frequent quizzes: Student preferences. *International Journal of Teaching and Learning in Higher Education, 21*(2), 181–186.

Westerkamp, A. C., Hiejne-Penninga, M., Kuks, J.B.M., & Cohen-Schotanus, J. (2013). Open-book tests: Search behaviour, time used and test scores. *Medical Teacher, 35*, 330–332.

Wiggins, G. (1998). *Educative assessment: Designing assessments to inform and improve student performance.* San Francisco: Jossey-Bass.

Wiggins, G., & McTighe, J. (2005). *Understanding by design, expanded* (2nd ed.). Alexandria, VA: Association for Supervision and Curriculum Development.

Williams, A. E., Aguilar-Roca, N. M., Tsai, M., Wong, M., Moravec Beaupré, M., & O'Dowd, D. K. (2011). Assessment of learning gains associated with independent exam analysis in introductory biology. *CBE-Life Sciences Education, 10,* 346–356. DOI: 10.1187/cbe.11-03-0025

Wilson, M. L. (2002). Evidence that extra credit assignments induce moral hazard. *Atlantic Economic Journal, 30*(1), 97.

Wollack, J. A., & Fremer, J. J. (2013). Introduction: The test security threat. In J. A. Wollack & J. J. Fremer (Eds.), *Handbook of test security* (pp. 1–13). New York, NY: Routledge.

Wyss, V. L., Freedman, D., & Siebert, C. J. (2014). The development of a discussion rubric for online courses: Standardizing expectations of graduate students in online scholarly discussions. *Tech Trends, 58*(2), 99–107.

Index